"Raymond F. Collins' study of the practice of celibacy in Latin Catholicism is a calm and critical assessment of the data that has generated this tradition. . . . Collins' skills as a New Testament scholar are well known; his skills as an interpreter of the patristic and early canonical tradition of the Latin Church become evident as this study opens and then unfolds. . . . This clearly written and well-documented study . . . deserves to become an essential point of reference for all future discussions of this question."

Francis J. Moloney, SDB, AM, FAHA
Senior Professorial Fellow
Australian Catholic University
Melbourne, Australia

"*Accompanied by a Believing Wife* is the definitive work on celibacy and the New Testament, with important implications for the church of our own day. Raymond F. Collins brings decades of experience and learning as a New Testament scholar to this project, and it is evident on every page. . . . His conclusions are often bold and challenging but always supported by careful investigation. . . . With a reputation for exemplary clarity, his writing is highly accessible to scholar, student, clergy, and layperson. Essential reading for all."

Margaret Y. MacDonald
Professor
St. Francis Xavier University
Nova Scotia, Canada

Accompanied by a Believing Wife

Ministry and Celibacy in the Earliest Christian Communities

Raymond F. Collins

A Michael Glazier Book

LITURGICAL PRESS
Collegeville, Minnesota

www.litpress.org

A Michael Glazier Book published by Liturgical Press

Cover design by Jodi Hendrickson. Cover photo: Thinkstock.

1	2	3	4	5	6	7	8	9

Library of Congress Cataloging-in-Publication Data

Collins, Raymond F., 1935–
    Accompanied by a believing wife : ministry and celibacy in the earliest Christian communities / Raymond F. Collins.
        pages   cm
    "A Michael Glazier book."
    Includes bibliographical references.
    ISBN 978-0-8146-8213-5 — ISBN 978-0-8146-8238-8 (e-book)
        1. Celibacy—History of doctrines—Early church, ca. 30–600.   2. Celibacy—Catholic Church—History.   I. Title.

BV4390.C64   2013
253'.2509015—dc23

                                                                    2013024504

For those who Search

For those who Sacrifice

For those who Strive

For those who Struggle

For those who Stumble

For those who Suffer

Contents

Preface

Each of the books that I have written during the past three decades has its own history and its own story. In many ways the story of this book began more than a half century ago when I was ordained a subdeacon in the Roman Catholic Church for the service of the diocese of Providence, Rhode Island. I made the requisite promises—namely, that I pray the daily office and commit myself to a life of celibacy. At the time I did not anticipate writing this book or any other book. I envisioned that I would be ordained to the priesthood the following year and then serve as a parish priest in my native diocese. Little did I know that in the mysterious ways of Divine Providence, the obedience I had promised to my bishop would lead to a life of teaching and writing about the New Testament, mixed with no small measure of academic and ecclesiastical administration.

In 1993 life as scholar and administrator brought me to The Catholic University of America in Washington, DC, where I was to become dean of the university's School of Religious Studies. My predecessor as dean was Professor William Cenkner, OP, whose academic interests focused on the religions of the East, particularly Hinduism. As dean, he formulated a three-year, three-faith conference on marriage and the family. The three faiths were Roman Catholicism, Judaism, and Islam.

The first year of the conference was devoted to the horizontal axis of the family, the relationship between husband and wife. The second year was devoted to the vertical dimension of the family, the relationships between parents and children, children and parents. The third year was devoted to the entire *gestalt*, the family circle. Each year included nine presentations, three each by scholars from the respective faith traditions. One presentation focused on the topic from the vantage point of the tradition's scriptures. Another presentation considered the topic from the standpoint of law and morality. The third presentation studied the topic from the point of view of its history and sociology.

Thus it was that when I came to Washington to discuss with Dean Cenkner some of the specifics of the position that I was about to assume, he asked me if I would be willing to speak on marriage in the New Testament during the conference that was to convene just three months into my deanship. I willingly consented, thus setting the stage for this book. In addition to the nine presentations, the conference had an open, public session. During this session, an Iranian imam pointedly asked me how I could claim to be a man of God when I so publicly flaunted God's law.

The question nonplussed me. I was startled. To this day I wish that I could remember my answer but I cannot. Many times I had been asked about priestly celibacy. Many times have I discussed the topic, particularly when I was a seminary rector in the 1970s. Never before had I been personally confronted with the idea that priestly celibacy was a violation of God's law. The imam's question led me to begin thinking about celibacy in a new way.

The imam's question obviously arose from his understanding of the Qur'an's vision of creation. "And among his Signs is this," says Surah 30:21, "that He created for you mates from among yourselves, that you may dwell in tranquility with them, and He has put love and mercy between your 'hearts.' Verily, in that are the Signs for those who reflect." Similarly, in a staccato-like series of reflections on creation, Surah 78:8 says, "And [have we not] created you in pairs?" No wonder then that Surah 24:32 commands, "Marry those among you who are single."

The Qur'an's vision of the creation of human beings with the consequent obligation that believers be married is most likely influenced by the idea of creation found in the first pages of Genesis. In any case, the visions are remarkably similar. The older narrative of creation, the Yahwist's tale, tells the imaginatively beautiful story of the creation of woman (Gen 2:18-24) because, in God's judgment, "It is not good that the man [*hadam*] should be alone" (Gen 2:18). In a parallel, and probably later account of creation, the Priestly narrative says, "In the image of God he created them; male and female he created them. God blessed them, and God said to them, "Be fruitful and multiply" (Gen 1:27b-28a). With a divine mandate, humans are to be God's representatives and agents within the world of creation.

While the imam's question personally challenged me and prompted me to reflect on the biblical origins of the Roman Catholic discipline of ecclesiastical celibacy in its Western Church, the Latin Church, my study of the New Testament led me to want to investigate the matter still further.

A little more than twenty years ago, Michael Glazier asked me to write a book on divorce in the New Testament.[1] In the course of studying the pertinent texts I came to realize how widely misused, in the discussion of Matthew 19:1-12 (Matthew's version of the dialogue between some Pharisees and Jesus on the subject of divorce), Jesus' words were: "And there are eunuchs who have made themselves eunuchs for the sake of the kingdom of heaven" (Matt 19:12c).

My study of Paul's First Letter to the Corinthians led me to question seriously the popular interpretation of some of the apostle's words, including, "It is well for a man not to touch a woman" (1 Cor 7:1), and, "To the unmarried and the widows I say that it is well for them to remain unmarried as I am" (1 Cor 7:8; cf. 7:7a).

I often wondered why my Roman Catholic tradition so often cites passages from the Pastoral Epistles, particularly First Timothy and Titus, as proof texts for a threefold ordering of ministerial leadership in the church—bishop, priest, and deacon—yet at the same time neglects these texts' inclusion of "married only once" among the qualities that bishops and deacons should have (cf. 1 Tim 3:2, 12).

In sum, this book has come into being because of my life experience as a Roman Catholic priest, an administrator of ecclesiastical institutions, and a New Testament scholar. The catalyst was a suggestion that this was a book that needed to be written and that I was a person who could write it. Retired from the university lecture hall, I had the time. Having lectured on the New Testament for more than forty years, I had the expertise, or so it was thought. Writing the book was a challenge. I have endeavored to meet the challenge as best I could.

The project could not have been completed were it not for the assistance of several persons. Let me begin with a word of thanks to Dr. Susan Harvey, then chair of the department of religious studies at Brown University, who not only promoted my appointment as a visiting scholar in the department but also introduced me to Dr. David Hunter, holder of the Cottrill-Rolfes Chair of Catholic Studies at the University of Kentucky, who has done no inconsiderable amount of study on the discipline of clerical continence, albeit at a later period of time than is the focus of my exegetical study.

I am indebted to the staff of Brown's Rockefeller Library, particularly the staff of its interlibrary loan service who procured several items for

---

[1] The book was published by Liturgical Press as *Divorce in the New Testament*, Good News Studies 38 (Collegeville, MN: Liturgical Press, Michael Glazier, 1992).

me, even from abroad. I am also grateful to Wouter Biesbrouck, a member of the Christian Self-Understanding and Interreligious Dialogue Group of the Faculty of Theology and Religious Studies of the Catholic University of Leuven, Belgium. From that university's vast theological research library, Wouter tracked down for me a number of journal articles that were seemingly unavailable in the United States.

I am grateful to Dr. Hunter, a patristic scholar, for the conversations that we have had in the past couple of years. He read much of the manuscript and offered a number of useful suggestions. I must also express my gratitude to Dr. Andrea Molinari, a former student and now president of the Rice Institute of Pastoral Studies of the Diocese of Venice. He not only allowed me the use of the institute's library but also proofread the text with an eagle's eye and provided me with some helpful advice and occasional criticism. One of his staff, Jack Conroy, PhD, read through the sections on Paul, his area of expertise, and prevented more than one *erratum* from making its way to the press. I am particularly grateful to Dr. Florence Morgan Gillman, professor of biblical studies at the University of San Diego and also a former student, who read the completed manuscript in its final stages. And I will be forever grateful to Dr. Amy-Jill Levine, professor of New Testament and Jewish studies at Vanderbilt University, who read the manuscript ever so carefully in an earlier draft and made many valuable comments and much incisive critique. With the help of these several people and a few unnamed others, I was able to improve the manuscript, both in content and in format. The errors that remain are of my own making.

Last but not least, I wish to express my thanks to Hans Christoffersen, publisher at Liturgical Press, who took an interest in the project from the start and encouraged me to complete it as well and as soon as possible. Under his leadership, I had the pleasure of working with Nikki Werner, copy editor at Liturgical Press, who read the manuscript ever so carefully and raised a number of queries for me to answer.

I offer this study as a contribution to the ongoing discussion of the role of celibacy in the Latin Church. It is dedicated to those who have striven to live a life of celibacy within the church and those who wonder whether continuation of the practice best serves the needs of the church of the twenty-first century.

Raymond F. Collins
Feast of St. Joseph the Worker
May 1, 2013

Abbreviations

AB	Anchor Bible
ABD	*Anchor Bible Dictionary.* 6 vols. New York: Doubleday, 1992.
ABRL	Anchor Bible Reference Library
ACCS	Ancient Christian Commentary on Scripture
ALGHJ	Arbeiten zur Literatur und Geschichte des hellenistischen Judentum
AnBib	Analecta biblica
ANF	*Ante-Nicene Fathers: The Writings of the Fathers Down to AD 325.* 10 vols. New York: T&T Clark, 1885–97.
ANTC	Abingdon New Testament Commentaries
ATR	*Anglican Theological Review*
AUSS	Andrews University Seminary Studies
AYB	Anchor Yale Bible
b.	Babylonian Talmud
BAGD	*Greek-English Dictionary of the New Testament and Other Early Christian Literature,* edited by W. Bauer, W. F. Arndt, F. W. Gingrich, and F. W. Danker.
BCNH	Bibliothèque Copte de Nag Hammadi. Section "Études"
BDF	*A Greek Grammar of the New Testament and Other Early Christian Literature,* edited by F. Blass, A. Debrunner, and Robert W. Funk. Chicago-London: University of Chicago Press, 1961.
BETL	*Bibliotheca ephemeridum theologicarum lovaniensium*
Bib	*Biblica*
BNTC	Black's New Testament Commentaries
BSac	*Bibliotheca sacra*
BTB	*Biblical Theology Bulletin*

CBET	Contributions to Biblical Exegesis and Theology
CBQ	*Catholic Biblical Quarterly*
CC	Corpus Christianorum. Turnhout, Belgium: Brepols, 1953–.
CH	*Church History*
CNT	Commentaire du Nouveau Testament
CSEL	Corpus scriptorium ecclesiasticorum latinorum. Salzburg, Austria: University of Salzburg, 1866–.
CTR	*Criswell Theological Review*
DJD	Discoveries in the Judaean Desert. 40 vols. Oxford: Clarendon Press, 1955–2008.
DSD	*Dead Sea Discoveries*
EBib	*Études bibliques*
ECC	Early Christianity in Context
EDNT	*Exegetical Dictionary of the New Testament*
EKKNT	Evangelisch-katholischer Kommentar zum Neuen Testament
EncJud²	*Encylopedia Judaica.* 22 vols. 2nd ed. Woodbridge, CT: Macmillan Reference, 2007.
Epist.	*Epistola* (letter)
EstBib	*Estudios biblicos*
FC	Fathers of the Church. Washington: Catholic University of America Press, 1947–.
frg.	fragment
FRLANT	Forschungen zur Religion und Literatur des Alten und Neuen Testaments
GCS	Die griechischen christlichen Schriftsteller der ersten Jahunderte. Leipzig: Hinrichs, 1897–.
GNS	Good News Studies
Hom.	*Homily*
ICC	International Critical Commentary
IVP	Intervarsity Press
JANT	*The Jewish Annotated New Testament*
JBL	*Journal of Biblical Literature*

JSJ	*Journal for the Study of Judaism in the Persian, Hellenistic, and Roman Periods*
JJS	*Journal of Jewish Studies*
JSNT	*Journal for the Study of the New Testament*
JSNTSup	Journal for the Study of the New Testament: Supplement Series
JSOT	*Journal for the Study of the Old Testament*
JTS	*Journal of Theological Studies*
KEK	Kritisch-exegetischer Kommentar über das Neue Testament
KJV	King James Version (Authorized Version)
LD	*Lectio Divina*
LS	*Louvain Studies*
LSJ	Liddell, Henry George, Robert Scott, and Henry Stuart Jones. *A Greek English Lexicon.* 9th ed. with revised supplement. Oxford: Clarendon, 1996.
LTP	*Laval théologique et philosophique*
m.	Mishnah
MM	*The Vocabulary of the Greek New Testament.* Edited by J. H. Moulton and G. Milligan.
N-A[28]	*Novum Testamentum Graece.* 28th rev. ed. Edited by Barbara and Kurt Aland et al. Münster: Deutsche Bibelgesellschaft, 2012.
N. S.	New Series
NAB	New American Bible
NCB	New Century Bible
NEB	New English Bible
New Docs	*New Documents Illustrating Early Christianity.* Edited by G.H.R. Horsley and S. Llewelyn. North Port, NSW: Macquarie University, 1981– .
NICNT	New International Commentary on the New Testament
NIDB	*New Interpreters' Dictionary of the Bible.* 5 vols. Nashville: Abingdon, 2006–9.
NIGTC	New International Greek Testament Commentary

NovT	*Novum testamentum*
NovTSup	Novum Testamentum Supplements
NTL	New Testament Library
NTS	*New Testament Studies*
NTTS	New Testament Tools and Studies
NPNF	*Nicene and Post-Nicene Fathers.* Series 1, 14 vols. Series 2, 14 vols. New York: T&T Clark, 1886–1900.
NRSV	New Revised Standard Version
Pap	Papyrus
Past	Pastoral Epistles
PE	Pastoral Epistles
PG	Patrologia graeca (=Patrologiae cursus completus. Series graeca). 162 vols. Edited by Jacques-Paul Migne. Paris: Imprimerie catholique, 1857–86.
PL	Patrologia latina (=Patrologiae cursus completus. Series latina). 217 vols. Edited by Jacques-Paul Migne, Paris: Imprimerie catholique, 1844–64.
Q	Qumran; *Quelle*, the Sayings Source for the Synoptic Gospels
R.	Rabbi
RB	*Revue biblique*
REB	Revised English Bible
RevQ	*Revue de Qumran*
RSV	Revised Standard Version
RTP	*Revue de théologie et de philosophie*
SBFLA	*Studii biblici Franciscani liber annus*
SBLABib	Society of Biblical Literature Academia Biblica
SBLDS	Society of Biblical Literature Dissertation Series
SBM	Stuttgarter biblische Monographien
SBS	Stuttgarter Bibelstudien
SCH	Studies in Church History
SNTSU	Studien zum Neuen Testament und seiner Unwelt
SP	Sacra Pagina
STDJ	Studies on the Texts of the Desert of Judah

SVTQ	St. Vladimir's Theological Quarterly
t.	Tosefta
TBT	The Bible Today
THKNT	Theologischer Handkommentar zum Neuen Testament
TLZ	Theologische Literaturzeitung
TSK	Theologische Studien und Kritiken
TynBul	Tyndale Bulletin
UBS	United Bible Societies
VC	Vigiliae christianae
VCSup	Supplements to Vigiliae christianae
WBC	Word Biblical Commentary
WUNT	Wissenschaftliche Untersuchungen zum Neuen Testament
ZNW	Zeitschrift für die neutestamentliche Wissenschaft und die Kunde der älteren Kirche
ZTK	Zeitschrift für Theologie und Kirche

Ancient Texts

Columella, *Rust.*	De re rustica
Gaius, *Inst.*	Institutiones
Herodotus, *Hist.*	Historiae
Lucian, *Eunuch.*	Eunuchus
Tacitus, *Ann.*	Annales
Xenophon, *Symp.*	Symposium

Jewish Texts

Dead Sea Scrolls

Typically the Dead Sea Scrolls are designated by a numeral (designating the cave in which they were found), the letter Q (for Qumran), and a number. Some scrolls have been named and are identified by an abbreviated form of the name.

1QH	Hodayot or Thanksgiving Psalms
1QM	Milḥḥamah or War Scroll
1QS	Serek Hayahad or Rule of the Community

1QSa	*Rule of the Congregation*, an appendix to 1QS [=1Q28a]
1QIsa[a]	Isaiah Scroll[a]
1QIsa[b]	Isaiah Scroll[b]
4QD[a]	*Damascus Document*[a] (=4Q266)
4QD[b]	*Damascus Document*[b] (=4Q267)
4QD[c]	*Damascus Document*[c] (=4Q268)
4QD[d]	*Damascus Document*[d] (=4Q269)
4QD[e]	*Damascus Document*[e] (=4Q270)
4QD[f]	*Damascus Document*[f] (=4Q271)
4QD[g]	*Damascus Document*[g] (=4Q272)
4QMMT	*Miqṣat Maʾaśê ha-Torah* (=4Q394), the Halakhic Letter
4QpapD[h]	Papyrus fragment of the *Damascus Document*[h] (=4Q273)
5QD	*Damascus Document* (=5Q12)
6QD	*Damascus Document* (=6Q15)
11QPs[a]	*Psalm Scroll* (=11Q5)
11QT[a]	*Temple Scroll*[a] (=11Q19)
11QT[b]	*Temple Scroll*[b] (=11Q20)
CD	Cairo Genizah Copy of the *Damascus Document*

Josephus

Ag. Ap.	*Against Apion (Contra Apionem)*
Ant.	*Jewish Antiquities (Antiquitates judaicae)*
J. W.	*Jewish War (Bellum judaicum)*
Life	*The Life (Vita)*

Mishnah

m. ʾAbot.	*Mishnah ʾAbot*
m. Giṭ.	*Mishnah Giṭṭin*
m. Ketub.	*Mishnah Ketubbot*
m. Qidd.	*Mishnah Qiddušin*
m. Yebam.	*Mishnah Yebamot*
m. Soṭah	*Mishnah Soṭah*

Old Testament Pseudepigrapha

2 Bar.	2 Baruch (Syriac Apocalypse)
4 Ezra	4 Ezra
T. Mos.	Testament of Moses

Testament of the 12 Patriarchs

T. Job	Testament of Job
T. Levi	Testament of Levi
T. Reub.	Testament of Reuben

Philo

Contempl. Life	On the Contemplative Life
Creation	On the Creation of the World
Good Person	That Every Good Person is Free
Heir	Who Is the Heir?
Joseph	On the Life of Joseph
Moses	On the Life of Moses
Rewards	On Rewards and Punishments
Spec. Laws	On the Special Laws

Rabbinic Works

Deut. Rab.	Rabbah Deuteronomy
E. H.	Evan ha-Ezer
Exod. Rab.	Rabbah Exodus
Gen. Rab.	Rabbah Genesis
Sifre Deut.	Sifre Deuteronomy
Tanḥ.	Tanḥuma

Talmud

b. ʾErub.	Babylonian Talmud ʾErubin
b. Ketub.	Babylonian Talmud Ketubbot
b. Ned.	Babylonian Talmud Nedarim

b. Pesaḥ.	*Babylonian Talmud Pesaḥim*
b. Qidd.	*Babylonian Talmud Qiddušin*
b. Sabb.	*Babylonian Talmud Sabbat*
b. Sanh.	*Babylonian Talmud Sanhedrin*
b. Yebam.	*Babylonian Talmud Yebamot*

Early Christian and Patristic Texts

Eusebius

| *Dem. ev.* | *Demonstration on the Gospels (Demonstratio evangelica)* |
| *Eccl. Hist.* | *Ecclesiastical History* |

Ignatius

Magn.	*Letter to the Magnesians*
Phld.	*Letter to the Philadelphians*
Pol.	*Letter to Polycarp*
Trall.	*Letter to the Trallians*

NT Apocrypha

| *G. Thom.* | *Gospel of Thomas* |

| Polycarp, *Phil.* | *Letter to the Philippians* |

Pseudo-Clementines

| *Hom.* | *Homilies* |
| *Recon.* | *Recognitions* |

1

A Methodological Introduction

When Cardinal Alfons Maria Stickler died on December 12, 2007, the Roman Catholic Church lost one of its staunchest defenders of clerical celibacy. During the course of recent decades many churchmen[1] have defended clerical celibacy, but, during his long academic career and a much longer life, the Austrian-born cardinal[2]—nearing one hundred years of age at the time of his death—was a staunch academic defender of the discipline of mandatory clerical celibacy for priests in the Western Church.

A member of the Salesians of Don Bosco, Stickler was successively professor of canon law, dean of the faculty of canon law, and rector of the Salesian University in Rome. Named cardinal in 1985, he served as archivist and librarian of the Church from then until his retirement in 1988. During his career, and even after he was raised to the cardinalate, he published a number of scholarly articles on the discipline of clerical celibacy.[3] A small volume that was published in English in 1995, *The Case*

---

[1] One of them is the emeritus pope, Benedict XVI, who used the occasion of a vigil service marking the end of the "Year of Priests" in Rome's St. Peter's Square on June 10, 2010, to defend the logic of priestly celibacy.

[2] Stickler was born on August 23, 1910.

[3] Many of these are cited in the bibliography given below. In addition to the studies cited in the bibliography, Stickler also published newspaper articles on the topic in *L'Osservatore Romano* (March 4, 1970) and *L'Osservatore della Domenica* (May 20, 1979).

for Clerical Celibacy: Its Historical Development and Theological Foundations,[4] represents the fruition of his study of the topic.

In this book and elsewhere, Stickler stresses the importance of using the tools of modern historiography in order to properly appreciate historical texts that speak about clerical celibacy, the development of what is often called clerical continence. The latter is the idea that ordained married men should forgo the sexual expression of their marriage. Stickler and other historians are right in affirming that ancient texts must be read in critical fashion if they are to be of use to us today as we try to understand the development of the Western ecclesiastical discipline of clerical celibacy.

Unfortunately, the historians of clerical celibacy apply the historical-critical method of studying ancient texts only to a point. That point lies somewhere after the texts of the New Testament were composed. These authors claim to embrace a rigorous historical methodology but they do not apply the methodology to the scriptural texts that they cite and examine. All too often they treat scriptural passages as if they were not also historical texts, subject to the vicissitudes of historical circumstances, whose true meaning can be discovered only if these Scriptures are likewise subject to the rigors of historical-critical examination.

It can be said of the work of these and other authors who use Scripture in their discourse about clerical celibacy that "the biblical quotations are not interpreted within the textual and historical contexts from which they are taken; rather, they are more or less used as isolated propositions and the biblical quotations are organized mainly according to dogmatic perspectives."[5]

An Appropriate Methodology

In the opening chapter of his book, devoted to "concept and method," Stickler rightly observes:

---

[4] Alfons Maria Stickler, *The Case for Clerical Celibacy: Its Historical Development and Theological Foundations* (San Francisco: Ignatius Press, 1995). The German original, *Der Klerikerzölibat: Seine Entwicklungsgeschichte und seine theologische Grundlagen*, was published in 1993 by the Kral Verlag in Abensberg, Germany.

[5] *The Biblical Foundations of the Doctrine of Justification: An Ecumenical Follow-Up to the* Joint Declaration on the Doctrine of Justification (Mahwah, NJ: Paulist, 2012), 3. The words are as applicable to the discussion of clerical celibacy as they are to the historical discussion of justification.

For a history of law, a knowledge of law and of its particular and proper methodology is also clearly fundamental.

Given this, we need to be conscious of the fact that the history of celibacy implies, with respect to its content and development, an understanding of both the law of the Church and of Catholic theology. Therefore, in establishing a correct hermeneutic of the relevant historical evidence (documents and facts), serious consideration must be paid to the method proper to both canon law and theology.[6]

This methodological observation is echoed in the course of the book. Accordingly, Stickler writes about "the rules of a sound historical-juridical methodology" and "a clear and precise scientific method."[7] His study devotes considerable attention to the historical context within which legislation pertaining to the discipline of celibacy[8] was promulgated, and he notes that "the glossators—of either the Roman or canon law—did not have the necessary critical approach for the study of the sources and the texts."[9]

Stefan Heid

Concern for a proper methodology in studying ancient texts on celibacy is also evident in the later study of Stefan Heid, *Celibacy in the Early Church: The Beginning of Obligatory Continence for Clerics in East and West.*[10] This German scholar does not devote a discreet section of his work to methodology, but he is nonetheless concerned with methodological issues.

For example, comparing texts of the third-century authors Tertullian and Hippolytus, and citing the importance of "methodological reasons," Heid observes: "The two texts must be treated separately. A critical reading

---

[6] Stickler, *Clerical Celibacy*, 15.

[7] Ibid., 41.

[8] See also Stickler, "The Evolution of the Discipline of Celibacy in the Western Church from the End of the Patristic Era to the Council of Trent," in *Priesthood and Celibacy*, ed. Joseph Coppens (Milan-Rome: Ancora, 1972), 503–97, 506–9, 585–88, etc.

[9] Ibid., 46; Cf. ibid., 98.

[10] Published in English by San Francisco's Ignatius Press in 2000, the German original appeared with the title *Zölibat in der frühen Kirche: Die Anfänge einer Enthaltsamkeitspflicht für Kleriker in Ost und West* (Paderborn, Germany: Ferdinand Schöningh GmbH, 1997).

will reveal, moreover, that they are to a great extent misleading on account of their polemical character."[11] Commenting on a passage in Tertullian's *Monogamy*,[12] Heid notes that "Tertullian is being polemical" and that some of his language is "merely rhetorical."[13]

Examining the writings of Cyprian on the topic of priestly celibacy, Heid notes that "Cyprian does not mince words."[14] Apropos what Cyprian wrote in the case of Fortunatianus,[15] Heid says that "Cyprian is not very reliable here. . . . This is generalizing, a rhetorical ploy."[16] With regard to a letter in which the third-century bishop of Carthage treated the case of Novatus,[17] Heid writes, "we are dealing with an unfounded allegation."[18] Taking issue with what he styles to be Peter Brown's slippery version of history,[19] Heid addresses the matter of Jerome's letter against Vigilantius, written in 404, which "is dated twenty years after the decretals of Siricius, and anyway, because of its blatantly polemical nature, it is to be enjoyed with the utmost caution."[20]

Emphasizing the importance of a critical method in studying ancient texts and further reflecting on the work of Jerome, Heid states:

> Of course, caution is required in regard to Jerome's statements. To be sure, his arguments were based on the writing of Vigilantius. But whether the latter really expressed therein his opinions about clerical continence is doubtful. Jerome, in any case, indicates that on this point he has the views of Vigilantius second-hand. That is already reason enough not to take Jerome simply at his word. Above all one must realize: Jerome actually wanted to give precisely this (false)

---

[11] Heid, *Celibacy in the Early Church*, 80.

[12] *De Monogamia* 12.3 (CC 2, 1247). The treatise was written ca. 217 CE.

[13] Heid, *Celibacy in the Early Church*, 81. Earlier, Jean-Paul Audet had cited Tertullian's "oratorical style." Cf. Jean-Paul Audet, *Mariage et célibat dans le service de l'Église: Histoire et orientations* (Paris: Éditions de l'Orante, 1967), 22.

[14] Heid, *Celibacy in the Early Church*, 139.

[15] *Epist.* 65.3 (FC 51, 128–30).

[16] Heid, *Celibacy in the Early Church*, 139–40.

[17] *Epist.* 52.2-3 (FC 51, 221–22).

[18] Heid, *Celibacy in the Early Church*, 140.

[19] In Peter Brown, *The Body and Society: Men, Women, and Sexual Renunciation in Early Christianity* (New York: Columbia University Press, 1988; republished in 2008 with a new introduction), 379–85. Heid's reference is to pages 364–68 of the German translation of this work, *Die Keuschheit der Engel: Sexuelle Entsagung, Askese und Körperlichkeit am Anfang des Christentums* (Munich-Vienna: Hanser, 1991).

[20] Heid, *Celibacy in the Early Church*, 247.

impression that hell had broken loose in Gaul. If historical criticism has any significance whatsoever, then it is to unmask such invective and to take literally texts that are handed down without first scrutinizing the way in which they present themselves. One should never make the mistake of further embellishing the exaggerations of the Scripture scholar from Bethlehem with one's own imaginings.[21]

In the conclusion to his work, Heid takes issue with those many scholars who hold that "a celibacy discipline arose from the fourth century on because, as a result of Constantine's Edict and the mass conversions to Christianity, pagan religious sentiments made their way into the Church and, with them, pagan notions of purity as well." He continues:

> Behind this there is the erroneous notion of a primitive Christian church of the elite, a biosphere completely closed off from its environment, teeming exclusively with Christians unaffected by the Jewish thought of late antiquity, where only later on the decadence of the masses broke in. But why should the Church suddenly in the fourth century fall victim to unchristian insinuations, when from the very beginning she stood in the midst of the Greco-Roman culture?[22]

Christian Cochini

Expressed concern for a proper methodology in the study of the history of ancient texts pertaining to the discipline of clerical celibacy and continence is also evident in some earlier studies on the topic. Stickler draws attention to three previous works[23] as being fundamental for the study of the history of clerical celibacy/continence. Among them is the

---

[21] Ibid., 270. Heid cites Edward Schillebeeckx as an example of someone who has done what he cautions against.

[22] Ibid., 335.

[23] Christian Cochini, *Apostolic Origins of Priestly Celibacy* (San Francisco: Ignatius Press, 1990); a 1969 doctoral thesis defended at the Institut catholique de Paris and then published as *Origines apostoliques du célibat sacerdotal* (Paris: Lethielleux, 1981); Filippo Liotta, *La Continenza di Chierici nel pensiero canonistico classico: da Graziano a Gregorio IX*, Quaderni di Studi Senesi 24 (Milan: Gioffrè, 1971); and Roman Cholij, *Clerical Celibacy in East and West* (Leominster, England: Fowler Right Books, 1988; 2nd ed., Leominster: Gracewing, 1990).

work of Christian Cochini.[24] Examining a passage in Eusebius' *Demonstration of the Gospel*, which begins with "It is fitting" (*prostēkei*),[25] Cochini observes: "It does not seem that in the mind of the *Demonstratio Evangelica's* author, the continence required from clerics be a corollary having, strictly speaking, force of law."[26] He then continues: "When we take a closer look, however, this manner of speaking seems to point to a certain obligation."[27] The closer look is based on what Cochini describes as "grammatical reasons." The study of the grammar of an ancient text, in its original language, is a basic element in any historical understanding of such texts.

The Hermeneutic of Historical Texts

The observations of these scholars are points well taken. A correct hermeneutic of historical documents is necessary if they are to be understood properly. That hermeneutic requires the interpretation of the texts within their individual historical contexts. Texts are not composed in "a biosphere completely closed off from its environment."[28] The culture within which ancient texts were written[29] is an important consideration, as is the date of their composition. Particular attention needs to be paid to the relative dating of the texts—that is, was a text under consideration

---

[24] Stickler lauds Cochini for "using a particular rigorous method" (Stickler, *Clerical Celibacy*, 20). He observes that in attempting "to reestablish the theory of the apostolic origin of celibacy, Cochini has appealed "to patristic, conciliar, and pontifical tradition" (ibid.), but there is no mention of Scripture.

Liotta's almost four-hundred-page study of the history of clerical celibacy during the century (1142–1241) that followed Lateran II's declaration of the nullity of marriage of clerics in major orders (1139) barely mentions the Scriptures. Apart from a reference to the *unius uxoris vir* clause in a letter of Pelagius I (bishop of Rome from 555 to 560) to the bishop of Florence (*Continenza di Chierici*, 14), Liotta makes incidental reference to 1 Corinthians 9:5 (ibid., 16, n. 38); 1 Corinthians 7:2 (ibid., 96–97); and Matthew 19:9 (ibid., 317–18). From Liotta's study it appears that Scripture played virtually no role in the canonical discussion of clerical celibacy in that crucial era.

Cholij's "Introductory Remarks on Methodology," in *Clerical Celibacy*, 69–71, promotes the argument of "cumulative evidence" but does not address the issue of the interpretation of particular texts.

[25] *Demonstration on the Gospel* 1.9 (PG 22, 82). The work was composed between 315 and 325.

[26] Cochini, *Priestly Celibacy*, 179.

[27] Ibid., 180.

[28] Heid, *Celibacy in the Early Church*, 270.

[29] Ibid.

written before, roughly at the same time as, or after another text being analyzed?[30] What are the historical circumstances within which individual texts were written?[31] Cochini warns against an anachronistic attitude in interpreting ancient texts.[32]

A correct hermeneutic also includes reflection on the language used in these texts; the denotation and connotations of words, along with any number of grammatical considerations, must be taken into account.[33] When is the language of ancient texts a generalization[34] or an exaggeration?[35] These are legitimate uses of language but *when* they come into play must be determined.

Due attention must also be paid to the literary genre of ancient texts. The language of law is one thing, the language of polemics another. Heid draws attention to Jerome's invective,[36] which engenders the obligation not to take these texts literally. He repeatedly mentions the polemical character of some of the texts that he studies.[37]

The historicity of events referenced in ancient texts is another factor to be weighed. Heid takes note of Cyprian's response to an unfounded allegation.[38] He, along with Cochini and Stickler, dismiss as "legend" the story of Paphnutius' intervention at the Council of Nicea (325),[39] a story that enjoyed a long day in the study of the history of the discipline of celibacy.

A Case in Point

The methodological observations of scholars such as Cochini, Stickler, and Heid point to elements that constitute the core of the historical-critical method of the study of ancient texts. Regrettably, as Stickler

[30] Ibid., 247.
[31] Cf. ibid., 80.
[32] Cf. Cochini, *Priestly Celibacy*, 43.
[33] Ibid., 180.
[34] Cf. Heid, *Celibacy in the Early Church*, 140.
[35] Ibid., 270.
[36] Ibid.
[37] Ibid., 80, 81, 247, 314.
[38] Ibid., 140.
[39] Ibid., 15–19, 297-305; Cochini, *Priestly Celibacy*, 24–26, 195–200; Stickler, *Clerical Celibacy*, 62–65. These authors also refer incidentally to the event as a legend. See also Stickler, "Evolution of the Discipline of Celibacy," 537, 541–42, and Cholij, *Clerical Celibacy*, 85–92, who provides the fullest account of the incident.

observes,[40] they were not available to the medieval glossators of texts of ancient Roman and early canon law. Authors from long ago did not have the advantage of the critical approach that is necessary for an accurate study of the sources and the texts. The early sources had not yet developed a method for the study of legal texts. Thus, the *Decretals of Gratian*,[41] so important for the history of canon law, uncritically accepted as fact the story of Paphnutius' intervention at Nicea and canon 13 of the Second Council of Trullo (Quinisext), which convened in Constantinople in 691 during the reign of Justinian III.

Canon 13 of Trullo II[42] is a forthright rejection of the practice of sexual continence within marriage for married priests and deacons: If someone is deemed worthy to be ordained subdeacon, deacon, or priest, it should not "be demanded that he promise at the time of his ordination to abstain from legitimate relations with his own wife; for otherwise he would insult marriage which was instituted by God and blessed by his presence."[43] In support of its legislation, canon 13 of Trullo II makes the claim that this is in conformity with "the ancient rule of strict observation and apostolic discipline." The framers of this canon claimed the support of "the Fathers gathered at Carthage" and the fifth apostolic canon.[44]

Subject to the rigorism of contemporary historical criticism, their claim is patently false. Trullo II misquoted the Council of Carthage. Cholij says that canon 13 cannot be connected with any earlier laws" and that "it does not fit in with the overall concept of the Trullan legislation."[45] Stickler speaks of the manipulation of texts and of changing the original

---

[40] Stickler, *Clerical Celibacy*, 46–47.

[41] Gratian's *Concordia discordantium canonum*, the oldest collection of canonical texts in the millennium, appeared in Bologna ca. 1142.

[42] The text of the canon can be found in English in Cochini, *Priestly Celibacy*, 405, and in both Greek and Latin in Cholij, *Clerical Celibacy*, 208–9.

[43] Canon 13 supports this legislation with harsh penalties. If a priest or deacon dismisses his wife, he is to be excommunicated. If anyone requires that a subdeacon, deacon, or priest renounce marital relations, he is to be deposed. The canon, nevertheless, maintains the practice of a cleric's sexual abstinence when he is assigned to liturgical practice.

[44] On this canon, ca. 375, see Roger Gryson, *Les Origines du célibat ecclésiastique du premier au septième siècle: Recherches et synthèses*, Section d'histoire 2 (Gembloux: Duculot, 1970), 101; Cholij, *Clerical Celibacy*, 98–99; Heid, *Celibacy in the Early Church*, 181–83.

[45] Heid *Celibacy in the Early Church*, 311, summarizing Cholij's study of the legislation.

sense of the texts.[46] Heid speaks about the juxtaposition, abbreviation, and combination of texts "in such a way that the result is exactly the opposite of what they originally asserted."[47] The canon was drafted in opposition to the Western discipline in regard to clerical celibacy. Heid rightly regards it as a polemic against the West and speaks of its "anti-Roman tongue-lashing"[48] and ultimately dismisses its significance as "one, single, little point—which is nonetheless momentous"[49]

The historical overview of the discipline of clerical celibacy reveals that it is really a history of a discipline of clerical continence whose by-product was the discipline of clerical celibacy as it is generally understood today—namely, the renunciation of marriage and with that a concomitant life of abstinence from sexual union and the procreation of children. In any case, the history of the discipline of clerical celibacy cannot be written on a straight line. A broad outline, over the course of more than a millennium, would be as follows: a ban on remarriage after the death of one's spouse, the prohibition of marriage by celibate clerics, the requirement that married clergy live in sexual continence, and the declaration that marriage of clerics is null and void.[50] According to Stickler, "The real meaning of celibacy . . . which in the first millennium and beyond was well known consists in this: complete abstinence with respect to the procreation of children even within the context of marriage."[51]

The actual prohibition of marriage generally remained in the background during the first millennium.[52] For the most part, ordination to the diaconate and priesthood[53] was conferred upon married men who

---

[46] Cf. Stickler, *Clerical Celibacy*, 75–77.

[47] Heid, *Celibacy in the Early Church*, 313.

[48] Ibid., 314.

[49] Ibid., 315. The discipline promulgated by canon 13 of Trullo II continues to be an important element in the ecclesiastical discipline of the East; see Cholij, *Clerical Celibacy*, 161–94.

[50] See Henri Crouzel, "Celibacy and Ecclesiastical Continence in the Early Church: The Motives Involved," in Coppens, *Priesthood and Celibacy*, 451–502, at 452.

[51] Stickler, *Clerical Celibacy*, 12–13. He also states (ibid., 12) that the first obligation of celibacy is "the commitment to continence in the use of marriage after ordination."

[52] Indeed Audet notes that until the final decades of the third century it was marriage, rather than continence or celibacy, that appeared to be the dominant reality in the pastoral service of the church. Cf. Audet, *Mariage et célibat*, 26.

[53] For purposes of this study, there is no need to enter into a discussion of subdeacons and those in lesser orders.

had already raised a family. Only later did the Church impose the prohibition of marriage on those celibates from whom virtually all candidates for sacred orders were exclusively recruited.[54]

In the beginning and generally throughout the first millennium, it was men who had experienced life, the so-called *viri probati*, who were called to orders,[55] sometimes against their will. Men married at a relatively young age. At a still relatively young age—at least by today's standards—they had fulfilled their essential responsibilities as spouses[56] and fathers. Thereafter, they could be ordained to the diaconate and priesthood. Accordingly, the Ecclesiastical Canons of the Holy Apostles (ca. 300) called only for married priests who were already "elderly."[57] Canon 11 of the Council of Neocaesarea (ca. 314–25) stipulated that no one was to be ordained before the age of thirty. Siricius, bishop of Rome from 384 to 399, identified thirty as the age for the ordination to the diaconate, thirty-five for priesthood, and forty-five for the episcopacy.[58] In 546, the Code of Justinian noted that priests should be at least thirty-five years of age.[59]

Scriptural Basis for the Practice of Clerical Continence

As was customary at the time, the Fathers of the Church and the early decretalists found support for the practice of clerical continence in Scripture.

---

[54] Cf. Stickler, *Clerical Celibacy*, 13.

[55] Cf. Heid, *Celibacy in the Early Church*, 323–25.

[56] The history of the spouses of the ordained is complex. The literature of the first millennium includes many references to women, the *virgines subintroductae*, who were allowed to live in the home of a priest. Some wives lived with their husbands in continence (cf. Leo the Great's response, ca. 458, to the third question posed by Bishop Rusticus of Narbonne (*Epist. Ad Rusticum Narbonensem episcopum, Inquis. III. Resp* [PL 54, 1204]); others went to the monastery. The fifth *Apostolic Canon*, cited by Trullo II, says that a bishop, priest, or deacon is to be excommunicated if he sends his wife away. On the other hand, referencing Ambrose, Heid writes, "Many a woman, too, occasionally found that it was a gift from God to be free at last as a result of her husband's ordination" (*Celibacy in the Early Church*, 324; cf. Ambrose, *De exhortatione virginibus* 3–4, 24 [PL 162, 358c]).

[57] *Constitutio ecclesiastica apostolorum* 18, 2. This and the following references are provided by Heid, *Celibacy in the Early Church*, 324.

[58] *Epist.* I, 9, 13 *ad Himerium* (PL 13, 1143a).

[59] *Codex Justinianus*, Novel 123, 11.

Unius uxoris vir

Given that the dominant practice was the choice of married men who had already raised their families, it is to be expected that among the texts most frequently cited are those that speak of the "husband of one wife," the famous *unius uxoris vir* in the Latin translation of 1 Timothy 3:2, 12 and Titus 1:6. In his overview, Stickler says, "Saint Paul, in writing to his disciples Titus and Timothy, prescribed that such candidates could be married only once."[60] Later canonical tradition held that the pope could not dispense from the prohibition of a second marriage because he could not dispense *contra apostolum*—that is, he could not act contrary to the Scripture.[61]

The *Wirkungsgeschichte*, the history of the interpretation of the *unius uxoris vir* passages, at least in documents pertaining to the discipline of clerical continence, consistently reflects the view that the apostolic prescription was formulated "because one must fear incontinence," *propter continentiam futuram*, in the words of Pope Siricius.[62] A second marriage was taken to be a sign of incontinence.[63] Among many possible witnesses to this interpretation of the scriptural passage, Stickler cites not only Siricius but also Pope Innocent I (401–17), the *Glossa Ordinaria* on the Decretals of Gratian, and the thirteenth-century decretalist Henry of Susa's (Hostiensis) commentary on the *Decretals* of Gregory IX.[64]

Commenting on Eusebius' *Demonstration of the Gospel*,[65] Stickler notes that according to this early Church historian, "the sense of the *unius uxoris vir* consists in this, that is, that those who have been consecrated and dedicated to the service of the divine cult must therefore properly abstain from sexual relations with their wives."[66] Other patristic authors

---

[60] Stickler, *Clerical Celibacy*, 12. Heid says that the prescription was an unequivocal order from Paul that simply cannot be evaded: clerics should be married only once (*Celibacy in the Early Church*, 83).

[61] Cf. Stickler, *Clerical Celibacy*, 92–93.

[62] See *Cor in unum* (PL 13, 1160).

[63] There was, however, a discussion with regard to marriages contracted before baptism.

[64] Cf. Stickler, *Clerical Celibacy*, 91–92.

[65] Specifically in reference to *Dem. ev.* 1.9 (PG 22, 82).

[66] Stickler, *Clerical Celibacy*, 92.

hold similar opinions, for example, Ambrose in the West[67] and John Chrysostom in the East, at least with regard to bishops.[68]

1 Corinthians 7

During the course of the centuries, other biblical texts, especially texts found in the New Testament, were introduced into the discussion on clerical celibacy[69] and priestly continence. One of the texts quoted most often was 1 Corinthians 7:5. Apropos this text, Pope Siricius'[70] decretal *Cor in unum* (386), a synodal text,[71] states: "Paul writing to the Corinthians, says, 'Abstain from one another so as to be free for prayer' (1 Cor 7:5). If continence is commanded for lay people so that their prayers may be heard, how much more must the priest be ready at any moment, in perfect purity and confidence, to offer sacrifice or to baptize."[72] Using a similar *a fortiori* argument, the Ambrosiaster's *Questions on the Old and New Testament*[73] affirms, "This is why the Apostle tells married couples that they should agree to abstain for a while from relations so as to free themselves for prayer (1 Cor 7:5)."[74] The Ambrosiaster echoes the predominant first-millennium interpretation of 1 Corinthians 7:5—namely, that the passage prescribed that married couples should abstain from sexual union in order to devote themselves to prayer.

In addition to the idea that 1 Corinthians 7:5 imposed a mandatory obligation for all married couples, an important issue in the interpretation of the text was the meaning of the apostle's "for a while." Heid

---

[67] Cf. Ambrose's letter to the church at Vercelli (*Epist.* 63, 62–63 [PL 16, 1257a]).

[68] See John Chrysostom's homiletic remarks on 1 Timothy 3:2 (*In epist. I ad Tim.* III, X 1–2 [PG 62, 549a]).

[69] In a chapter titled "Methodological Precisions," Cochini writes, "celibacy in the early Church, was understood as a prohibition to marry (or to remarry) *after* the reception of major Orders." *Priestly Celibacy*, 180; his emphasis.

[70] Siricius' decretal, written to Bishop Himerius of Tarragona in 385, was the first decree on clerical celibacy.

[71] See Heid, *Celibacy in the Early Church*, 241.

[72] Heid's translation. Cf. PL 13, 1160.

[73] The name of the author of this text is unknown. For centuries, that is, until the time of the work of Erasmus, his writings were assumed to have been written by Ambrose of Milan. Hence, the unknown author is known as Pseudo-Ambrose or the Ambrosiaster. His commentaries appear to have been written between 380 and 384.

[74] *Questions on the Old and New Testament*, 127, 35 (CSEL 50, 414–15 pp.; PL 35, 2213–386). See also, *Comm. In 1 Tim.* 3:12–13 (CSEL 81, 3 268, 17–270 2).

responds: "This is not to be understood as a few days but rather in terms of weeks and months that accompanied prolonged fasting"[75]

Two other Pauline passages of some importance in the discussion on clerical continence are also found in the seventh chapter of Paul's First Letter to the Corinthians. These are 1 Corinthians 7:7, "I wish that all were as I myself am"[76] and 1 Corinthians 7:29, "Let even those who have wives be as though they had none." Innocent I references 1 Corinthians 7:7 in a February 20, 405, letter to Exupery of Toulouse on the subject of deacons and priests who have not kept the disciple of clerical continence.[77] Canon 25 of the Seventeenth Council of Carthage (419) cites Aurelius, the bishop of Carthage and president of the council, as referencing 1 Corinthians 7:29 in support of the sexual continence of deacons, bishops, and priests,[78] while Leo the Great's Letter to Anastasius of Thessaloniki (ca. 446) argues that 1 Corinthians 7:29 applies to subdeacons and, *a fortiori*, to bishops, priests, and deacons.[79]

A few years later, the First Council of Tours (461) stated, "If the faithful are advised to observe chastity, according to the doctrine of the Apostle, 'so that those who have a wife be as if they did not have one,' how much more the priests of God and deacons, attached to the service of the divine altar must practice it."[80] For his part, John Chrysostom reiterated the opinion that the injunction of 1 Corinthians 7:29 applies to bishops who were not freed from ties to their wives.[81] A closely related passage that Chrysostom brought into his discussion of bishops was 1 Corinthians 7:32-33 about being free from anxieties, a passage in which the apostle cites the married man as someone who is anxious to please his wife.[82]

---

[75] Heid, *Celibacy in the Early Church*, 322.

[76] For purposes of easy reference, the English translation of scriptural passages is that of the NRSV. This translation/interpretation is not always consistent with that found in various patristic writings. When patristic and canonical writings cite the Scripture, the translation of Scripture in this study will be that found in the published translations of the ancient texts.

[77] Cf. *Epist. Ad Exuperium episcopum Tolosanum* I, 2 (PL 20, 496–98).

[78] Cf. Cochini, *Priestly Celibacy*, 285; Stickler, *Clerical Celibacy*, 27.

[79] Cf. *Epist. ad Anastasium Thessalonicensem episcopum* IV (PL 54, 672–73).

[80] CC 1478, 143.

[81] *In epist. I ad Timotheum*, III, homily X, 1–2 (PG 62, 649). Cf. Cochini, *Priestly Celibacy*, 292, 420.

[82] Cf. *In epist. I ad Timotheum*, III, homily X, 1–2 (PG 62, 547–50); see also Isidore of Seville, *De ecclesiasticis officiis* 2.9.11; 10.2, 20; 3.10.13; 1, 18, 9–10 (PL 83, 790b, 790c–791a, 810a, 812b, 813c–814a, 765b–757a).

1 Corinthians 9:5

Yet another passage from 1 Corinthians that entered into the discussion of clerical continence was 1 Corinthians 9:5, "Do we not have the right to be accompanied by a believing wife, as do the other apostles and the brothers of the Lord and Cephas?" Responding to Jovian, Jerome wrote in regard to this verse, "The Apostle was talking about the other holy women who, according to Judaic custom, assisted their masters with their goods. . . . It is clear that [they] must not be seen as wives but, as we have said, as women who assisted them with their goods."[83] Augustine interprets Paul in similar fashion,[84] but Severian, bishop of Gabala, suggested in his commentary on the letter that the female traveling companion, "whether she was a wife or not," was a woman who desired instruction from the apostle.[85] Relating the accompanying women to the ministry of Paul, but in a fashion different from that suggested by Jerome, was Clement of Alexandria, who saw these women as fellow ministers of the Gospel "to the [other] women of the household, so that the gospel would reach them without causing a scandal."[86]

In a similar vein, Bishop Isidore of Pelusium wrote to the deacon Isidore (ca. 435) that if women accompanied the apostles, "it was not in order to procreate children or to lead with them a common life but, in truth to assist them with their goods, to take care of feeding the heralds of poverty." And if Paul called them sister-women, *adelphoi gynaikes* in Greek, it was "because by the word *sister* he wanted to show that they were chaste, while describing their nature with the word *women*."[87]

Commenting on such passages, Cochini writes:

> There is . . . a consensus among the Fathers about the interpretation of the Pauline passage relative to *adelphoi gynaikes*. This would not mean, in their minds, women with whom the apostles went on living a conjugal life, but persons of the feminine sex who were attached

[83] Jerome, *Adversus Jovinianum* I, 26 (PL 23, 245). The text dates to 393. Cf. David G. Hunter, *Marriage, Celibacy, and Heresy in Ancient Christianity: The Jovinianist Controversy*, Oxford Early Christian Studies (Oxford: Oxford University Press, 2007), 15–50.

[84] See *The Work of Monks* 2, 10 (FC 16, 338, 341).

[85] *Homilies on 1 Corinthians* (PG 65). Cf. Judith L. Kovacs, *1 Corinthians Interpreted by Early Christian Commentators*, The Church's Bible (Grand Rapids, MN: Eerdmans, 2005), 146–47.

[86] *Miscellanies* III.53.3 (FC 85, 289).

[87] *Epist.* III, 176 (PG 78, 865d–868c); *Adversus Jovinianum* I, 26 (PL 23, 246).

to their service for the needs of the ministry. In the case where one of these women was indeed the wife of an apostle, it is to be understood that she then lived with her husband "as a sister."[88]

Stickler makes reference to three texts in the Synoptic Gospels—namely, Matthew 19:12 and Luke 18:29 and 14:26 as indicating the context, "especially in its significance for ecclesiastical celibacy"—within which Paul's words on the relationship of the unmarried to God are to be understood.[89] Arguing with Heinz-Jürgen Vogels's interpretation of Matthew 19:11-12, Heid discusses the charismatic nature of clerical continence within the context of a discipline of obligatory continence.[90]

Married Apostles?

A related issue was whether or not the apostles were married. In this regard, Tertullian claimed, "Peter is the only one I found to have been married because of his mother-in-law. . . . The others, whom I did not find to be married, were perforce either celibate [eunuchs] or continent."[91] Two centuries later, Jerome wrote a letter in which he said, "The Apostles were either virgins or married."[92] Certainly one of the better students of the Scripture during the patristic era, Jerome affirms that the only apostle whom Scripture affirms to have been married is Simon Peter.[93] The affirmation is based on the fact that Matthew, Mark, and Luke concur in stating that Peter had a mother-in-law whom Jesus healed.[94]

There was, however, another tradition on the subject of the marriage of the apostles. Notwithstanding the absence of any supporting evidence, the Ambrosiaster affirmed, "All the apostles, with the exception of John

---

[88] Cochini, *Priestly Celibacy*, 81.

[89] Cf. Stickler, *Clerical Celibacy*, 98.

[90] See Heid, *Celibacy in the Early Church*, 327–31. Cf. Heinz-Jürgen Vogels, *Priester dürfen heiraten: Biblische, geschichtliche und rechtliche Gründe gegen den Pflichtzölibat* (Bonn: Köllen, 1992), 23–36.

[91] *Monogamy* 8, 4 (CC 2, 1239). Tertullian was referring to what he found or did not find in Scripture. In regard to this passage, Audet remarks that Tertullian was writing from his Montanist perspective. Cf. Audet, *Mariage et célibat*, 70.

[92] *Epist.* 49.21.3 (CSEL 54, 386, 20–37, 1).

[93] *Epist.* 118, 4.

[94] Cf. Mark 1:30-31; Matt 9:14-15; Luke 4:38-39.

and Paul were married."[95] Two second-century bishops, Papias of Hieropolis toward the beginning of the century and Polycratus of Ephesus toward the end of the century, affirm that the apostle Philip was married and had a number of daughters.[96] In the early third century, Clement of Alexandria says that both Philip and Peter had children.[97] In the fourth century Ambrose affirmed that the brothers Peter and Andrew had married a pair of sisters.[98] In the same century, the Cappadocian Basil of Caesarea said that all the apostles were married.[99] In the early fifth century, Epiphanius suggests that because Peter, Andrew, Matthew, and Bartholomew were married, the unmarried John was entrusted with care of the mother of Jesus.[100] Eusebius of Caesarea and Augustine of Hippo concur in using Psalm 109:9 to infer that Judas Iscariot was married and had children.[101]

As for the possibility that Paul, an apostle[102] though not one of the Twelve, was married, almost from the very beginning different ideas were held by various Church Fathers. Origen suggests that there were two possibilities, one that Paul was married and one that he was not.[103] Methodius of Olympus,[104] in the third-century East, and Ambrose,[105] in the fourth-century West, using 1 Corinthians 7:7-8, thought that Paul was a widower. Clement of Alexandria had previously expressed the

---

[95] *In epist. B. Pauli ad Corinthios secundam* XI, 2 (PL 17, 320).

[96] Cf. Eusebius, *Ecclesiastical History* III, 39, 8–9 (for Papias); III. 31, 2–3 (for Polycratus).

[97] Cf. *Miscellanies* III.6.52–53. He is quoted by Eusebius in *Eccl. Hist.* III, 30, 1.

[98] Cf. *Expositio evangelii secundum Lucam*, 4 (CC 14, 128).

[99] *De renunciatione saeculi*, 1 (PG 31, 628).

[100] Cf. *Refutation of All Heresies*, 78, 10 (PG 42, 714).

[101] Cf. Eusebius, *Dem. ev.*, 10 (PG 22, 740); Augustine, *Ennarations on the Psalms*, 108, 11 (CC 40, 1590).

[102] Paul first uses the designation of himself in 1 Thessalonians 2:7. Later, it will be the title that he ascribes to himself in writing his Letter to the Romans, his first and second Letters to the Corinthians, and the Letter to the Galatians. Cf. Eph 1:1; Col 1:1; 1 Tim 1:1; 2 Tim 1:1; Titus 1:1.

[103] *Comm. on Rom 1*, 1 (PG 14: 839bcd). Interpreting 1 Corinthians 7:8, placing Paul among the *agamoi*, rather than among those who espoused virginity, Origen seems to suggest that Paul would have been married at one time in his life. Cf. Claude Jenkins, "Origen on I Corinthians, III," *JTS* 9 (1908): 500–514, esp. 504. Gryson (*Origines*, 18, n. 6) interprets this to mean that Paul separated from his wife.

[104] *Symposium* XII, 82–83 (PG 18, 80).

[105] *Virginity* 18 (PL 16, 315; cf. Cochini, *Priestly Celibacy*, 76).

opinion that Paul was married.[106] He thought that, because of his itinerant ministry, Paul did not take his wife along with him on his travels.[107] Clement based his ideas on the apostle's reference to a person identified as his loyal companion (*gnēsie syzyge*) in Philippians 4:3. Paul's *syzyge* is the vocative form of the Greek adjective *syzygos*, which means "yoked together." Paul uses the word as a noun[108]—a substantivized adjective—with the (literal) meaning of "yoke mate," someone with whom a person (or animal) is "yoked together." In Greek, the substantivized adjective was occasionally used to speak about a wife; used in this sense, the term was basically a rich metaphor.

Subsequently both John Chrysostom and Theodoret of Chyrrus, in their respective exegetical works on Paul's Letter to the Philippians,[109] rejected Clement's interpretation of "Syzyge." They must be counted alongside of Jerome who, in no uncertain terms, states that Paul was not married. Citing three key passages from 1 Corinthians 7:7; 7:9; and 9:5-6, Jerome writes that we should pay no heed to those who claim that Paul had a wife, "because when he writes about continence and advises perpetual chastity, he argues from his own case."[110]

With regard to the marital status of the Twelve, two passages from the Synoptic Gospels are frequently cited in the literature.[111] These are the words of Peter in Matthew 19:27, "We have left everything and followed you," and the words of Jesus from Luke 18:28-30: "Then Peter said, 'Look, we have left our homes and followed you.' And he [Jesus] said to them, 'Truly I tell you, there is no one who has left house or wife or brothers or parents or children, for the sake of the kingdom of God, who will not get back very much more in this age, and in the age to come eternal life.'" These words are cited to support the idea that the apostles abandoned

---

[106] Cf. *Miscellanies* III, 6 (GCS 52, 220). See also Eusebius who references Clement in *Eccl. Hist.* III, 30, 2.

[107] Cf. 1 Cor 9:5-6.

[108] The word could be treated as a proper noun and transcribed as Syzyge.

[109] John Chrysostom, *In epist. ad Philippenses argumentum et homiliae* 1–15, 13, 3 (PG 62, 279); Theodoret, *Commentary on the Epistle to the Philippians* 4, 3 (PG 82, 585). Cf. Theodore of Mopsuestia, in Henry Barclay Swete, *Theodori episcopi mopsuesteni: In epistolas B. Pauli commentarii*, 1 (Cambridge: Cambridge University Press, 1880), 245–46.

[110] *Epist.* 20, the *Letter to Eustachium*, 22, 20 (CSEL 54, 170–71); see also *Adversus Jovanianum* I, 34 (PL 23, 258).

[111] Cf. Stickler, "Tratti salienti nella storia del celibato," *Sacra Doctrina* 60 (1970): 585–620, esp. 587; Cochini, *Priestly Celibacy*, 43, 82–83.

their wives and embraced a life of sexual continence after they were called to discipleship. Augustine, for example, uses Matthew 19:27 in his interpretation of 1 Corinthians 7:29.[112]

A Methodology for Studying Scriptural Texts

In their interpretation of the scriptural texts cited in the discussion of clerical continence, the writings of the Fathers are generally devoid of the kinds of considerations that contemporary biblical scholars, with their historical-critical methodology, bring to bear on these texts.[113] One notable exception is John Chrysostom who brings considerations of literary genre and the circumstances of composition to bear on the interpretation of 1 Timothy 3:2, with its *unius uxoris vir* passage that figured so strongly in the development of the discipline of clerical continence.

With regard to the nature of the text, Chrysostom writes: "He [Paul] does not say this as a law, as though it were the only thing allowed, but rather he restrains immoderation thereby. It was in fact permitted to the Jews to marry a second time and to have two wives at the same time."[114] In this passage, the bishop of Constantinople draws attention to one element in the historical situation of the passage, namely, the traditional allowance of a second marriage in the Jewish tradition. Later in his commentary on the same epistle, he observes that it was appropriate to ordain married men since it was incumbent upon Paul to fill episcopal sees.[115] Surprisingly, Jerome concurred with this opinion.[116] Jerome also interprets 1 Timothy 3:2 in the context of Jewish practice, even, says Jerome, "among priests."[117]

---

[112] Cf. *Sermon* 161.11 (PL 38, 884).

[113] One of the few scholars who recognized this deficiency in texts dealing with clerical celibacy was Henri Crouzel. Crouzel writes: "The Early Church understood its Scripture texts in the light of its contemporary culture. It is this that has sometimes caused the Fathers to falsify the sense of certain passages, or to add to the motives furnished by the gospels and epistles regarding virginity certain others supplied by the ritual continence of Graeco-Roman cults and by Stoic and neo-Platonic Philosophy." See Crouzel, "Celibacy and Ecclesiastical Continence in the Early Church: The Motives Involved," in Coppens, *Priesthood and Celibacy*, 451–502, esp. 452.

[114] *Hom.* 10, 1 in 1 Tim 3:1-4 (PG 62, 547).

[115] Ibid. (PG 62, 550).

[116] See *Adversus Jovinianum* I, 26 (PL 232, 268b).

[117] See *Epist.* 69, 5, 1–2 (CSEL 54, 686, 18–687, 5).

While few are the patristic authors who try to elucidate the historical circumstances of the scriptural texts, most of them take the texts out of their literary contexts, citing only the words that they want to use. Augustine and the Ambrosiaster,[118] most likely close contemporaries and both influenced by Ambrose, are among the few fathers who cite more than the words "let even those who have wives be as those who had none" from 1 Corinthians 7:29. The verse begins "I mean, brothers and sisters, the appointed time has grown short." Augustine and Ambrose cite the introductory words but other patristic authors typically omit Paul's reference to the impending eschaton in their use of the verse. The Fathers generally use the scriptural texts in proof text fashion. Paul's reference to a specific historico-theological context, indicated by the words, "the appointed time has grown short," is conveniently omitted from the use of the verse in the discussion on clerical celibacy.

If it can be said that the medieval glossators on canonical texts did not have the necessary critical approach for the study of the sources and the texts,[119] *a fortiori* ought it to be said that the glossators and the authors of the patristic and canonical texts cited in the study of the history of the discipline of clerical celibacy/continence did not possess a critical approach to the scriptural texts that they cite. This is not surprising. The historical-critical approach to the Scriptures had not yet been developed when they wrote. What is surprising, however, is that the historians of the discipline of clerical celibacy/continence do not apply to the interpretation of the passages of Sacred Scripture the same critical methods that they use in their interpretation of patristic and canonical texts.

A Necessary Methodology

The use of a historical-critical method is, however, as necessary for the interpretation of Scripture as it is for the interpretation of later historical texts. An important document of the Pontifical Biblical Commission, whose preface was written by Cardinal Joseph Ratzinger, then-prefect of the Congregation for the Doctrine of the Faith and later Pope Benedict XVI, says:

---

[118] On Augustine, Ambrosiaster, *In epist. B. Pauli ad Corinthios primam* (CSEL 81.3.83–84).

[119] Stickler, *Clerical Celibacy*, 46; cf. ibid., 98.

> The literal sense of Scripture is that which has been expressed directly by the inspired human authors. Since it is the fruit of inspiration, this sense is also intended by God, as principal author. One arrives at this sense by means of a careful analysis of the text, within its literary and historical context. The principal task of exegesis is to carry out this analysis, making use of all the resources of literary and historical research, with a view to defining the literal sense of the biblical texts with the greatest possible accuracy.[120]

In accordance with this hermeneutical principle, *The Interpretation of the Bible in the Church*, presented to Pope John Paul II in April 1993, and published in late November 1993, affirmed:

> The historical-critical method is the indispensable method for the scientific study of the meaning of ancient texts. Holy Scripture, inasmuch as it is the "word of God in human language," has been composed by human authors in all its various parts and in all the sources that lie behind them. Because of this, its proper understanding not only admits the use of this method but *actually requires it*.[121]

The historical-critical method of the interpretation of Scripture "studies the biblical text in the same fashion as it would study any other ancient text and comments upon it as an expression of human discourse."[122] The historical-critical method begins with the establishment of the text itself, the work of textual criticism. Along the same lines, historians of the discipline of clerical celibacy/continence draw attention to the fact that some ancient texts exist only in fragmentary form, only insofar as they have been quoted, or, sometimes, only in translation.

A second step in the use of the historical-critical method of interpretation focuses on the language of the text under consideration. The text must be "submitted to a linguistic (morphology and syntax) and semantic analysis, using the language derived from historical philology."[123] A whole range of philological and grammatical issues, such as those

---

[120] *The Interpretation of the Bible in the Church* II.B.1, published in *Origins* 23 (1994) 497, 499–524, 512.

[121] My emphasis. Cf. ibid. I.A, *Origins* 23, 500.

[122] Ibid. I.A.2, *Origins* 23, 501.

[123] Ibid. I.A.3, *Origins* 23, 501.

raised by Cochini in his interpretation of Eusebius' *Demonstration of the Gospel*,[124] must be taken into consideration.

A third step is genre criticism that seeks "to identify literary genres, the social milieu that gave rise to them, their particular features and the history of their development."[125] This is the matter of how the texts present themselves. Thus, the historians of the celibacy/continence discipline distinguish between patristic writings and canonical texts. They distinguish letters from decretals. They note that some texts are written in response to another text of a given situation, even if that should be an unfounded allegation. These kinds of distinctions pertain to the macro-genre of ancient texts (the genre of an entire composition or major part thereof), but there are also considerations of what might be called the *micro-genre*, which come into play in the interpretation of ancient texts. Historians of patristic and canonical text note the presence of invective and generalization in the texts that they study. They note the hortatory nature of some texts while other passages seem to have the force of law.

The proper understanding of a text, ancient or modern, requires an identification of the text as a whole but it also requires the identification of the literary form of the component parts of the text.[126] This is of major importance in the interpretation of Pauline texts, such as those quoted in the long history of the discipline of clerical celibacy/continence. All of them appear in documents that have the form of a letter. Their opening words are similar in form to the opening words of Hellenistic letters, with the identification of the sender, followed by the identification of the recipient, and a stereotyped greeting. In Paul's letters, each of these elements is given a decidedly Christian cast. In this form they are found at the beginning of Paul's writings in such a way that the texts are readily identified as letters.

Paul's letters end with closing conventions, again similar to those found in Hellenistic letters but likewise expressed in typical Christian language and expressing thoughts that are part of the Christian message. Between the opening conventions and the closing conventions comes the body of the letter, generally beginning with a thanksgiving that takes

---

[124] Cf. Cochini, *Priestly Celibacy*, 180.

[125] *The Interpretation of the Bible in the Church* II.A.3, *Origins* 23, 501. Cf. Vatican Council II, *Dei Verbum*, 12.

[126] Cf. Raymond F. Collins, *Introduction to the New Testament* (New York: Doubleday / London: SCM, 1983), 156–95.

the place of the health wish more commonly found in Hellenistic letters.[127]

The proper understanding of any one of Paul's letters requires that due attention be paid to the genre, that is, the micro-genre, of the individual parts of the letter. Paul's letters not only include thanksgivings but also confessional material, hortatory material, apocalyptical material, catalogues of virtues and vices, and so forth. Merely to say that what Paul writes is a letter is not enough for the proper interpretation of any one of his missives.

Epistolary Criticism

Paul's missives have the literary form of a letter and must be understood as letters. In recent years, biblical scholars—especially Pauline scholars—have studied Paul's letters from the vantage point of what is known as epistolary criticism. There is an interrelationship between the form and function of any text. What does an author's use of any given literary form intend to do? What is the function of a letter? What does it mean that Paul has written letters? How do his letters function?

First of all, letters are essentially one-time compositions. They are *ad hoc* documents. Letters are written to their recipients in a particular set of circumstances. It is true that all literary compositions are circumstantial but this is particularly true of letters. The circumstances at hand dictate the contents of a letter. The circumstance of the death of a friend or acquaintance is an integral part of the function of a letter of sympathy. Circumstances dictate what is said and what is not said; they also dictate *how* things are said.

When commentators write about the circumstances in which letters are written, they are generally concerned with the particular circumstances that gave rise to a given letter. That should not and generally does not mean that a commentator can overlook the broader political, social, and religious circumstances in which a letter is written. Paul's letters were written in the Greco-Roman culture of his time—that is, the culture was Hellenistic, the political power Roman. Moreover, the interpreter of Paul's letters must take into consideration the fact that Paul

---

[127] Cf. Raymond F. Collins, "A Significant Decade: The Trajectory of the Hellenistic Epistolary Thanksgiving," in *Paul and the Ancient Letter Form*, ed. Stanley E. Porter and Sean A. Adams, Pauline Studies (Past) 6 (Leiden: Brill, 2010), 159–84.

himself was bicultural. He was a Hebrew and a Hellenist. His letters were written to churches that were for the most part Hellenistic but also contained a number of Jewish Christians.

An important element regarding the issue of the circumstances in which an ancient letter was written is an issue that has sometimes been overlooked, though hardly so in recent studies of the Pauline corpus. This issue is that of the authenticity of ancient letters. Were they really written by the person whose name they bear? Many readers of the Pauline letters uncritically assume, as did the Fathers of the Church and the decretalists, that the apostle himself wrote all of the letters in the New Testament that bear his name.

However, the phenomenon of pseudepigraphy, writing something in the name of someone else, was not unknown in antiquity. Indeed, Tertullian of Carthage (ca. 160–225 CE) wrote, "It is allowable that that which disciples publish should be regarded as their master's work."[128] In the secular sphere, Porphyry, a third-century CE Neoplatonic philosopher and logician, examined the large body of works attributed to Pythagoras, the sixth-century BCE mathematician and philosopher who founded the Pythagorean religion. Porphyry distinguished Pythagoras' works from those that had been forged. Of the two hundred eighty authentic works, Porphyry claims that eighty came from Pythagoras himself. Rhetoricians such as Cicero[129] and philosophers such as Plato[130] espoused the idea of the noble falsehood. The latter considered deception to be a useful and human means of communicating.

Since God speaks to human beings in human fashion in the inspired Scripture, the interpreter of Paul's letters may not assume that they were written by Paul just because they bear his name. The possibility of pseudepigraphy must be taken into consideration.[131]

---

[128] Tertullian, *Against Marcion*, IV. 5 (PL 2, 567).

[129] Cf. Cicero, *Brutus*, 11. 42

[130] Cf. Plato, *Statesman*, II. 282c, 382d–III. 383a.

[131] Contemporary Pauline scholars are in agreement that Romans, 1–2 Corinthians, Galatians, Philippians, 1 Thessalonians, and Philemon were surely written by Paul. These seven letters constitute the body of undisputed Pauline letters. The other letters in the Pauline corpus, Ephesians, Colossians, 2 Thessalonians, 1–2 Timothy, and Titus are the subject of scholarly dispute as to their authorship. These six texts are generally referred to as the disputed letters. On this issue, see Raymond F. Collins, *Letters That Paul Did Not Write: The Epistle to the Hebrews and the Pauline Pseudepigrapha*, GNS 28 (Wilmington, DE: Glazier, 1988).

The essentially circumstantial nature of letters calls for two additional considerations. The first can almost be taken for granted. That is the letter writer is away from the recipient of the letter. A letter is a way of being present when one is physically absent. Accordingly, Heikki Koskenniemi considered *parousia*, "presence," to be the first function of a Hellenistic letter.[132] Moreover, the presence-absence theme (*parousia/apousia*) is a common motif in ancient letters as it is in Paul's correspondence.[133]

The absence of the letter writer from the recipient does not mean that the recipients are unknown to the letter writer. There are exceptions, of course, but for the most part letters are written to people with whom the letter writer has a shared experience. This is true of all Paul's undisputed letters, even the Letter to the Romans,[134] which is a kind of letter of introduction. This means that a letter can express more than it actually says. Its wording often alludes to the shared experience of writer and recipient, an experience often unappreciated or unknown to a third party.

That letters are written in particular sets of circumstances led the ancients who study letters, the epistolographers, to speak of letters as one-half of a conversation, part of a dialogue. Sometimes the dialogue continues and we have an exchange of letters but this is not always the case. But it is always the case that the letter is a kind of conversation with the person(s) to whom it is written, particularly in the ancient world where letters were generally dictated by their authors and read aloud by or to[135] their recipients.

The Letter's Dialogical Nature: A Few Corollaries

The dialogical nature of a letter has a number of important corollaries. Among them is that the circumstances in which the letter was written and the circumstances to which it responds must be taken into consideration if the letter is to be properly understood. In the case of Paul's

---

[132] Heikki Koskenniemi, *Studien zur Idee und Phraseologie des griechischen Briefes bis 400 n. Chr.* Annales Academicae scientiarum Fennicae, Series B, 102, 2 (Helsinki: Suomalaisen Tiedeakatemia, 1956), 38–42.

[133] See the use of the contrasting participles *apōn*, "absent," and *parōn*, "present," in 1 Cor 5:3; 2 Cor 10:1, 11.

[134] See especially the list of greetings in Romans 16.

[135] This is sometimes true in the modern world but it was almost always true in the ancient world where literacy was minimal. On average, about 5 percent of the population appears to have been able to read and write during the first century CE. There was a higher rate of literacy in the large cities than there was in more rural areas.

letters, this issue is problematic. More often than not, Paul's letters are the only source of information that we have to enlighten us about the situation. Sometimes Paul tells us how he learned about the situation to which he responds and what that situation was,[136] but that is not usually the case. For the most part we must infer what the situation was from the reading of the letters.[137] That is not always easy to do as the difference of opinion among the interpreters of Paul's letters indicates ever so clearly.

An integral element in the circumstances of a letter is the relationship between the partners in dialogue. Sometimes Paul speaks as an apostle;[138] sometimes he chooses not to.[139] Sometimes he speaks as a stern father;[140] more often he writes as a loving brother.[141] Sometimes he invokes the authority of the Lord;[142] more often he does not do so explicitly; at other times he cannot do so.[143] The overall and circumstantial nature of Paul's relationship with those to whom he is writing bears mightily on the interpretation of what he writes.

Another corollary of the dialogical nature of the ancient letter, and of Paul's letters, is that it dictates the language that is used in the letter. In the ancient world, as in ours, there are standard epistolary formulae that are used. When we write "Dear Tom," we are using an epistolary formula that does not necessarily express particular endearment for a man named Tom.[144] We are using a formula that is usually just a polite way to address the person to whom we are writing. The letter of condolence generates

---

[136] Cf. 1 Cor 1:11; 5:1.

[137] From this point of view, modern interpreters of Paul's letters are at a decided disadvantage in comparison with those who "read"—that is, *heard*—them for the first time. Not only would they have had a shared experience with Paul but one of the roles of a letter carrier in the ancient world was to provide additional information about the contents of the letter. It appears most likely that Paul's letters were delivered by travelling missionaries who had spent some time with Paul and were able to fill in the gaps, as it were.

[138] Cf. 1 Cor 9:2; Gal 1:1.

[139] Cf. 1 Thess 2:7.

[140] Cf. 1 Cor 4:14-21.

[141] Cf. 1 Cor 15:58.

[142] Cf. 1 Cor 7:10.

[143] Cf. 1 Cor 7:12.

[144] There might well be a deep relationship between the author of the letter and Tom as, for instance, in a love letter, but that cannot be inferred immediately from the use of the customary formula. The intensity of the relationship between the writer and Tom can be gleaned only from the contents of the letter or from other knowledge that a person might have about the relationship.

a particular kind of language. We write about sadness and about loss. Ancient letters, including Paul's, typically made use of the epistolary formulae in common use in their day.

Yet another way in which the dialogical nature of the letter contributes to its formulation is that some of the language is "borrowed" from the other partner in the conversation. The writer of a letter picks up and appropriates the language that he/she has heard or read. This is apparent to anyone who has read a letter that was written in response to a letter received. Sometimes the respondent makes this clear by writing "you said" or "you wrote." At other times the use of borrowed language can be determined only when the two letters are compared with one another. On occasion the respondent's use of language that is unusual for him or her is a sign that the language has been borrowed.

In the case of Paul's letters, we do not have a copy of the letter to which he responds, not even when he tells us that he is responding to a letter that he has received.[145] So a comparison between the language of Paul's letters and that of his interlocutors is impossible. On the other hand, we do have a number of letters that come from the hand of Paul. A comparison of these letters allows us to determine that Paul sometimes uses language that is unusual for him to use. This creates the possibility, and sometimes the likelihood, that Paul has appropriated the language of those to whom he is writing.

For example, writing to the Thessalonians, Paul says, "When they say 'There is peace and security [*asphaleia*],' then sudden destruction will come upon them" (1 Thess 5:3). In this case, Paul clearly indicates that he is referencing what others have said but the fact that "security" (*asphaleia*) does not appear in any of his other letters, not even those whose authorship is disputed, provides a clue that he is using borrowed language. The language is, in fact, the language of Roman political slogans of that era.

In recent years, students of Paul's First Letter to the Corinthians have become increasingly aware that part of the language of this letter is the language of slogans that have circulated among the Corinthians, even among Corinthian believers. Paul sometimes uses direct and indirect quotations when he writes.[146] Sometimes the quotations may be Paul's own summary of ideas that were being bandied about.[147] This, of course,

---

[145] Cf. 1 Cor 7:1.

[146] Cf. 1 Cor 15:12, 35.

[147] The technique is common in diatribe, a kind of rhetoric with which Paul was familiar and occasionally uses.

means that the quotation is cast in Paul's own language. Sometimes Paul's use of an introductory phrase such as "someone will ask" lets the reader know that Paul is making some sort of quotation. This is most apparent when Paul quotes Scripture. He typically uses an introductory formula, most often "it is written" (*gegraptai*).[148]

But there are other times when Paul alludes to Scripture or even quotes Scripture verbatim without any formal introduction. For example, Paul writes in 1 Corinthians 5:13, "Drive out the wicked person from among you." Modern English translations put these words within quotation marks, indicating that they are a quotation, which indeed they are. The words of the exhortation come from Deuteronomy 17:7, but Paul does not formally introduce the exhortation as a Scriptural exhortation. Some among those who listened to the reading of the letter might have recognized the exhortation to have been scriptural, but others—probably the great majority—would not have done so. We recognize the words as a quotation because they appear within quotation marks but quotation marks were not used in ancient times. They do not appear in any of the ancient manuscripts of Paul's letters.

Since Paul is directly interacting with the Christian community at Corinth, responding to their issues and their questions, it is perhaps more likely in this than in any other of his extant letters that he would quote the Corinthians. Accordingly scholars have identified "All things are lawful for me" (1 Cor 6:12)[149] and "Food is meant for the stomach and the stomach for food" (1 Cor 6:13) as pithy sayings that summarize the opinions of some Corinthians. In similar fashion, "It is well for a man not to touch a woman" (1 Cor 7:1) is seen to be a Corinthian slogan, whose popularity within the community was problematic and an issue about which some of the Corinthians wrote to Paul. The fact that the verb "touch" (*haptō*) appears in no other letter of Paul, except in a quotation of Psalm 94:14 in 2 Corinthians 6:17,[150] provides a clue as to its alien provenance.

---

[148] Cf. 1 Cor 9:9, for example. Far less common is the "it is said" (*phēsin*, literally, "they say") of 1 Cor 6:15.

[149] Cf. 1 Cor 10:23.

[150] The quotation of Psalm 94 occurs in a passage, 2 Corinthians 6:14–7:1, that many authors consider to be a later interpolation into the letter but that issue need not detain us here. Were the passage from 2 Corinthians not to be of Pauline authorship, then the appearance of *haptō* in 1 Corinthians 7:1 would be its only known use by Paul. See, however, its appearance in Colossians 2:21, a text whose authorship is

Another consequence of the dialogical nature of a letter is that the language used in the dialogue must be understood by each of the partners in the dialogue. In many respects, this goes without saying but it is especially important for the understanding of the letters of Paul. Paul wrote his letters in response to particular situations as a way of expressing the Gospel in the defined set of circumstances. As a preacher who used the letter-form to express the Gospel,[151] Paul wanted his message to be understood. He had no option available to him other than to use language that people could understand.

Effectively this means that the language of his letters is the ordinary language of the people to whom he is writing. The meaning of his words is best understood not only by looking at how those words were used in the specific literary context of an individual letter but also by looking at how they were used in the Hellenistic literature of his day. To be sure, Paul was a bicultural person so it is not to be excluded that the connotation of some of his idioms were influenced by his Jewish background, but he wrote to largely Gentile communities whose language was that of the Koine Greek of the time.

Rhetoric

The aforementioned document of the Pontifical Biblical Commission cites rhetorical analysis as a new method of literary analysis though observing that in itself it is not a new method.[152] Historians of clerical celibacy/continence frequently call attention to weighing the quality of the rhetoric of an ancient text. *A fortiori*, attention must be paid to the rhetoric of Paul's letters. Rhetoric, as defined by *The Interpretation of the Bible in the Church*, is

> The art of composing discourse aimed at persuasion. The fact that all biblical tests are in some measure persuasive in character means that some knowledge of rhetorical should be part of the normal scholarly equipment of all exegetes. Rhetorical analysis must be carried out in a critical way, since scientific exegesis is an undertak-

---

disputed, where it appears in a slogan with which the author of the epistle takes issue.

[151] As the oldest texts in the New Testament, Paul's letters are the oldest written form of the Gospel, the Good News of salvation accomplished in, through, and by Jesus Christ.

[152] Cf. *The Interpretation of the Bible in the Church* I.B.1, *Origins* 23, 502.

ing which necessarily submits itself to the demands of the critical mind.[153]

Use of the method is particularly important in the studies of Paul's letters, as is realized when consideration is given to two fundamental realities. The first is that Paul is, if anything at all, a preacher of the Gospel.[154] The apostle's words were meant to persuade, to bring people to accept the truth of the Gospel of Jesus Christ. His letters were a continuation of his preaching. They were a means that the apostle adopted to convince people the Gospel was relevant to the circumstances of their lives even after he had physically departed from them. His letters, to reprise the wording of *The Interpretation of the Bible in the Church*, were "aimed at persuasion."[155]

A second fundamental reality is that, in Paul's day, the art of letter writing was taught in schools of rhetoric. I do not claim that Paul had studied in a Hellenistic school of rhetoric.[156] The steadfast Pharisaism of his youth[157] may well have prevented him from doing so. On the other hand, it may well be that some upper-class Hellenistic Jews were educated in the Hellenistic system as Philo seems to imply in *Special Laws* 2.229–30. Thus, some authors think that Paul was indeed formally educated in the art of rhetoric.[158] In any case, Paul was fully immersed in the Hellenistic culture to which he belong and proved himself to be a master rhetorician—not to mention that he was obviously a skilled letter writer. Accordingly, now for more than a quarter of a century, students of Paul's letters have increasingly had recourse to rhetorical analysis in order to understand more fully what Paul wrote to his various churches. The Fathers of the Church were sometimes polemical when they wrote; Paul too occasionally adopted a polemical manner of speaking as he dictated his letters to a nearby scribe.

---

[153] Ibid.

[154] Cf. 1 Cor 1:17.

[155] This, of course, does not mean that the rhetorical genre of each and every sentence that Paul dictated is to be classified as a unit of deliberative rhetoric.

[156] Cf. 2 Cor 11:6.

[157] Cf. Phil 3:5.

[158] See the discussion in Jerome Murphy-O'Connor, *Paul: A Critical Life* (Oxford: Clarendon, 1996), 47–51; cf. Marcus J. Borg and John Dominic Crossan. *The First Paul: Reclaiming the Radical Visionary Behind the Church's Conservative Icon* (New York: Harper One, 2009), 61–62.

In Conclusion

This brief overview is hardly an adequate analysis of the historical-critical method of studying ancient scriptural texts nor has it attempted to be a full study of the considerations that can be gathered together under the rubric of epistolary criticism. What it has intended to be is a brief survey of the highlights of the methodological considerations that must be brought to bear on the letters in the Pauline corpus if they are to be properly understood.

Other methodological considerations would be highlighted if the majority of texts studied in this work had come from New Testament texts whose macro-genre was other than epistolary. The historical-critical method of studying passages in Matthew, Mark, Luke, and John requires that considerable attention be paid to redaction criticism,[159] in consideration of the way in which these texts were composed, and to narrative criticism,[160] in the light of the fact that each of the four gospels is, in its own way, a story about Jesus. Elements of each of these methodologies will be brought to bear when we study such texts as Matthew 19:12, Luke 14:26, and Luke 18:29.[161]

Within the Pauline epistolary corpus, the crucially important texts in the history of the development of clerical celibacy are three passages in Paul's response to a letter that he had received from the Corinthians, 1 Corinthians 7:5, 7, and 29, a passage in Paul's exposition of his own *exemplum* in 1 Corinthians 9:5, and the *unius uxoris vir* phraseology, originally in Greek, of 1 Timothy 3:2, 12 and Titus 1:6.

The meaning of these ten and a few related texts[162] in their original New Testament contexts is the burden of the present study. To begin at the beginning, we will look at the situation in first-century Palestine—the socioreligious situation of Jesus' proclamation of the Gospel and of his choice of followers, one of whom is known to have had a mother-in-law (Matt 8:14; Mark 1:30; Luke 4:38). Before we do so, we must take a look at the socioreligious circumstances in which Jesus called his first disciples.

---

[159] Cf. *The Interpretation of the Bible in the Church* I.A.3, *Origins* 23, 501.

[160] Cf. ibid., I.B.2, *Origins* 23, 503–4.

[161] Parallels to this verse are found in Matthew 19:29 and Mark 11:29, passages that have been all but overlooked as the discipline of clerical celibacy/continence developed throughout the centuries.

[162] Cholij, for example, states that 1 Corinthians 7:33 "was a classic text traditionally used in the Church (both East and West) for defending and promoting virginity and priestly celibacy" (*Clerical Celibacy*, 111; cf. 200–201).

The Time of Jesus

Some years ago, in a lecture that he gave in the School of Theology of the Catholic University of Leuven (Belgium) where I was teaching, the late David Flusser, professor of early Christianity and Judaism of the Second Temple Period at the Hebrew University of Jerusalem, remarked that the parables of Jesus are a very important source for understanding the life and times of people living in first-century Palestine. In the absence of much other information, Jesus' little stories allude to many of the ways in which people in his society lived their daily lives.

Jesus spoke about the lamp on the lampstand that "gives light to all in the house" (Matt 5:14), preserving for us the memory of the people who lived in one-room houses in Jesus' day. From the triple tradition in which Jesus is quoted as saying, "Those who belong to this age marry and are given in marriage but those who are considered worthy of a place in that age and in the resurrection from the dead neither marry nor are given in marriage" (Luke 20:34-35[1]), we learn that in first-century Palestine, Jewish men married and Jewish women were married. Other people, their parents or their clan, took the initiative in seeing that women were married.

[1] Cf. Matt 22:30.

There was, indeed, a remarkable amount of truth in Flusser's observation. History is generally written from above and deals with institutions and their instruments. It contains very little history from below. This must be put together from occasional remarks and reconstituted on the basis of archeological evidence.

The Sources

We are fortunate to still possess three multivolume works of the first-century CE Jewish historian Flavius Josephus (37–ca. 100 CE). These are his *Jewish Antiquities* (*Antiquitates judaicae*), *Jewish War* (*Bellum judaicum*), and *Against Apion* (*Contra Apionem*), to which can be added his autobiography, *The Life* (*Vita*). All of these works were written in Greek. All of them reflect Josephus' personal biases, including his desire to please Roman authorities, a bias especially evident in *Jewish War*. Josephus' writings, as valuable as they are, represent history from above. They have little to say about ordinary life in first-century Palestine.

Another valuable source of information about first-century Judaism is the multiple works of Philo of Alexandria, an early contemporary of Josephus, but, as the geographic designation suggests, he was not a Palestinian. Moreover, most of his works are not historical. Probably more valuable are the Dead Sea Scrolls, the Qumran texts, the first of which were discovered in a cave near the western coast of the Dead Sea in 1947. These provide some information, but the Judaism that they reflect is of a sectarian nature. They shed light on life in first-century Palestine from a point of view on the fringes.

Rabbinic Texts

Yet another source for understanding the situation in first-century Judaism are rabbinic writings. Since rabbinism attempts to faithfully pass along the established tradition, the Mishnah and other rabbinic texts are valuable sources for knowing about life in first-century Palestine. The interpreter who uses the Mishnah and other rabbinic works to know about life in Palestine at the time of Jesus works, however, under a double caveat. First of all, the rabbinic writings are late. They were written some decades, even centuries, after the time in which Jesus and his Jewish contemporaries lived. So, the question necessarily arises as to how faithful to previous times are the traditions that have been handed down. Secondly, the Mishnah, written about 200 CE and probably the oldest of the rabbinic texts, contains *halakah*, norms of conduct. It is a text that concerns the Law and its interpretation. So, the question arises as to how faithfully people lived according to these norms. Were they a kind of ideal for good behavior rather than a reflection on how people actually lived?

Nevertheless, within the parameters set out by the pair of caveats, the discussion between the disciples of Shammai and the disciples of Hillel is often cited as a witness to the background of the question about divorce posed by some Pharisees to the Matthean Jesus: "Is it lawful for a man to divorce his wife for any cause?" (Matt 19:3).[2] The question pertains to the interpretation of Deuteronomy 24:1-2, "Suppose a man enters into marriage with a woman, but she does not please him because he finds something objectionable about her, and so he writes her a certification of divorce, puts it in her hand, and sends her out of his house; she then leaves his house and goes off to become another man's wife."

In regard to the interpretation of this classic biblical text on divorce, the Mishnaic tractate *Giṭṭin* ("Bills of Divorce") 9:10, reports:

> The School of Shammai say: "A man may not divorce his wife unless he has found unchastity in her, for it is written, *Because he hath found in her* indecency *in anything*." And the School of Hillel say: "[He may divorce her] even if she spilled a dish for him, for it is written, *Because he has found in her indecency in* anything. R. Akiva says: "Even if he found another fairer than she, for it is written, *And it shall be if she find no favor in his eyes*."[3]

This report reveals that the disciples of Shammai were more rigorous in their interpretation of the Law than were the disciples of Hillel, among whom Rabbi Akiva was perhaps the most prominent. Akiva (ca. 15–135 CE) was active during the second-century CE Bar Kokhba rebellion. His

---

[2] The earlier Markan version of the discussion between the Pharisees and Jesus describes them as asking a less nuanced question, "Is it lawful for a man to divorce his wife?" (Mark 10:3). Matthew's editorial modification is deemed to stem from a discussion within Palestinian Judaism in the late first century CE.

[3] This and all following English language translations of the Mishnah are taken from Herbert Danby, *The Mishnah Translated from the Hebrew with Introduction and Brief Explanatory Notes* (London: Oxford University Press, 1933).

mentor, Hillel, was born in Babylon (ca. 110 BCE) and died in Jerusalem (ca. 10 CE). His most famous halakic opponent was his younger contemporary Shammai (ca. 50 BCE–ca. 30 CE). Modern rabbinism derives from the School of Hillel. Disputes between the two rabbinic schools were legendary in early Judaism, as were rabbinic disputations between the two rabbis themselves. Many of them are recorded in the Mishnah.

The present study does not intend to pursue the investigation of divorce in first-century Palestine. The Mishnah's account of the rabbinic debate between the disciples of Shammai and Hillel has been introduced only to make the point that if the Mishnah's account of the divorce debate is a legitimate source for the interpretation of one New Testament text, it is likewise legitimate to use the Mishnah as a source of light for other situations addressed in the New Testament.

The passage in *m. Giṭṭin* 9:10 nonetheless calls for three further reflections. First of all, the quotation is in the form of a *sugya*, a kind of debate between rabbinic authorities. The debate is a literary creation rather than a report of an actual debate between members of the two schools. The dialectic form of presentation leaves the discussion open-ended. It does not resolve the issue one way or the other.[4] Second, the rabbis referenced in this passage are tannaim, that is, Palestinian rabbis who lived until the early third century CE. The two most important of the early Palestinian rabbis were Hillel, who died in Jerusalem in 10 CE, and Shammai, who founded his own school and died in 30 CE. Third, the Mishna can be tendentious. Its compiler, Rabbi Yehudah ha Nasi, redacted the text in the early third century CE in order to preserve for posterity the oral tradition of his people. Not only had some of the material been modified in the course of transmission but the redactor preserved the tradition in accord with his own concerns and interests.[5]

---

[4] Cf. Daniel Boyarin, *Carnal Israel: Reading Sex in Talmudic Culture* (Berkeley: University of California Press, 1993), 26.

[5] Thus, Bruce D. Chilton and Jacob Neusner write: "No critical scholar today expects to open a rabbinic document, whether the Mishnah of ca. 200 CE or the Talmud of Babylonia (Bavli) of 600 CE, and to find there what particular sages on a determinate occasion really said or did. Such an expectation is credulous." See Bruce D. Chilton and Jacob Neusner, "Paul and Gamaliel," in *In Quest of the Historical Pharisees*, ed. Jacob Neusner and Bruce D. Chilton (Waco, TX: Baylor University Press, 2007), 175–223, 175.

Genesis 1:28, "Be Fruitful and Multiply"

Apropos the interpretation of the first *mitzvah* recorded in the Torah, "Be fruitful and multiply" (Gen 1:28),[6] the Mishnaic tractate *Yebamoth* ("Sisters-in-Law"[7]) 6:6, for instance, says:

> No man may abstain from keeping the law, *Be fruitful and multiply*, unless he already had children: according to the School of Shammai, two sons; according to the School of Hillel, a son and a daughter, for it is written, *Male and female created he them.*

Given the influence of the School of Hillel on later rabbinic tradition, it is not surprising that the Babylonian Talmud's commentary on the tractate *Yebamot* interprets Genesis 1:28 as being fulfilled if a Jewish man fathers a son and a daughter.[8]

The Babylonian Talmud, the Bavli, is one of two versions of the Talmud. The other is the Jerusalem Talmud, the Yerushalmi. As the canonical gospels, each of the compilations was redacted in the light of then-contemporary concerns and the redactor's own interests. Both Talmuds were written from a male perspective and for the upper- and educated classes.

Of the two, the Yerushalmi is the older, having been compiled in Galilee around 425 CE. The Yerushalmi is a partial commentary on the Mishnah redacted on the basis of interpretive tradition of sages, the Palestinian amoraim—rabbis who lived and taught between the redaction of the Mishnah and the composition of the Talmud. These traditions, the Gemara, had been compiled into books a few decades before the Yerushalmi was redacted. The redactor of the Jerusalem Talmud combined the Gemara with passages from the Mishnah. For purposes of this study, it is important to note that the Yerushalmi was more influenced by Hellenistic thought, especially Jewish Hellenistic thought, than was the Babylonian Talmud.

---

[6] See Jeremy Cohen, *"Be Fertile and Increase, Fill the Earth and Master It": The Ancient and Medieval Career of a Biblical Text* (Ithaca, NY: Cornell University Press, 1989), 158–65, where he examines the binding force of the blessing in the rabbinic tradition.

[7] Danby's edition of the Mishnah gives "Sisters-in-Law" as the English language title of the tractate. The term *Yebamoth* literally means levirate marriages. It is derived from *ymb*, "perform a levirate marriage" (cf. Gen 38:8; Deut 25:5, 7).

[8] Cf. *b. Yebam.* 61b.

The Gamara incorporated into the Yerushalmi were traditions that originated in the land of Israel. There were, however, other interpretive traditions, especially those that were developed and handed down in the Jewish academies in the Babylonian cities of Sura and Pumbedita. These were compiled around 500 CE. The combination of these Western traditions, derived from the Babylonian amoraim, with passages from the Mishnah resulted in the redaction of the Babylonian Talmud sometime between 500 and 700 CE.[9] It too is only an incomplete commentary on the Mishnah.

Since the Bavli was considered by medieval rabbinic Jewish authorities to be the authoritative interpretation of the Mishnah, it is more widely quoted than is the Yerushalmi and is often simply referred to as the Talmud. For purposes of this study, it can be noted that with regard to family law and sexual relationships, the Bavli was more concerned with sexual propriety[10] whereas the Yerushalmi was more focused on the establishment of households.

The Mishah's account of the dispute between the schools of Shammai and Hillel recounted in *Yebamoth* 6:6 pertains to how the commandment can be fulfilled; there is neither dispute between them concerning the commandment itself nor a dispute about its obligatory force. The obligation of the Law that a Jewish man marry and have at least two children derives from the fact that the two verbs in the biblical commandment "be fruitful" (*perû*) and "multiply" (*rebû*), are in the Qal plural imperative forms of the respective Hebrew verbs (*pârâh* and *râbab*). That the verbs are in the plural number suggests that a man must be "fruitful and multiply" more than once. The question is whether a man's fathering a female counts toward the total of at least two children. The command was repeated in the Genesis account of the restoration of humanity after the flood.[11] "God blessed Noah and his sons," recounts Genesis 9:1, "and said to them, 'Be fruitful and multiply.'"

---

[9] The oldest complete manuscript of the Bavli, the Munich Talmud, dates from 1342.

[10] The Bavli's insistence on early marriage was similar to the opinions of the surrounding Zoroastrian culture that view early marriage as the only antidote for sexual temptation. To some extent, the Bavli's insistence on marriage and the use of sexual activity can also be seen as a reaction to an increasingly sexual asceticism in Christianity.

[11] The Genesis 9:1-17 account is a priestly narrative as is the creation story in Genesis 1.

The dispute as to the number of children that a man must have was not the only rabbinic disputation apropos the fulfillment of the commandment found in Genesis 1:28. What if, for example, a man's children should die? On this issue there was disagreement, as the Babylonian Talmud reports: "If a man had children and they died, he has fulfilled, said R. Huna, the duty of propagation. R. Johanan said: He has not fulfilled it" (*b. Yebam.* 62d).[12]

Another issue was that of a man remarrying in his old age. With regard to this question, the Bavli, the Babylonian Talmud, says: "If a man married in his youth, he should marry again in his old age; if he had children in his youth, he should also have children in his old age; for it is said, *In the morning sow thy seed and in the evening withhold not thy hand . . .*"[13] (*b. Yebam.* 62b).

And what about a man who had children before he became a Jewish proselyte? Had he fulfilled the obligation to be fruitful and multiply? Rabbis were not in agreement on the issue:

> It was stated: If a man had children while he was an idolater and then he became a proselyte, he has fulfilled, R. Johanan said, the duty of propagation of the race; and Resh Kakish said: He has not fulfilled the duty of the propagation of the race. R. Johanan said: He has fulfilled the duty of propagation since he had children. And Resh Lakish said: He has not fulfilled the duty of propagation because one who became a proselyte is like a child newly born. (*b. Yebam.* 62a)

The commandment "increase and multiply" was considered to be universally binding. Boyarin observes that "there was an absolute demand on everyone to marry and procreate."[14] There was, however, a dispute as to the gender of those on whom it was incumbent, as the text of Genesis 9:1 might intimate. A record of this dispute is recorded in the conclusion to the Mishnah's *Yebamot* 6:6:

---

[12] The English translation comes from Flavius Josephus, *Jewish Antiquities XVIII–XIX*, trans. Louis H. Feldman, Loeb Classical Library 433 (Cambridge, MA: Harvard University Press, 1965).

[13] The citation comes from Qoh 11:6.

[14] Boyarin, *Carnal Israel*, 165; cf. Michael Satlow, *Jewish Marriage in Antiquity* (Princeton, NJ: Princeton University Press, 2001), 32.

The duty to be fruitful and multiply falls on the man but not on the woman. R. Johanan b. Baroka says: Of them both it is written, *And God blessed them and God said unto them, Be fruitful and multiply.*

The prevailing opinion, that of an unnamed teacher whose view was accepted as Jewish Law, to which Johanan ben Baroka, an early second-century rabbi, a tanna, offered a demurer, was that males were required to observe the *mitzvah* but females were not. Jewish men were under the obligation to "be fruitful and multiply" but Jewish women were not so obligated.[15] This is in keeping with the view that the precepts of the Torah were addressed to Jewish males—an opinion that may have been inferred from a strict reading of Genesis 9:1. An incident recounted in the Babylonian Talmud confirms the prevailing opinion:

Judith, the wife of R. Hiyya,[16] having suffered in consequence agonizing pains of childbirth, changed her clothes [on recovery] and appeared in her disguise before R. Hiyya. "Is a woman," she asked, "commanded to propagate the race?" "No," he replied. (*b. Yebam.* 65b)[17]

The idea that a man should marry and have children in order to fulfill the divine commandment continued to be emphasized in rabbinic tradition. For example, Joseph B. Ephraim Caro writes in the sixteenth-century *Shulhan Arukh* that "every man is obliged to marry in order to fulfill the duty of procreation, and whoever is not engaged in propagating the race is as if he shed blood, diminishing the Divine image and causing His presence [the Shekinah] to depart from Israel" (*Evan ha-Ezer* 1:1). This harsh judgment on the man who does not marry and have children is based on the Babylonian Talmud's commentary on the Mishnaic tractate *Yebamot* (*b. Yebam.* 63b–64a).

[15] The tradition rejected the interpretation of Rabbi Johanan ben Baroka cited in *m. Yebam.* 6:6. On the other hand, "in respect of conjugal union all agree that the [wife who refuses] is to be regarded as rebellious" (*b. Ketub.* 63b). This and subsequent English language translations of the Babylonian Talmud's tractate Ketubbot are taken from Samuel Daiches and Israel W. Slotki, *The Babylonian Talmud: Seder Nashim,* vols. 3–4, ed. Isidore Epstein (London: Soncino, 1936).

[16] Hiyya was an early fourth-century rabbi.

[17] English-language translations of the Bavli are given according to Isidore Epstein's Soncino edition (London, 1936).

The Talmud was harsh on men who did not marry, who violated the first commandment in the Law. With regard to a man who had not married, a Talmudic commentary on the tractate *Yebamot* recounts that: "R. Eleazar[18] said, Any man who has no wife is no proper man; for it is said, *Male and female created He them and called their name Adam*"[19] (*b. Yebam.* 63a). And "R. Tanhum[20] stated in the name of R. Hanilai: Any man who has no wife lives without joy, without blessing, and without goodness"[21] (*b. Yebam.* 62b). The man who is still an unmarried man by the age of twenty is one who "spends all his days in sinful thoughts" and is deemed to be a sinner (*b. Qidd.* 29b).[22]

The Mishnah reports that Rabbi Judah ben Tema, a late second-century tanna, taught that a man is fit for marriage at the age of eighteen,[23] but the age of twenty is considered to be the crucial age by which a man must marry.[24] Otherwise, he is cursed by God. In this regard the Talmud reports, "Raba[25] said, and the School of R. Ishmael taught likewise: Until the age of twenty, the Holy One, blessed be He, sits and waits. 'When will he take a wife?' As soon as one attains twenty and has not married, He exclaims, 'Blasted be his bones!' " (*b. Qidd.* 29b).[26]

---

[18] Eleazar ben Shammua, one of the sages of Jabneh and one of the five disciples of Akiva, was a fourth-generation rabbi who lived in the second century CE. He is often cited in rabbinic literature, generally without mention of his patronymic.

[19] Cf. Gen 1:27; 5:2. In a footnote to *b. Yebam.* 63a, the translator Israel W. Slotki comments, "*Adam* = man. Only when the male and female were united were they called *Adam*" (*The Babylonian Talmud. Seder Nashim. Yebamot* I, 419, n, 10).

[20] Rabbi Tanhum was a Palestinian Amora who lived in the second half of the fourth century CE.

[21] Scriptural grounds for these three deprivations were found in Deuteronomy 14:26; Ezekiel 44:30, and Genesis 2:18, respectively.

[22] This and subsequent English language translations of the Babylonian Talmud's tractate *Qiddušin* are taken from Harry Freedman, *The Babylonian Talmud: Seder Nashim*, vol. 8, ed. Isidore Epstein.

[23] Cf. *m. ʾAbot* 5. 21.

[24] The *Shulhan Arukh* says that the courts can compel a man to marry if he has not married by the age of twenty (cf. *E. H.* 1:3).

[25] "Raba," Abba ben Joseph bar Hama, was a fourth-century Babylonian amora. He is often cited in the Bavli, the Babylonian Talmud. In the vast majority of disputed issues, his opinion held sway.

[26] The Talmud immediately adds that the proud Rabbi Hisda said, "The reason that I am superior to my colleagues is that I married at sixteen. And had I married at fourteen, I would have said to Satan, An arrow in your eye."

Marriage and Sex

It is a man's responsibility to respond faithfully to the first *mitzvah* in the Torah. This requires not only that he marry but also that he have sex with his wife. Without sexual intercourse, the commandment would not be fulfilled. Hence, the Babylonian Talmud also addresses the matter of sex within marriage. Recalling rabbinic tradition, the tractate *Yebamot* says:

> R. Joshua b. Levi[27] said: Whosoever knows his wife to be a God-fearing woman and does not duly visit her is called a sinner; for it is said, *And thou shalt know that thy tent is in peace*,[28] etc.
> R. Joshua b. Levi further stated: It is a man's duty to pay a visit to his wife when he starts on a journey. (*b. Yebam.* 62b)

The frequency of sexual intercourse within marriage was also a subject for rabbinic discussion.[29] Thus the Mishnaic tractate *Ketubbot* says:

> If a man vowed to have no intercourse with his wife, the School of Shammai say: [She may consent] for two weeks. And the School of Hillel say: for one week [only]. Disciples [of the Sages] may continue absent for thirty days against the will [of their wives] while they occupy themselves in the study of the law; and laborers for one week. The *duty of marriage* enjoined in the Law is: every day for them that are unoccupied;[30] twice a week for laborers; once a week for ass-drivers; once every thirty days for camel drivers; and once every six months for sailors. So R. Eliezer. (*m. Ketub.* 5:6[31])

The prescribed frequency clearly depends on the husband's occupation. Sailors are assumed to be away from their wives during longer journeys than are camel drivers. And the journeys of camel drivers are thought to be generally longer than the journey of those who drive donkeys. In

---

[27] Joshua ben Levi was a Palestinian amora of the first half of the third century CE.

[28] Cf. Job 5:24.

[29] Cf. *m. Ketub.* 5:6.

[30] In a footnote, n. 35, the translator, Samuel Daiches, comments that the expression refers to "men who have no need to pursue an occupation to earn their lives and are able 'to walk about' idly."

[31] See the commentary in *b. Ketub.* 61a–63b.

respect to scholars, the Talmud asks, "How often are scholars to perform the marital duties?" The answer: "Rav Judah in the name of Samuel replied, Every Friday night" (*b. Ketub.* 62b).[32]

Parental Responsibility

The onus of fulfilling the commandment set out in Genesis 1:28 falls on Jewish men who were obliged to marry but it falls on Jewish men in yet another way—namely, in their fulfillment of their paternal duties. This obligation is to be seen within the context of a society in which clans or individual parents arranged for the marriage of their offspring. An oft-quoted passage in the Babylonian Talmud cites the traditional rabbinic teaching of a father's responsibilities in regard to his son:

> We thus learnt [here] what our Rabbis taught: The father is bound in respect of his son, to circumcise, redeem, teach him Torah, take a wife for him, and teach him a craft. Some say, to teach him to swim too. (*b. Qidd.* 29a)

Commenting on the obligation "to take a wife for him," the Talmud asks, "How do we know it?" and answers "Because it is written, 'Take ye wives, and beget sons and daughters; and take wives for your sons, and give your daughters to husbands'"[33] (*b. Qidd.* 30b).

The Talmud reports that Rav Judah was criticized because he had not found a wife for his grown son. He claimed that he had not done so because he was concerned about the genealogical purity of his family but his interlocutor countered the argument by saying that in the light of Lamentations 5:1, no one could be sure of the purity of his family's lineage.[34]

There was, however, a discussion as to whether an obligation to find a wife for one's son was also incumbent upon the son's mother. To this question, the Talmud responds with a clear "no."[35] Another discussion

---

[32] Rav Judah, Judah bar Ezekiel (220–99 CE) was a second-generation Babylonian amora. After the death of his mentor, Rav, he studied under Samuel of Nehardea and founded the academy in Pumbedita.

[33] The Scripture is Jer 29:6.

[34] Cf. *b. Qidd.* 71b.

[35] Cf. *b. Qidd.* 30b.

bears on the sequence of the faithful son's response to the father who both teaches him Torah and finds a wife for him, to wit:

> Our Rabbis taught: If one has to study Torah and to marry a wife, he should first study and then marry. But if he cannot [live] without a wife, he should first marry and then study. Rab Judah said in Samuel's name, "The halachah is, [A man] first marries and then studies." R. Johanan[36] said, "[With] a millstone around the neck, shall one study Torah!" Yet they do not differ: the one refers to ourselves [Babylonians]; the other to them [Palestinians]. (*b. Qidd.* 30b)

The sugya indicates that the contradictory demands of marriage and study of the Torah was one of the great unresolved dilemmas of rabbinism.[37]

As far as a girl is concerned, the Babylonian Talmud says that a father's responsibility is to "Let her be dowered, clothed and adorned, that men should eagerly desire her" (*b. Qidd.* 30b). If her father has not found her a husband while she is still relatively young,[38] twelve or so years old, she may become unchaste and he will have violated the *mitzvah* found in Leviticus 19:29, "Do not profane your daughter by making her a prostitute."[39]

This rapid overview of the developing rabbinic tradition[40] shows that the tradition spawned a series of halakoth as well as a number of halakic disputes with regard to the observance of the first mitzvah in the Torah, "Increase and multiply." The obligation to fulfill the commandment fell primarily on Jewish men and secondarily on their fathers who were expected to obtain wives for their sons. Eventually the age of twenty was seen to be the age by which a Jewish man should be married.[41] Those

---

[36] R. Johanan, Johanan ben Zakai (ca. 30–90 CE) was one of the most important among the Palestinian tannaim.

[37] See the lengthy discussion in Boyarin, *Carnal Israel*, 134–64.

[38] Cf Sir 7:25.

[39] Cf. *b. Sanh.* 76a. Cf. Harry Freedman, trans., *The Babylonian Talmud: Seder Nezikin*, vol. 6, ed. Isidore Epstein.

[40] See also Harvey McArthur, "Celibacy in Judaism at the Time of Christian Origins," AUSS 25 (1987): 163–81.

[41] Satlow observes that early marriage is the ideal expressed in the Babylonian Talmud. The reality might have been quite different, especially in the Palestine of an earlier period. See Michael Satlow, *Jewish Marriage in Antiquity* (Princeton, NJ: Princeton University Press, 2001), 104–11.

who were not married by that age were deemed to be sinners and were looked on with scorn.

Furthermore

The practice of celibacy was alien to this tradition.[42] A well-known exception was R. Simeon ben Azzai[43] who responded to Eleazar ben Azariah's criticism that there was a contradiction between what he said and what he did, that he preached well but did not act well because he had not married, by saying, "What shall I do, seeing that my soul is in love with the Torah; the world can be carried on by others" (*b. Yebam.* 63b).[44] It may be that Ben Azzai married afterward.[45] The tractate *Ketubbot* in the Bavli suggests that he married the daughter of Rabbi Akiva.[46] Celibacy seems to have been considered incompatible with personal and

---

[42] Boyarin says, "the Rabbis disallowed virginity in principle," while David Novak observes, with reference to *b. Yeb.* 63b, which, in turn, references Gen 9:6-7, "the rabbinic tradition regarded the commandment to marry and have a family to be without exception." See Boyarin, *Carnal Israel*, 41; David Novak, "Jewish Marriage: Nature, Covenant and Contract," in *Marriage, Sex, and Family in Judaism*, ed. Michael J. Broyde and Michael Ausubel (Lanham, MD: Rowman & Littlefield, 2005), 61–87, 79. See further Elliott N. Dorff, "The Jewish Family in America: Contemporary Challenges and Traditional Resources," in *Marriage, Sex, and Family*, 214–43, 214, 225.

[43] Simeon ben Azzai, sometimes cited simply as Ben Azzai, was a tanna of the first third of the second century. Van der Horst comments that Ben Azzai: "In spite of Gen. 1:28 and in spite of the social pressure of his co-religionists, purposefully renounces marriage and the founding of a family in order to enable himself to pursue a higher goal with all the more determination: i.e., greater knowledge of the Torah and hence a better understanding of God's will." Pieter W. van der Horst, "Celibacy in Early Judaism," *RB* 109 (2002): 342–90, 392–93. Boyarin calls him a "complicated hypocrite" while Diamond styles him "the exception that proves the rule." See Boyarin, *Carnal Israel*, 135; Eliezer Diamond, " 'And Jacob Remained Alone': The Jewish Struggle with Celibacy," in *Celibacy and Religious Traditions*, ed. Carl Olson (New York: Oxford University Press, 2008), 41–64, 53.

[44] Cf. *Gen. Rab.* 34:14.

[45] Another case that is sometimes cited is that of the third-century Babylonian rabbi, Hamnuna. When he was introduced to R. Huna, he appeared without a headdress. His bareheadedness prompted the question "Why have you no head-dress? Hanuhna responded, "Because I am not married." "Thereupon he [Huna] returned his face away from him. 'See to it that you do not appear before me [again] before you are married' " (*b. Qidd.* 289b.). Apparently Hamnuna did marry later on. The Talmud reports that he had a good relationship with Huna. See *b. ʾErub.* 63a.

[46] Cf. *b. Ketub.* 63a.

ethnic holiness. The Bible stipulated that the High Priest be married (Lev 21:13) and the rabbis used the term *Qiddušin*,[47] holiness, to describe marriage.[48]

The rabbinic interpretive tradition of Genesis 1:28—among other things, the failure to marry and procreate was often seen as a diminishment of the image of God or as if the celibate had spilled blood[49]—developed under the influence of the great rabbi Hillel but the Mishnah reports that there had been a dispute between the earliest generations of his disciples and the disciples of his successor, Shammai, as to the minimal observance of the commandment. The disciples of Hillel claimed that the commandment was essentially satisfied if a man fathered a son and a daughter; the disciples of Shammai held that the commandment required a man to beget two sons in order to satisfy the mitzvah. That the commandment could be satisfied in this fashion allowed at least one exegetical tradition, at least as old as Philo, to hold that Moses, God's great prophet, eventually forsook the conjugal life in order to speak regularly with God and therefore be able to lead God's people.[50]

Why Marry?

The Mishnah's retrospective view of the debates among authorities as to how and by whom the first *mitzvah* was to be obeyed suggests that the observance of the commandment was considered to be obligatory in first-century Judaism despite the disputes as to the precise nature of the obligation. To put the rabbinic tradition in its proper light, one must not overlook the fact that the rabbis did not base the obligation to marry solely on obedience to the first commandment in the Torah. Anthropological considerations and respect for God's creation also came into play.

[47] There is, however, no evidence that the rabbis reflected on the use of the term *Qiddusin*. The Hebrew term may be a loan term from the Greek. Authors such as Plato and Aristotle used the word *ekdosis* in reference to the handing over of a bride in marriage. Cf. Satlow, *Jewish Marriage*, 77.

[48] What Paul writes to the Thessalonians in 1 Thessalonians 4:3-8 reflects this tradition. In this first of his extant letters Paul writes about marriage in a passage devoted to sanctification and holiness.

[49] Cf. Diamond, " 'And Jacob Remained Alone,' " 41.

[50] Cf. Naomi Koltun-Fromm, *Hermeneutics of Holiness: Ancient Jewish and Christian Notions of Sexuality and Religious Community* (New York: Oxford University Press, 2010), 9–10.

Rabbi Tanhum,[51] for instance, said that the unmarried man was someone "without joy, without blessing, and without goodness"[52] (*b. Yebam.* 62b). That the unmarried man is without goodness is based on the Scripture, "It is not good that the man should be alone" (Gen 2:18). Rabbi ben 'Ulla[53] said concerning the man who is not married that he is "without peace, for it is written, *And thou shalt know that thy tent is in peace; and thou shalt visit thy habitation and shalt miss nothing*"[54] (*b. Yebam.* 62b). And, basing himself on scriptural description of the creation of humankind, the oft-quoted Eleazar[55] said that the unmarried man is not a complete man for it is said, "*Male and female created He them*[56]" (*b. Yebam.* 63a). As for a man who is childless, "R. Joshua b. Levi said, A man who is childless is accounted as dead, for it is written, *Give me children or else I am dead*" (*b. Ned.* 64b).[57]

All things considered, there appears to be remarkable consistency in the rabbinic treatment of marriage and sexuality during the Tannaitic and Amoraic periods.

A View from the Margins

The canonical gospels tell us nothing about the Essenes, whose "philosophy" the historian Josephus describes as the third form of Jewish philosophy.[58] According to Josephus, the first form of Jewish philosophy is that of the Pharisees, a group that is often mentioned in the gospels. The second form is that of the Sadducees, cited eight times in Matthew, just once in Mark and Luke, and not at all in the Fourth Gospel.[59] The Essenes represented a third form of the Jewish tradition.

---

[51] Tanhum ben Hiyya was a collector of the saying of third-century CE Palestinian sages.

[52] Scriptural grounds for these three deprivations were found in Deuteronomy 14:26; Ezekiel 44:30; and Genesis 2:18, respectively.

[53] Ben 'Ulla was a third- or fourth-century Palestinian amora.

[54] The Scripture is Job 5:24. The rabbis took "tent" as a reference to a man's wife.

[55] Eleazar ben Azaria was a first-century CE Palestinian tanna.

[56] Cf. Gen 1:27.

[57] The Scripture is Genesis 30:1. In a footnote, n. 14, H. Freedman, the translator, says, "Possibly the inclusion of the poor and childless (in addition to the leper and the blind man) was directed against the early Christian exaltation of poverty and celibacy."

[58] Cf. *J. W.* 2:119.

[59] Cf. Matt 3:7; 6:1, 6, 11, 12 [2x]; 22:23, 34; Mark 12:18; Luke 20:27.

Prior to the discovery of the Dead Sea Scrolls in 1947, little was known about the Essenes apart from what Flavius Josephus (ca. 37–100 CE) wrote about them in book two of the *Jewish War*[60] (J. W. 2:120–161). Briefer but earlier mentions of the Essenes appear in the writings of the Roman historian Pliny the Elder (23–79 CE) and the Hellenistic Jewish philosopher, Philo of Alexandria (ca. 15 BCE–ca. 45 CE).

Pliny's short account in the *Natural History* 5.73, is based on the work of Marcus Vipsanius Agrippa, who wrote about 15 BCE. As his predecessor, Pliny locates the Essenes at Ein Gedi, a site on the western shore of the Dead Sea. He says that the Essenes, who had existed for thousands of generations, have no wives, renounce venal pleasure, have no money, and live in the company of palm trees.

Flavius Josephus

Josephus claims to have had first-hand experience of the Essenes.[61] The experience was apparently a rather brief one since the historian chose to be a Pharisee rather than an Essene. Nevertheless, the experience, as brief as it might have been, allowed Josephus him to have first-hand knowledge of the Essenes. Strikingly, he begins his description of this "sect" with a description of their views on marriage, so much different from those of the dominant Pharisees and Sadducees:

> The Essenes have a reputation for cultivating peculiar sanctity.[62] Of Jewish birth, they show a greater attachment to each other than do the other sects. They shun pleasures as a vice and regard temperance and the control of the passions as a special virtue. Marriage they disdain, but they adopt other men's children, while yet pliable and docile, and regard them as their kin and mold them in accordance with their own principles. They do not, indeed, on principle condemn wedlock and the propagation thereby of the race, but they wish to protect themselves against women's wantonness, being

[60] J. W. 2:120–161.

[61] See *Life* 10–11. Josephus says that he made a thorough investigation of the three sects in order to "be in a position to select the best."

[62] The Greek word is *semnotēta*. H. St. John Thackeray, the editor of the Loeb edition of this work, notes that the Greek could be translated as "solemnity." It should be noted that the first sentence in the English translation is a subordinate clause in Greek, where it is found in par. 119.

persuaded that none of the sex keeps her plighted troth to one man. (*J. W.* 2:120–121)[63]

William Loader comments, "the grounds for their [the Essenes[64]] espousing celibacy are . . . not ascetic nor any hesitation about engaging in sexual intercourse for procreation, nor any taboo about sacred space and time, such as might apply to prophets (a role for which only some of them trained), or the especially holy, but rather their fear of women's infidelity."[65] According to Josephus, the Essenes have a very negative view of women. They are an ascetic and tightly disciplined group,[66] as Josephus continues to tell his readers. The Essenes were, nonetheless, not entirely uniform in their thinking, especially in their views on marriage, as Josephus shares with his readers:

> There is yet another order of Essenes, which, while at one with the rest in its mode of life, customs, and regulations, differs from them in their view on marriage. They think that those who decline to marry cut off the chief function of life, the propagation of the race, and, what is more, that, were all to adopt the same view, the whole race would quickly die out. They give their wives, however, a three years' probation, and only marry them after they have by three[67] periods of purification given proof of fecundity. They have no intercourse with them during pregnancy, thus showing that their motive in marrying is not self-indulgence but the procreation of children. In the bath the women wear a dress, the men a loin-cloth. Such are the usages of this order. (*J.W.* 2.160–161)

---

[63] English-language translations of book 2 of *The Jewish War* are taken from Flavius Josephus, *The Jewish War Books 1–2*, trans. H. St. John Thackeray, Loeb Classical Library 203 (Cambridge, MA: Harvard University Press, 1927).

[64] That is, the Essenes in Josephus' view of them.

[65] William Loader, *Philo, Josephus, and the Testaments on Sexuality: Attitudes towards Sexuality in the Writings of Philo and Josephus and in the Testaments of the Twelve Patriarchs* (Grand Rapids, MI: Eerdmans, 2011), 337.

[66] Josephus says that the number of men (*andres*) in the group is more than four thousand. See Josephus, *Ant.* 18.20. Philo, *Good Person*, 75, gives a similar number. Both authors report that the Essenes were held in high regard by the rulers of Palestine, by Herod, as Josephus reports (*Ant.* 15.10.5), or, more generally, as Philo, who speaks of the admiration of the Essenes by commoners and great kings, asserts (*Hypothetica* 11. 18).

[67] In a footnote, the editor of the Loeb edition observes that "the text can hardly be right; the Lat. has '*constanti purgatione*.'"

These are the final words in the *Jewish War*'s description of the Essenes, thus highlighting by means of a literary *inclusio* Josephus' view that what is really remarkable about the sect is their view of marriage and their sexual practices. Nevertheless, Josephus's mention of individual Essenes, such as Judas (*J. W.* 1.78–80), Simon (*J. W.* 2.113), John (*J. W.* 2.567; 3.11), and Manaemus (*Ant.* 15.373–379), all of whom engaged in prophecy, makes no reference to their marital status. Those Essenes who lived in community were not or no longer married in Josephus's view.

The historian gives another, a later and much shorter description[68] of the sect in *Jewish Antiquities* 18.18–22.[69] This short description includes but a brief reference to the Essenes' marital customs, to wit, "They neither bring wives into the community nor do they own slaves, since they believe that the latter practice contributes to injustice and that the former opens the way to a source of dissension" (*Ant.* 18.21).[70]

Philo of Alexandria

Josephus' somewhat younger contemporary, Philo of Alexandria, also gives a description of the Essenes. It is found in *Every Good Person Is Free*, 75–91, but the passage has nothing to say about the Essenes' marital customs except what might be inferred from his assertion that their love of virtue includes their freedom from love of pleasure (*aphilēdonon*)[71] and the statement that "no one's house is his own in the sense that it is not shared by all, for besides the fact that they dwell together in communities, the door is open to visitors from elsewhere who share their convictions."[72]

In a work titled *Hypothetica*, an "Apology for the Jews," two large extracts of which are preserved by Eusebius, Philo speaks explicitly and

---

[68] Introducing the short description of the three sects, Josephus refers his readers to the longer descriptions in book 2 of the *Jewish War*. Cf. *Ant.* 18.11. Josephus mentions only three sects in both the *Jewish War* and *The Life* but adds a fourth in the brief overview given in the *Jewish Antiquities*. The fourth is that of Judas the Galilean about which Josephus is hesitant to say very much. Cf. *Ant.* 18.23–25.

[69] See also *Ant.* 15.10.4–5.

[70] The English translation comes from Flavius Josephus, *Jewish Antiquities XVIII–XIX*, trans. Louis H. Feldman, Loeb Classical Library 433 (Cambridge, MA: Harvard University Press, 1965).

[71] Cf. Philo, *Good Person*, 84.

[72] Philo, *Good Person*, 85. This translation is taken from *Philo Volume IX*, trans. F. H Colson (Loeb Classical Library 363. Cambridge, MA: Harvard University Press, 1941).

at greater length about the marital customs of the Essenes.[73] His first observation is rather short but it is revelatory of their sexual asceticism:

> No Essene is a mere child nor even a stripling or newly bearded, since the characters of such are unstable with a waywardness corresponding to the immaturity of their age, but full grown and already verging on old age, no longer carried under by the tide of the body nor led by the passions, but enjoying the veritable, the only real freedom. (*Hypothetica* 11.3)

A longer description of the Essenes by Philo talks about their avoidance of marriage and their exclusion of women. Their communal life demands that marriage be avoided. The importance of the virtue of self-control (*enkrateia*) comes into play.[74] The reasons for the avoidance of marriage, as alleged by Philo, are quite misogynist[75] and less than appreciative of children:

> They eschew marriage because they clearly discern it to be the sole or the principal danger to the maintenance of the communal life, as well as because they continually practice continence (*enkrateian*). For no Essene takes a wife, because a wife is a selfish creature, excessively jealous and an adept at beguiling the morals of her husband and seducing him by her continued impostures. For by the fawning talk which she practices and the other ways in which she plays her part like an actress on the stage she first ensnares the sight and hearing, and when these subjects as it were have been duped she cajoles the sovereign mind. And if children [*paides*] come, filled with the spirit of arrogance and bold speaking she gives utterance with more audacious hardihood to things which before she hinted covertly and under disguise, and casting off all shame she compels him to commit actions which are all hostile to the life of fellowship. For he who is either fast bound in the love lures of his wife or under the stress of nature makes his children [*teknōn*] his first care ceases to be the same to others and unconsciously has become a different man and has passed from freedom into slavery. (*Hypothetica* 11.14–17)

---

[73] The second abstract, *Hypothetica* 8.11.1–18, is a description of the Essenes.

[74] Interestingly, however, Philo's description of the Essenes who lived in Palestinian Syria has nothing to say about sexual matters. See Philo, *Good Person*, 75–91.

[75] Philo's description of the Essenes negative views on women far exceeds that given by Josephus in *Ant.* 2.161.

The Dead Sea Scrolls

Much more is known about the Essenes since the discovery of the Dead Sea Scrolls in 1947. Although not all scholars agree, most observers hold that the documents come from a community of Essenes. Among the finds are about 215 "biblical" manuscripts, including several of the book of Genesis. All twenty-four of the Genesis manuscripts that have been found are fragmentary.[76] These manuscripts include a fragmentary reading of Genesis 1:28. Texts from the book of Genesis are used in the same way the other books in the Torah are used.[77] A striking exception to the general practice is the citation of Genesis 1:27 in the *Damascus Document*.[78] The Genesis citation serves as an argument in favor of monogamy in what seems to be a polemic against the Pharisees who allowed polygamy. The *Damascus Document* says that these latter "are caught twice in fornication: by taking two wives in their lives even though the principle of creation is 'male and female he created them.' "[79]

Around the time that the Dead Sea Scrolls were first unearthed at Qumran, a cemetery was discovered nearby. Initially the cemetery was thought to contain the bones of males only. Indeed, Satlow asserts that "the only evidence outside of the Greek sources that the Qumran community did not marry is archeological."[80] On further investigation some of the bones, admittedly relatively few, were judged to be those of fe-

---

[76] 1QIsa[a] and 11QPs[a] are among the rare exceptions of scrolls containing an entire book of the Bible. As far as Genesis 1:28 is concerned, 4Q1 (4QGen[b]), frg. 2; 4Q10 (4QGen[k]), frg. 3; and 4Q483 (4QpapGen) have portions of Gen 1:28, but together they yield only this text: "And [God] blessed [them, and God said to them, 'Be fruitful and multiply,] and replen[ish the earth, and subdue it; and have dominion over the fish of the sea, and over the birds of the heavens, and over every living thing that moves upon the earth.]' " Cf. Martin Abegg, Jr., Peter Flinch, and Eugene Ulrich, *The Dead Sea Scrolls Bible: The Oldest Known Bible Translated into English for the First Time* (San Francisco: Harper, 1999), 7.

[77] Maimonides' identification of the 613 commandments likewise does not include any commandments in Genesis, not even Genesis 1:28.

[78] Only fragments of this document were found in the caves around Qumran. See also Mayer I. Grubner, "Women in the Religious System of Qumran," in *Judaism in Late Antiquity, 5: The Judaism of Qumran: A Systemic Reading of the Dead Sea Scrolls 1: Theory of Israel*, ed. Alan J. Avery-Peck, Jacob Neusner, and Bruce Chilton (Leiden: Brill, 2000), 173–96, esp. 178–89.

[79] CD 4:20–21; 6QD, frg. 1. On this text, see Koltun-Fromm, *Hermeneutics of Holiness*, 61.

[80] Satlow, *Jewish Marriage*, 22.

males.[81] A few beads, clearly the adornment of women, have also been been found in the cemetery.[82]

Hence, an important question arises. Did the Essenes really avoid marriage as Pliny, Josephus,[83] and Philo contend? The texts found in the environs of Qumran reinforce the importance of the question.

Marriage and Women

The *Rule of the Congregation* (1QSa) set forth some regulations on the education of children and on marriage, to wit:

> And this is the rule of all the congregation of Israel in the final days, when they gather. . . . When they come, they shall assemble all those who come, including children and women, and they shall read into *their* ears all the precepts of the covenant, and shall instruct them in all their regulations, so that they do not stray in *the*ir errors. . . . And this is the rule for all the armies of the congregation, for all native Israelites. From *his* yo*uth they shall edu*cate him in the book of HAGY, and according to his age, instruct him in the precepts of the covenant, and he will *receive* his *ins*tructions in their regulations; during ten years he will be counted among the children. At the a*ge* of twenty ye*ars, he will transfer to* those enrolled, to enter the lot among his fam*i*ly and join the holy commu*nity*. He shall not *approach* a woman to know her through carnal intercourse until he is fully twe*nty* years old, when he knows *good* and evil. (1QSa 1:1–11)[84]

Strikingly, this passage in the Rule of the Congregation continues with a reference to a wife being allowed to provide testimony with regard to her husband's fulfillment of the laws of the Torah.[85]

---

[81] Cf. Joseph E. Zias, "The Cemeteries of Qumran and Celibacy: Confusion Laid to Rest?," *DSD* 7 (2000): 220–53. The bones of five females about thirty years old were found.

[82] A whorl of a spindle has also been discovered on site.

[83] Josephus had, nonetheless, observed that there was another order of Essenes whose members married. See *J. W.* 2.160–61, above, p. 47.

[84] In the Martínez-Tigchelaar edition of the Scrolls, 1:101, the italicized letters are enclosed between brackets. These letters come from the editors' reconstruction of the text.

[85] Cf. 1QSa 1:11–12.

Another Qumran text contains rules for a father giving his daughter in marriage as well as a man who would take a woman in marriage. Among other things this text says:

> And if a *man gives his daughter to someone* else, he should recount all her blemishes to him, lest he bring upon himself the judgment *of the curse which he said*, "whoever leads a blind man astray from the path." [86] And he shall not give her to anyone who is not fit for her. . . . No one should bring *a woman . . . the holy . . .* who has experience in doing the act, who has either done *the act in* her father's *house*, or as a widow who slept *with someone* after she was widowed. And every woman *who has had* a bad *reput*ation during her maiden-hood in her father's house, no one should take her . . . and if he takes her, he should proceed in accordance with the regulation. (4Q271, frg. 3, 7–15)[87]

Although there appears to have been minimal physical presence of women at Qumran, Moshe Bernstein observes that there is abundant textual presence of women at Qumran. The scrolls contain a significant number of texts that deal with marriage, sexual activity, women's vows, and women's witness, and purity issues concerning women.[88] In addition to the texts from the Rule of the Congregation and from 4Q271, the Temple Scroll (11QT^a) has a considerable amount of things to say about women and marriage.[89] Moreover, 4Q502, termed a "Ritual of Marriage" by its original editor Maurice Baillet,[90] describes a liturgy in which women are clearly involved.

---

[86] Cf. Deut 17:18.

[87] Again in the Martínez-Tigchelaar edition of the Scrolls, 1:619, the italicized letters are enclosed between brackets. The text belongs to the *Damascus Document* and has been studied by David Rothstein ("Gen 24:12 and Marital Law in 4Q271:3: Exegetical Aspects and Implications," *DSD* 12 [2005]: 189–204); and Aharon Shemesh ("4Q271.3: A Key to Sectarian Matrimonial Law," *JJS* 49 [1998]: 244–63). An expanded version of Shemesh's study was published in Hebrew, in Jerusalem, 2001.

[88] Cf. Moshe J. Bernstein, "Women and Children in Legal and Liturgical Texts from Qumran," *DSD* 11 (2004): 191–211.

[89] Cf. Lawrence H. Schiffman, "Laws Pertaining to Women in the Temple Scroll," in *The Dead Sea Scrolls: Forty Years of Research*, ed. Devorah Dimant and Uriel Rappaport, STDJ 10 (Leiden: Brill and Jerusalem: Magnes Press and Yad Ben Zvi, 1992), 210–28.

[90] Cf. Maurice Baillet, DJD 7 (1982), 81–105.

The first of the Temple Scroll's reference to things marital speaks of fathers accepting non-Jewish wives for their sons (11QT^a 2:14–15). The danger of idol worship that might come from "your daughter or the woman who lies in your embrace" is addressed in 11QT^a 54:19–21.[91] Should it prove to be true that a woman (or a man) does evil in the sight of God, breaks the covenant, and engages in idol worship, the woman (or the man) shall be stoned with stones (11QT^a 55:15–21). In a passage on sorcery and the like, men are warned against making their sons or daughters pass through fire (11QT^a 60:17–18).

In war, enemy men are to be killed but women and children are to be captured (11QT^a 62:9–10). It may be that a man sees "among the prisoners a woman of beautiful appearance" and, desiring her, marries her. In which case there are procedures to be followed (11QT^a 63:10–15). The scrolls echo biblical directives[92] in setting down the procedure that is to be followed in the case of a man who marries a woman, disliking her, and then accuses her of not being a virgin at the time of the marriage (11QT^a 65:7–15).[93]

Royal marriages come in for particular scrutiny. The king "shall not multiply wives to himself, lest they turn his heart from me" (11QT^a 56:18–19; cf. Deut 17:17). The king "shall not take a wife from among all the daughters of the nations, but instead take for himself a wife from his father's house, from his father's family." He is to marry only once but if his wife should die, he is to take another wife from his father's house (11QT^a 57:15–19).

The scroll sets out purity regulations for men who have a nocturnal emission;[94] these are followed by the regulations for "a man who lies with his wife, and has an ejaculation" (11QT^a 45:7–12).[95] Similarly, there are purity regulations for menstruating women and women who have given birth (11QT^a 48:15–17). And there are extensive purity regulations for a woman whose child dies in utero (11QT^a 50:10–18).[96]

---

[91] Cf. 11QT^b 16:1–7.
[92] Much of the material in the Temple Scroll follows the Torah rather closely.
[93] Cf. Deut 22:13–21.
[94] Cf. 11QT^b 13:2.
[95] Cf. 11QT^b 12:4–5.
[96] Cf. 11QT^b 14:17–21.

In reference to the temple the scroll proscribes any woman or boy from entering one of the temple's courtyards (11QT[a] 39:7–8).[97] A third courtyard is to be made "for their daughters and for foreigners" (11QT[a] 40:5-6). Regulations are set down for vows made by women under a man's authority, particularly with regard to the possibility of the annulment of vows by a father or husband (11QT[a] 53:16–20; 54:2–3)[98] as well as for vows made by widows and divorcees (11QT[a] 54:4–5).

The text speaks about a man who is disobedient to his parents and does not accept their correction. In that case the man's father and mother are to testify against him before the elders of the city and he is to be stoned.

The last column of the Temple Scroll (11QT[a] 66) is entirely devoted to things marital and sexual. It sets down regulations for punishing a man who rapes a woman, setting down different prescriptions for a rape that takes place in a city from those in force when a rape occurs in the country (11QT[a] 66:1–8).[99] When a man seduces an unmarried woman, on payment of the stipulated bride price of fifty silver shekels, she is to become his wife (11QT[a] 66:8–11).[100] The final extant text in the Temple Scroll prohibits incest, sometimes coupled with adultery. Among the women prohibited to a man are his father's wife,[101] his brother's wife,[102] his sister, his aunt,[103] and his niece (11Q19 66:12–16).

In addition to the many passages that speak about women and marriage, the Temple Scroll makes a number of generic references to groups that would certainly include women and children. The most common of these expressions is "the children of Israel" (11QT[a] 26:11; 27:2, 4; 29:5; 37:12; 42:14; 46:7; 51:6, 7; 57:2; 58:19; 64:6, 10). The scroll speaks of the heads of families (11QT[a] 42:1–4) and makes references to the cities in which they live (11QT[a] 47:3, 8–9; 48:13–14; 64:4, 5; 66:1, 3, 5). The Temple Scrolls, 11Q19 and 11Q20, Temple Scroll[a] and Temple Scroll[b], are among the longer texts found at Qumran.

---

[97] As is the case with all the scrolls, the Temple Scroll has deteriorated; numerous pieces of the scroll are no longer extant. Sometimes the lacunae were such that the editors could not reconstruct the full text.

[98] Cf. Num 30:7-9; 4Q271, frg. 4. 10–12.

[99] Cf. Deut 22:22-27.

[100] Cf. Deut 22:13-21; Lev 18:8.

[101] Cf. Deut 22:30.

[102] Cf. Lev 18:16.

[103] Cf. Lev 18:12-14.

Three of the caves at Qumran yielded fragmentary pieces of a document known to scholars since its discovery in the genizah of a Cairo synagogue at the end of the nineteenth century.[104] After its discovery the document was known by several different names. The discovery of the fragmentary 4Q266 (4QD^a),[105] 4Q267 (4QD^b), 4Q268 (4QD^c), 4Q269 (4QD^d), 4Q270 (4QD^e), 4Q271 (4QD^f), 4Q272 (4QD^g), 4Q273 (4QpapD^h), 5Q12 (5QD), and 6Q15 (6QD) enabled scholars to determine the origin of the enigmatic document, now known as the *Damascus Document*. The ten fragments are part of that document.[106]

As has been noted, the *Damascus Document* cites Genesis 1:27, "male and female he created them," in apparent argument with Pharisees, the builders of the wall, who take two wives in their lives.[107] The text[108] indicates that the prohibition of bigamy as well as the prohibition of a man marrying his niece are two things distinguishing the sectarians from other Jews.

Those who entered the new covenant in the "land of Damascus" are to refrain from fornication (*zenut*) in accordance with the regulation,[109] but "if they reside in camps in accordance with the rule of the land, and take women and beget children, they shall walk in accordance with the law . . . and according to the regulation of the teachings, according to the rule of the law, as he said: 'Between a man and his wife and between a father and his son' " (CD 7:6–8; 19:2–5; cf. Num 30:17).[110] The contrast suggests that there were two groups of Essenes, those in the land of Damascus who abstained from sexual relations and groups that resided

---

[104] Cf. Solomon Schechter, *Documents of Jewish Sectaries*, vol. 1 (Cambridge: University Press, 1910).

[105] Of the ten fragments, 4QD^a contains the largest portion of the *Damascus Document*. It consists of eleven individual fragments, several of which contain more than one column.

[106] Columns 1–16 of the *Damascus Document* belong to a tenth-century document (CD^a); columns 19–20 (CD^b) belong to another document, coming from the twelfth century. While some of the material in the Qumran fragments supplements these documents; other material is found in the later texts. For the reconstituted text, see David Hamidovic, *"Écrit de Damas": Le manifeste des esséniens*, Collection de la Revue des Études Juives, 51 (Leuven: Peeters, 2011).

[107] Cf. CD 4:20–5:1; 6QD frg. 1, 1–3.

[108] CD 4:20–5:11.

[109] CD 7:1–2.

[110] Questions can be raised as to the pertinence of such texts. Do they simply rehearse Pentateuch laws, do they present a vision for a renewed Israel, or do they reflect actual life among the Essenes?

elsewhere and were married. This would support the view of the Essenes offered by Josephus.[111] In contemporary terms we might think of a celibate monastic community and of a third order whose members adhere to the founder's charism but otherwise live normal lives.

It would be for this latter group that the *Damascus Document* sets out rules for the possible annulment of a woman's oath by her husband or father (CD 16:9–12).[112] The document says that a wet-nurse should not pick up a baby in her arms and go in and out on the Sabbath and that not only the manservant but also the maidservant should not be compelled to work on the Sabbath (CD 11:11).[113] Men are enjoined from sleeping with women in the city of the temple (CD 12:1–2).[114] The Inspector (*mebeqer*) of the camp shall be consulted when men marry. It is his responsibility to assure the education of the children of men who have divorced (CD 13:16–19).[115]

In addition to the several stipulations with regard to women and marriage that are set out in the previous paragraph, all of which also appear in the fragments of the *Damascus Document* found in the cave, the tenth-century text has a few other regulations on marriage and sexuality. Citing Deuteronomy 17:17, the *Damascus Document* reiterates the law of royal monogamy (CD 5:1–2). Men who sleep with a woman during her menses or who violate the laws on incest are considered to have violated the temple (CD 5:6–9). And the laws of incest pertain "equally to females" (CD 5:9–11).

There are, however, a large number of statements concerning marriage, women, and sexuality[116] in the ten fragments of the *Damascus Document* found among the Dead Sea Scrolls that do not appear in the tenth-century version of the text.[117] Fragment three of 4QD[a] makes an enigmatic reference to those who make widows their spoils and murder orphans.[118] The

---

[111] Cf. *J. W.* 2.160–161, cited above, p. 47.

[112] Cf. 4QD[f], frg. 4, 2:10–12.

[113] Cf. 4QD[e], frg. 6, 5:16–17; 4Q271, frg. 5, 1:7–8.

[114] Cf. 4QD[f], frg. 5, 1:17–18.

[115] Cf. 4QD[a], frg. 9, 3:4–7.

[116] That is, in addition to the five statements in 4QD[a], frg. 9, 3:4–7; 4QD[e], frg. 6, 5:16–17 (=4QD[f], frg. 5, 1:7–8); 4QD[f], frg. 4, 2:10–12; 4QD[f], frg. 5, 1:17–18; and 6QD frg. 1, 1–3, all of which are replicated in CD[a].

[117] The corpus of statements pertaining to women in the *Damascus Document* has been studied by Cecilia Wassen, *Women in the Damascus Document*, SBLABib 21 (Leiden, Boston: Brill, 2005).

[118] Cf. 4QD[a] frg. 3, 2:22.

tattered sixth fragment of the scroll talks about menstruating women, women who have given birth, and wet-nurses.[119] Qumran's 4QD[b] imposes a ban on a man who has illegal sex with his wife.[120] In 4QD[d], frg. 9, 1–7, there are stipulations for a father who gives his daughter in marriage and speaks about eligible women who have had sexual experience while they were unmarried or widows. This fragment also mentions women who had a bad reputation while living in their father's house. These are to be scrutinized by trustworthy women appointed by the Inspector. These stipulations are also found in 4QD[e], frg. 5, 14–10 and 4QD[f], frg. 3, 7–15. This fragment gives the most complete text of the regulations.

The scroll designated 4QD[e] reprises the matter of the unmarried woman who has a bad reputation and also speaks about widows who sleep with someone else and men who approach their wives at inappropriate times.[121] In addition, 4QD[e] speaks about men who have intercourse with pregnant women, with their fraternal nieces, or with other men, as one sleeps with a woman.[122] The text also speaks about a woman who uses rape as a defense when she has been accused of sexual infidelity.[123] Thereafter the badly mutilated fourth fragment of 4QD[e] mentions kings, a ban on sleeping with certain women, the slave girl, and fathers giving a bride to their sons.[124] Qumran's 4QD[e] also includes passages that have been previously referenced in this overview of the Dead Sea Scrolls.[125] All told, 4QD[e] contains six passages that speak about women and sexual intercourse.

Manuscript 4QD[f] contains four passages that speak about women and sexual activity. All of them replicate material found in other scrolls.[126] Manuscript 4QD[g] contains purity regulations for menstruating women.[127] Finally, the scroll found in cave six (6QD) contains material found in

---

[119] Cf. 4QD[a] frg. 6, 2:1–13.

[120] Cf. 4QD[a] frg. 98, 6:4–5; 4QD[e] frg. 7, 1:12–13.

[121] Cf. 4QD[e] frg. 2, 1:1–18

[122] Cf. 4QD[e] frg. 2, 2:15–17 (= 6QD frg. 5, 2–4).

[123] Cf. 4QD[e] frg. 4, 1:1–7.

[124] Cf. 4QD[e] frg. 4, 1:9–19.

[125] Cf. 4QD[e] frg. 6, 5:16–17 (=4QD[f] frg. 5, 1:7–8; CD 11:11) and 4QD[e] frg. 7, 1:12–13.

[126] Cf. 4QD[f] frg, 3, 7–15 (= 4QD[d] frg. 9, 1–7; 4QD[e] frg. 5, 14–10); 4QD[f] frg. 4, 2:10–12 (= CD 16:9–12); 4QD[e] frg. 6, 5:16–17; 4QD[f] frg. 5, 1:7–8 (= 4QD[e] frg. 6, 5:16–17; CD 11:11); and 4QD[f], frg. 5, 1:17–18 (= CD 12:1–2).

[127] Cf. 4QD[g] frg, 1, 2:6–17 (cf. 4QD[a] 6, 2:1–4).

other scrolls—namely, the ban on two marriages[128] and the prohibition of sexual intercourse with a pregnant woman, a fraternal niece, or a male.[129]

In sum, not only does the *Damascus Document* speak about women, marriage, and sexual intercourse but so, too, do seven of the ten muti-lated scrolls of the document found at Qumran.[130] This abundance of evidence indicates that, while the community of Essenes at Qumran may have been celibate,[131] not all Essenes were.

Why Celibacy?

Why, then, did the members of the monastic-like community observe celibacy? The texts themselves provide no clear answer. Scholars[132] have offered various suggestions as to the motivation of their sexual absti-nence. Koltun-Fromm says: "The evidence . . . does not suggest that the Qumranites were necessarily a mindfully celibate community but, rather, that they developed a heightened sense of semen pollution." She con-tinues, "proper sexuality plays a different role in protecting holy or "hyper-pure" space. In the early Yahad's strident construct of holy space, active sexual relations and women are distanced from the center of activity—the Temple—as a precaution against semen pollution." [133] On the other hand, van der Horst[134] suggests that the sexually abstaining Qumranites were aware of a need to be in a constant state of readiness for an eschatological war.[135] That required the observance of the biblical rules[136] for sexual abstinence in a war situation. Other scholars opine that the Qumranites were celibate because of their study of the Law, which they considered to be a cultic activity.

---

[128] Cf. 6QD frg. 1, 2–3 (= CD 4:20–21).

[129] Cf. 6QD frg. 5, 2–4 (=4QD^e frg. 2, 2:15–17; 4QD^f frg. 2, 2:15–17).

[130] The exceptions are 4QD^c, 4QpapD^h, and 5QD.

[131] Koltun-Fromm, *Hermeneutics of Holiness*, 71.

[132] The contemporaries of the Qumranites, Philo and Josephus attributed the sexual continence of the Essenes to their negative regard for women. Cf. Philo, *Hypothetica* 11:14; Josephus, *J.W.* 2.121. Philo also sees celibacy as necessary for life in common.

[133] Ibid., 72.

[134] Cf. Van der Horst, "Celibacy," 397.

[135] Cf. 1QM; 4Q491–496.

[136] Cf. Deut 23:10-15; 1 Sam 21:5-6; 2 Sam 11:11-13.

In any case, there were other Essenes. These were those who lived in the cities, in "camps," were married, as was the population at large. They may have subjected themselves to a more rigorous sexual discipline than other Jews, but there were men, women, and children—and marriage—in the religious movement to which the community at Qumran belonged. There is no need for this study to examine the texts in detail.[137] For our purposes, the texts have been passed quickly in review to establish the fact of marriage among the Essenes.

Reviewing the evidence, Moshe Bernstein has said that the absence of a mention of women in Qumran's "Rule of the Community," the so-called "Manual of Discipline" (1QS), was an anomaly. When all the documents are taken into consideration, Bernstein is right on target.[138] The publication of the Rule, along with the War Scroll (1QM), the Hymns (1QH), and the Isaiah scrolls (1QIsa[a], 1QIsa[b]), coupled with the views of Philo, Josephus,[139] and Pliny and the presence of predominately male bones in the cemetery at Qumran gave rise to the widely popular view that the Essenes were a celibate community.[140] That, however, was not the way of life for all Essenes. It was certainly not the lifestyle of the Essenes who lived in towns. There is no evidence that celibacy was practiced by city-dwelling Essenes, a Jewish religious group whose particular textual legacy includes Genesis 1:28, "Increase and multiply," among its relatively few citations of the book of Genesis.

And from Another Culture

Rabbinic tradition, particularly those based on the sayings of the tannaim, provides us with some insights into marital customs and obligations in first-century Palestine. The scrolls found near the shores of the

---

[137] For such a study, see William Loader, *The Dead Sea Scrolls on Sexuality: Attitudes towards Sexuality in Sectarian and Related Literature at Qumran* (Grand Rapids, MN: Eerdmans, 2009).

[138] Bernstein, "Texts from Qumran."

[139] Josephus remarks about another order of Essenes was largely overlooked (*J. W.* 2.160–61). He mentions that this other group is "at one with the rest in its mode of life, customs, and regulations" but "differs from them in their view on marriage" (*J. W.* 2.160). Nevertheless it is at Qumran, apparently the location of "the rest," that texts pertaining to marriage have been found.

[140] There is no need here for me to consider the issue as to whether the name "Essene" should be reserved for the monastic community or whether it was equally apropos of city-dwellers who shared their views of Judaism.

Dead Sea reflect the marital views and practices of a group of sectarian Jews, some of whom apparently lived in a monastic community at Qumran[141] while others lived in enclaves around Palestine.

There is yet another source that might prove to be helpful in determining how first-century Jews might have expressed their sexuality. That source is the writings of a pair of Hellenistic Jewish authors, Philo of Alexandria and Flavius Josephus.

Philo

To some extent, Philo of Alexandria represents another subculture in first-century Judaism. He lived in Egypt where there had been a significant Jewish presence for centuries. The most remarkable witness to this presence may well be the Elephantine papyri, dating from the fifth century BCE. Elephantine[142] is an island in the upper Nile, where Jewish soldiers were stationed during the Persian period (495–399 BCE). Archeological excavations have revealed the presence of a Jewish temple on the island. The papyri, written in Aramaic and discovered during the nineteenth century, include divorce documents, personal letters to family members, and contracts. Among other things the papyri tell us about Ananiah, an official in the Jewish temple, who married a former slave owned by a Jewish master, Meshullam. The story of Ananiah and the Egyptian Talmut is a witness to the existence of interracial and intercultural marriage and is an indication that the kind of endogamous culture that characterized Judaism of the Maccabean and subsequent eras[143] was not a factor in the life of fifth-century BCE Jews who formed the Jewish colony at Elephantine.

Philo lived centuries after the heyday of the Jewish community in Elephantine. He was born in Alexandria ca. 20 BCE to a wealthy and aristocratic Jewish family who enjoyed Roman citizenship. Well educated and privileged, he once visited the Temple in Jerusalem[144] and was a

---

[141] Some years ago Hans Hübner expressed the view that scholars may have exaggerated the celibacy of the Qumran community. He held that its members might have embraced temporary sexual abstinence for special reasons. Cf. "Zölibat in Qumran?," *NTS* 17 (1971): 153–67.

[142] At the time the island was called Yeb.

[143] Philo of Alexandria, for example, was opposed to intermarriage. See *Spec. Laws* 3.29.

[144] Cf. *Providence* 2.64.

member of an Alexandrian Jewish delegation to the Emperor Caligula in 40 CE that sought to ease tensions between Jews and Romans in the imperial capital. Philo's nephew Tiberius was for a time governor of Judea and was Titus' chief of staff in suppressing the Jewish revolt (66–70 CE). Philo himself died ca. 50 CE, so he was a contemporary of Jesus and his disciples but his writings are of limited value for understanding marriage in first-century Palestine. Not only was Philo from Egypt, he was also of the upper class and his writings evidence a curious mixing (by our contemporary standards) of Hellenistic philosophy and the Jewish biblical tradition.

His views on sexuality and marriage[145] are colored by his Hellenistic philosophical tradition. As often as not, what the Scriptures say about sex and marriage serve as a basis for Philo's allegorical exposition. Thus, his treatment of Genesis 1:27, "God created humankind in his image, in the image of God he created them; male and female he created them,"[146] points to an asexual creation. William Loader correctly observes that Philo's interpretation of the biblical text is not to be understood as positing the idea that the sexual is to be abandoned, thus creating an ideological ground for the practice of celibacy. Philo never uses the Scripture in this way.[147]

It is well known that Philo considered women inferior to men in several respects.[148] On the other hand, he says that, "everything which is without a woman is imperfect and homeless."[149] As for marriage, a "woman changes her habitation from her family to her husband."[150] As for sex, Philo often warns against excessive passion but sexual intercourse in itself is good. Philo uses the imagery of sexual intercourse to speak about the soul's intercourse with God.[151] This is, in fact, an important motif in Philo's writings.[152]

---

[145] Cf. Richard L. Baer, *Philo's Use of the Categories Male and Female*, ALGHJ 3 (Leiden: Brill, 1970); William Loader, *Philo, Josephus*.

[146] Cf. *Creation* 134; *Heir* 164.

[147] Cf. Loader, *Philo, Josephus*, 16.

[148] See, for example, *Questions and Answers on Genesis* 1.27.

[149] *Questions and Answers on Genesis* 1.26.

[150] *Questions and Answers on Genesis* 1.27.

[151] Cf. *Questions and Answers on Genesis* 4.18.

[152] Cf. Richard A. Horsley, "Spiritual Marriage with Sophia," *VC* 33 (1979): 30–54, esp. 32.

It is, nonetheless, clear that, for Philo, the purposes of sexual union is procreation. He writes that men and women, "in the course of nature come together for the procreation of children"[153] and that marriage laws "are intended to promote the generation of children."[154] What he writes about the marriage of Isaac illustrates well his attitude toward sexual passion and the procreative purpose of sexual union: "It was not for the sake of irrational sensual pleasure or with eagerness that he had intercourse with his wife but for the sake of begetting legitimate children."[155]

Philo's brand of sexual restraint does not require sexual continence.[156] Moses is, however, a special case. Exodus 34:28 says that Moses, "was there with the LORD forty days and forty nights; he neither ate bread nor drank water." To Moses' fast, Philo added an affirmation that Moses also abstained from sex.[157] Moses, he wrote,

> Had to be clean, as in soul so also in body, to have no dealings with any passion, purifying himself from all the calls of mortal nature, food and drink and intercourse with women [*tēs pros gynaikias physiōs*]. This last he had disdained for many a day, almost from the time when, possessed by the spirit, he entered on his work as a prophet, since he held it fitting to hold himself always in readiness to receive the oracular messages. (Moses 2.68–69)[158]

Moses was, however, an exception, the only such exception that appears in Philo's extensive writing.[159] And Moses had already fulfilled the command to increase and multiply before he embraced, in Philo's view, a life of sexual continence for the sake of his prophetic mission.[160] Richard

---

[153] *Cherubim* 43.

[154] *Spec. Laws* 1.112.

[155] *Questions and Answers on Genesis* 4.154; cf. 4.86; *Moses* 1.28–29.

[156] Cf. Horsley, "Spiritual Marriage," 39; Loader, *Philo, Josephus*, 109.

[157] Philo may have been influenced in his portrayal of Moses' sexual abstinence by Exodus 19:15.

[158] The translation is taken from *Philo Volume VI*, trans. F. H Colson, Loeb Classical Library 289 (Cambridge, MA: Harvard University Press, 1962).

[159] The tradition that Moses abstained from sexual intercourse during this period of his life appears in later rabbinic literature. See *b. Yebam.* 62a; *b. Sabb.* 87a; *b. Pesaḥ.* 87b cf. *Sifre* on Num 2:1-2 (= 99–100); *Exod. Rab.* 46:3.

[160] Extant literary witness to the rabbinic tradition includes a couple of passages that point to Zipporah's displeasure with the idea of prophetic continence. Cf. *Avot of Rabbi Nathan* 9:22, a fairly late text, and the much earlier *Sifre* on Num 11:26-30.

Horsley observes that "although he [Philo] emphasizes the deeper, spiritual meaning of Scripture discerned through allegorical interpretation, he still retains a sense of the validity and importance of the Jewish Law as it bears on social life. Thus, he sees the human practice of sexual intercourse as Nature's mode of reproduction according to natural, hence divine law."[161] Philo's vision of the future, says Loader, "envisages a proper place for sexual desire, expressing itself in the pleasure of sexual intercourse in marriage for procreation, a reflection of what he insists should be the norm in the present."[162]

The philosopher's description of Moses who took up a life of sexual continence so as to be in union with God and be ready to receive oracular messages is remarkably similar to his description of the so-called Therapeutae and Therapeutrides, who

> When they have divested themselves of their possessions and have no longer aught to ensnare them they flee without a backward glance and leave their brothers, their children, their wives, their parents, the wide circle of their kinsfolk, the groups of friends around them, the fatherlands in which they were born and reared, . . . pass their days outside the walls pursuing solitude in gardens or lonely bits of country. (*Contempl. Life* 18, 20)[163]

The group is acceptable to a Jew like Philo because the men already had wives and children and therefore had fulfilled the command of Genesis 1:28.[164] Subsequently they embraced a life characterized by *enkrateia*, the virtue of self-control, in this case in the form of sexual abstinence, in order to devote themselves to the contemplation of the divine. Drawn from affluent and well-educated circles,[165] they lived in clustered houses outside of town, each of which had a small room, a "sanctuary," devoted to meditation. So that the inhabitants would not be distracted, their

---

Sifre says that Miriam, Moses' sister, thought that he was neglecting the divine command in Gen 1:28. See the discussion in Boyarin, *Carnal Israel*, 159–64.

[161] Horsley, "Spiritual Marriage," 39.

[162] Cf. Loader, *Philo, Josephus*, 133, with reference to *Rewards* 108–10.

[163] The translation is taken from *Philo, Volume IX*, trans. F. H Colson, Loeb Classical Library 363 (Cambridge, MA: Harvard University Press, 1941).

[164] Cf. Joan E. Taylor, *Jewish Women Philosophers of First Century Alexandria: Philo's Therapeutae' Reconsidered* (London: Oxford University Press, 2004), 264.

[165] See Taylor, *Jewish Women Philosophers*, 103.

houses were not as close to one another as were houses in town.[166] The best example of such a community, says Philo, was a group that lived near the shores of Lake Mariout,[167] fairly close to Alexandria. The group included women, "most of them aged virgins."[168] The order of reclining in their festal gatherings was based on their seniority in their community. The men gathered on the right, the women by themselves on the left.[169]

Philo's overarching concern was to present Judaism in a way that made it comprehensible to and accepted by his Hellenistic readers. His desire in this regard is most evident in his allegorical interpretation of the Jewish Scriptures. It may be that his eagerness to be in dialogue with Hellenists may have colored his description of the Therapeutae and Therapeutrides as an ideal expression of religious devotion. It could be that the exposition of his ideas was influenced by the cult of Isis' linking of sexual continence to the exercise of the cult[170] or by his desire to show that Jews were at least as virtuous as those who espoused the sexual abstinence put forth as an idea by the increasingly popular Stoic and Cynic philosophies.[171] One might even question whether the Therapeutae and Therapeutrides ever existed. They may have been a product of the philosopher's fertile imagination, a fictive contemplative community whose way of life represents what he considered to be an idyllic kind of human existence.[172]

Josephus

Having acknowledged his dependence on Moses—that is, the Torah—as his source, the historian, Flavius Josephus, begins his story of the

---

[166] Cf. *Contempl. Life* 24–25.

[167] During the twentieth century the lake, known in antiquity as Lake Mareotis, was reduced in size to less than twenty square miles, about one quarter of its size at the beginning of the century.

[168] *Contempl. Life* 68.

[169] Cf. *Contempl. Life* 67, 69.

[170] See Taylor, *Jewish Women Philosophers*, 256–57.

[171] See Joan E. Taylor, "Philo of Alexandria on the Essenes: A Case Study on the Use of Classical Sources in Discussion of the Qumran-Essene Hypothesis," *The Studia Philonica Annual* 19 (2007): 1–28, esp. 24.

[172] Cf. Boyarin, *Carnal Israel*, 40; Troels Engberg-Petersen, "Philo's *De Vita Contemplativa* as a Philosopher's Dream," *JSJ* 30 (1999): 40–64; Ross Shepherd Kraemer, "Spouses of Wisdom: Philo's Therapeutrides, Reconsidered," chap. 3 in *Unreliable Witnesses: Religion, Gender, and History in the Greco-Roman Mediterranean* (New York/ Oxford: Oxford University Press, 2011), 57–116.

Jewish people with the story of creation. Coming to the sixth day of creation, he writes simply, "the sixth day He [God] created the race of four-footed creatures, making them male and female; on this day also He formed man [*anthrōpon*]" (*Ant.* 1.32). Josephus makes no mention of the creation of gendered humanity nor does he cite Genesis 1:28's "Increase and multiply." He also omits the command in Genesis 9:1 from Genesis' narrative of the aftermath of the flood (Gen 9:1).[173] Josephus does, however, say of Adam that he "longed for children, and was seized with a passionate desire to beget a family."[174]

Josephus' story of the noble history of his people passes in review many of the sexual episodes in the biblical narrative and touches on the marital escapades and sexual practices of the Herodians, but his account of Moses on Sinai refers only to his abstinence from food.[175] There is no reference to Moses' sexual abstinence, as there was in Philo.

Tracing his ancestral story, Josephus comments on the heroes and heroines as well as the antiheroes, making abundant references to their marital and sexual experiences. His accounts include an element of romantic love, undoubtedly under the influence of the Hellenistic[176] culture in which he lived. The historian comments as well on the laws of his people, including the various laws on marriage, sexuality, and ritual purity. He affirms that marriage is for the sake of procreation[177] but he says nothing about a divine ordinance to that effect.

For Josephus marriage appears to be the normal form of social life throughout history, including the period in which Jesus lived. The singular exception that he mentions is a small group of Jewish men who were so suspicious of women[178] that they gathered together in a males-only community whose members embraced a life of sexual continence.

Within the Empire

While we may be inclined to consider the marital situation in first-century Palestine solely from a Jewish religious-cultural perspective, we ought not forget that at the time of Jesus Palestine was under the imperial

---

[173] Cf. *Ant.* 1.109–12.

[174] *Ant.* 1.67.

[175] Cf. *Ant.* 3.339.

[176] Cf. Louis H. Feldman, *Josephus's Interpretation of the Bible* (Berkeley: University of California Press, 1998), 185.

[177] Cf. *Ant.* 4.259, 261, 290; 5:168; *Ag. Ap.* 2.199.

[178] Cf. Philo, *Hypothetica* 11:14.

domination of the Roman Empire. The laws and policies of Rome were not without import for people living in the empire.

With regard to marriage,[179] the principal laws at the time were the *Lex Iulia de maritandis ordinibus* (18 BCE),[180] the *Lex Iulia de adulteriis coercendis* (18 BCE), and the *Lex Papia Poppaea* (9 CE). Caesar Augustus was successful in getting the consuls to sponsor this latest legislation.[181] The earlier laws addressed the issue of the low rate of reproduction among Roman citizens while the latter was chiefly concerned with promiscuity. The *Lex Papia Popaea* emended the earlier *Lex Iulia de maritandis ordinibus* which Augustus had passed by means of his tribunician power (*tribunicia potestas*). Together the two laws were popularly known as the *Lex Iulia et Papia Poppaea*.[182]

The laws were aimed at restoring the moral basis of society and were intended to promote marriage and procreation.[183] As such, they had a sociopolitical purpose. The Julian laws punished adultery and penalized those who were not married or were childless.[184] Men between the ages of 25 and 60 were bound[185] by the law, as were women between 20 and 50. Those whose spouse had died and who had divorced were granted a short period of time in which to bring their lives into conformity with the law.

Men were penalized if they did not marry.[186] For example, bachelors were not allowed to receive inheritances or legacies. Since betrothal was considered as marriage for purposes of the law, some men who did not

---

[179] See Susan Treggiari, *Roman Marriage: Iusti Conjuges from the Time of Cicero to the Time of Ulpian* (Oxford: Oxford University Press, 1991).

[180] For the history of this law, see Giovanni Rotondi, *Leges publicae populi Romani: Elenco cronologica con una introduzione sull' attività legislativa dei comizi romani* (Hildesheim: Georg Olms, 1966, a photographic reproduction of the 1912 Milan edition), 443–45.

[181] Cf. P. A. Brunt and J. M. Moore, *Res Gestae Divi Augusti: The Achievements of the Divine Augustus* (London: Oxford University Press, 1967), 11, 47.

[182] Cf. Biondo Biondi, *Storia di Roma*, 20: *Il Diritto Romano* (Bologna: Licinio Cappelli, 1957), 322. Rotondi notes that it is impossible completely to distinguish the two laws from one another. Cf. *Leges publicae*, 445.

[183] Cf. Biondi, *Il Diritto Romano*, 322, 348; see also Tacitus, *Ann.* 3.25.

[184] Cf. Jane F. Gardner, *Family and Familia in Roman Law and Life* (Oxford: Clarendon, 1998), 128, 226.

[185] Cf. Biondi, *Il Diritto Romano*, 322.

[186] Plutarch used the expression *agamiou dike* to describe the legal action taken against a bachelor for not marrying. Cf. Plutarch, *Lysander*, 30.

want to marry entered into a long-term betrothal. The *Lex Papia Poppaea* closed this loophole by limiting the engagement to two years and forbidding betrothal to young girls. If a couple had no children, the surviving spouse could inherit only 10 percent of the deceased's estate.

Divorced women were granted a period of eighteen months within which to remarry. For widows, the grace period was two years. Nevertheless, they were required to wait twelve months before remarrying to make sure that they had not become pregnant by their former husbands.[187] The purity of the family line was a most important consideration in the Julian laws on marriage.

The Julian legislation provided benefits for those who had large families.[188] Privileges were accorded to those who had three children (*iustos tres liberos*[189]). According to Aulus Gellius, among the privileges accorded to the person who had more children than his colleague was priority in taking the fasces to the consul.[190] Former slaves, freedmen, were encouraged to form traditional familiae.[191] Female Roman citizens who had three live births and freedwomen who had four lives births, all of whom had to be born after she was freed, were exempt from male guardianship.[192] They were allowed to conduct business and legal affairs without a tutor and thus were able, for example, to initiate divorce proceedings.

These laws were principally enacted to counteract a falling birthrate, principally among the upper classes.[193] The legislation was neither entirely

---

[187] Cf. Bonnie Bowman Thurston, *Women in the New Testament: Questions and Commentary*, Companions to the New Testament (New York: Crossroad, 1998), 22.

[188] In a society in which the rate of infant mortality was high, an infant who survived until its naming day, generally eight days after the birth, was considered a live birth for purposes of the Law. Cf. Lynn H. Cohick, *Women in the World of the Earliest Christians: Illuminating Ancient Ways of Life* (Grand Rapids, MN: Baker Academic, 2009), 109, n. 24.

[189] Gardner discusses the implications of the phrase. Did it mean only legitimate children? Did it include adoptive children? Did it refer only to living children? Cf. Gardner, *Family and* Familia, 47–55.

[190] Cf. *Noctes Atticae* 2.25.4. Gellius references chapter 7 of the *Lex Julia*. See Gardner, *Family and* Familia, 47.

[191] Cf. ibid., 182.

[192] Cf. Gaius, *Inst.* 1.145, 171.

[193] Cf. Brunt-Moore, *Res gestae*, 46–47. In this regard, one might note that the *Lex Iulia et Papia Poppaea* prohibited marriage with a person of lower social rank. Cf. Biondi, *Il Diritto Romano*, 339.

popular[194] nor fully successful but it was the law of the Empire. To what extent they were enforced in a far-off territory like Palestine remains a moot question. They were, nevertheless, the pertinent laws of the Empire under which Jesus and his disciples lived.[195]

Conclusion

Although we have no direct evidence of any legal or social obligation that first-century Palestinian Jewish men marry, an abundance of circumstantial evidence warrants the conclusion that Palestinian men of that era did marry in fidelity to their Jewish tradition and in order to propagate their race.

The rabbinic tradition, with roots in first-century Palestine, linked the requirement of marriage to the fulfillment of the first mitzvah in the Law, "Increase and multiply." The tradition gives no clear examples of any observant Jewish men who were not married. The inherent conservatism of the tradition allows its reflections of the obligation to marry to be retrojected onto the situation in first-century Palestine.

Thanks to the discovery of the Dead Sea Scrolls, scholars are now much more aware of the diversity in first-century Palestinian Judaism than they once were. "Normative Judaism" as a cipher for rabbinic Judaism is now past history. The discovery of the scrolls along with the nearby archeological digs at Qumran have confirmed the existence of a monastic community of Jews whose members embraced sexual continence but that also confirmed the existence of like-minded sectarians who married and lived in the cities in faithful observance of the Jewish Law. It is not beyond the realm of possibility that the Qumranites were men who had fulfilled the first commandment in the Law before retreating to a life of prayer and study or fulfilled in locations outside the monastic environ-

---

[194] In this regard, Brunt-Moore (*Res gestae*, 47) remarks, "One may suspect that Augustus was not entirely frank when he said that the senate wished him to pass it [the legislation]."

[195] More than thirty years ago, Corrado Marucci demonstrated the importance of the Julian laws on marriage, adultery, and divorce for the "exception clause" in Matthew 5:32; 19:9. Under Roman law in effect at the time, a man was required to divorce his wife if he suspected her of adultery. See Marucci, *Parole di Gesù sul divorzio: ricerche scritturistiche previa ad un risonsamento teologico, canonistico e pastorale della dottrina cattolica dell' indissolubilità del matrimonio*, Aolisiana 16 (Naples: Morelliana, 1982).

ment where cultic obligations and the avoidance of pollution required an absence from women.[196]

What Philo, Josephus, and Pliny said about the Essenes now appears to be descriptive of a monastic community rather than of a broader movement. At most, its existence was an exception to a general rule. With respect to celibacy, the views of the Hellenistic authors, Philo, Josephus, and Pliny, on the Essenes do not concur with what the texts found at Qumran actually say. Rather, they conform to a philosophic ideal of a religious community. These writers' distorted views of the Essenes' sexual mores were influenced by their own peculiarly Hellenistic views of human sexuality.

To quote a recent study, "Neither the Essenes nor some segments of their group were celibate; they did not disdain marriage or non-procreative sexual activity."[197] Heger notes, "I would . . . hesitate to impose on the Torah-centered Essene/Qumran group a way of life fundamentally in conflict with the divine command to the first humans to multiply."[198]

As David W. Chapman writes, marriage and procreation were "duties for most Jewish people."[199] First-century Jewish men considered it to be among their primary obligations to marry and raise a family. Such was the situation when Jesus of Nazareth appeared on scene, proclaiming, "The time is fulfilled, and the kingdom of God has come near; repent, and believe in the good news" (Mark 1:15).

---

[196] Van der Horst suggests that the development might possibly have been in the other direction, namely, from a "strictly celibate movement towards a situation in which gradually married couples were also tolerated or accepted" ("Celibacy," 394).

[197] Paul Heger, "Celibacy in Qumran—Hellenistic Fiction or Reality? Qumran's Attitude Toward Sex," *RevQ* 101 (2013) 21–90, 90.

[198] Heger, "Celibacy in Qumran," 60.

[199] David W. Chapman, "Marriage and Family in Second Temple Judaism," in Campbell, *Marriage and Family*, 182–240, 215.

3

Jesus and the Disciples

Mark's is the oldest of the canonical narratives about Jesus. After the important preliminaries to Jesus' ministry have been described, the evangelist describes the inauguration of Jesus' ministry: "After John was arrested, Jesus came to Galilee, proclaiming the good news of God, and saying, 'The time is fulfilled, and the kingdom of God has come near; repent, and believe in the good news'" (Mark 1:14-15).[1] This announcement of the proximity of the coming of the kingdom gives rise to much of the content and urgency of the sayings of Jesus, even in the form in which they are now preserved in the canonical gospels.[2]

What impact did Jesus' proclamation of the Good News and the proximate coming of the kingdom of God mean for Jesus with regard to marriage? What impact did Jesus' proclamation of the kingdom of God and the proximate coming of the kingdom of God mean for those whom he called to be disciples, people who lived in a religious society in which "be fruitful and multiply" was considered to be an important expression of the will of God? Among other things, what did Jesus mean when he

---

[1] Cf. Matt 4:12-17; Luke 4:15-16.

[2] See, for example, Glenn Holland, "Celibacy in the Early Christian Church," in *Celibacy and Religious Traditions*, ed. Carl Olson (New York/Oxford: Oxford University Press, 2008), 65–84, 67.

told his disciples, "There are eunuchs who have made themselves eunuchs for the sake of the kingdom of heaven"[3] (Matt 19:12c)?

The Call of the First Disciples

After the programmatic scene at the beginning of his gospel, Mark's narrative moves to a first episode in the ministry of Jesus—namely, the calling of the first disciples (Mark 1:16-18). Jesus' ministry would not be complete were he not to have disciples.

The Fishermen

According to Mark, the first disciples were two pairs of fishermen. Walking by the Sea of Galilee, in northern Palestine, Jesus saw the brothers Simon and Andrew casting their net into the waters and said to them, "Follow me and I will make you fish for people" (Mark 1:17). With few modifications the narrative is reprised in Matthew 4:18-19. In both of these gospels, the two brothers are portrayed as accepting Jesus' challenging invitation. Discipleship, following Jesus, demands a significant gesture.[4] Immediately, the pair of brothers left their nets and followed him.[5] The immediacy of their response points to the power of Jesus' invitation[6] and perhaps adds a note of eschatological urgency[7] to the scene. Jesus, who preached that the Kingdom of God has come near, now receives an immediate response from those whom he calls to be his first disciples.

With his predilection for literary duality,[8] Mark adds a parallel account, the call of another pair of brothers, James and John, sons of Zebedee (Mark 1:19-20). In this Mark is again followed by Matthew (Matt 4:21-22).

---

[3] "Kingdom of heaven" is Matthew's paraphrase of "kingdom of God."

[4] Cf. John 4:28.

[5] Adela Collins infers from Mark's account of the cure of Simon's mother-in-law (Mark 1:30-31) that Simon may have left his wife and perhaps other family members to follow Jesus. Cf. Adela Yarbro Collins, *Mark*, Hermeneia (Minneapolis: Fortress, 2007), 481.

[6] Morna Hooker attributes the immediacy of the brothers' response to the force of Jesus' personality. Cf. Morna D. Hooker, *The Gospel According to Saint Mark*, BNTC (Peabody, MA: Hendrickson, 1991), 39.

[7] Cf. Mark 1:10, 12, 20, 21, 23, 29, 30.

[8] Cf. Frans Neirynck, *Duality in Mark: Contributions to the Study of the Markan Redaction* (Leuven: Peeters-Leuven University Press, 1988).

As the first pair of brothers, this pair also responds immediately. They leave their father and his boat behind as they depart to follow Jesus. This parallel account differs from the first in the image used to portray the immediacy of the response. Simon and Andrew left their nets. James and John left their father and his hired hands. This suggests that Jesus' call involves a choice on his part. Jesus addresses his invitation, almost a command, only to the pair of brothers, not to their father, Zebedee, nor to his hired hands (Mark 1:20).

The paradigmatic account of the call to discipleship is intended to portray the claim of the Kingdom of God, mediated through Jesus, on those whom he calls. The eschatologically qualified response of Peter and Andrew receives dramatic response in their leaving their nets, their means of employment, to follow Jesus (Matt 4:20; Mark 1:18). The similarly qualified response of James and John is expressed in their leaving the boat and their father (Matt 4:22; Mark 1:20).

The evangelists' accounts of the dramatic immediate response of the first disciples to Jesus' invitation to follow him does not mean that the two pairs of brothers totally abandoned their means of providing for themselves.[9] The narrative is not intended to portray the practical details of their lives, specifically their employment; rather, it was intended to express their eager response to the invitation that they had received.

Luke has not taken over the Markan story about the call of the first disciples but he has included in his narrative an episode that features a disciple of Jesus catching people (Luke 5:1-11). The story focuses on Simon Peter, to whom alone Jesus says, "From now on you will be catching people" (Luke 5:10).[10] The Lukan account presupposes that Peter had previously met and somehow accepted Jesus, whom he calls "Master" (*epistata*, Luke 5:5).

[9] Focant notes that the call narratives in Mark 1:16-20 "neither confirm nor inform that the disciples left everything to follow Jesus." The possibility of their doing so was simply not mentioned. Cf. Camille Focant, *The Gospel according to Mark: A Commentary* (Eugene, OR: Pickwick, 2012), 416.

[10] The verbal expression (*esē zōgrōn*) is in the singular. In the parallel accounts, at Matthew 4:19 and Mark 1:17, the noun "fishers" (*alieis*) in Jesus' words to Peter and Andrew is in the plural. Luke 5:1-11 makes no mention whatsoever of Andrew. In many ways, the narrative found in Luke 5:1-11 is Luke's account of the primacy of Peter (cf. Matt 16:16-19), complemented by that segment of Jesus' farewell discourse in which he says, "Simon, Simon, listen! Satan has demanded to sift all of you like wheat, but I have prayed for you that your own faith may not fail; and you, when once you have turned back, strengthen your brothers" (Luke 22:31-32).

Having previously accepted Jesus as his Master, Peter continues to own a boat and work together with other fishermen. Only after the miraculous catch of fish and Jesus' primatial words to Simon Peter does Luke add "When they had brought their boats to shore, they left everything [*aphentes panta*] and followed him" (Luke 5:11).[11]

The Tax Collector

All three Synoptic authors tell the story of Jesus' calling of another disciple—a tax collector, a man employed in the collection of custom duties.[12] This tax collector is variously identified in the three accounts but Mark and Luke agree in calling him Levi.[13] In all three accounts, Jesus addresses the invitation to "follow me" to the tax collector. In response, the tax collector "got up and followed him."[14]

Luke, however, adds a preliminary remark to this description, namely, that the tax collector "left everything" (*katalipōn panta*[15]) and then got up and followed Jesus. Although he had "left everything," the tax collector was nonetheless able to host a dinner for Jesus and other guests in his own house (*en tē oikia autou*).[16] This suggests that, in fact, the tax collector had not really abandoned all that he had. Apparently all that he had left was his previous profession. On reading the call narratives it appears that the motif of leaving everything is a Lukan idea. The tax collector left everything (Luke 5:28) as did Simon Peter (Luke 5:11).

"We Have Left Everything and Followed You"

In Mark's story about Jesus, just prior to the account of the passion, Mark recounts that Peter, on behalf of the other disciples, said to Jesus,

[11] The plural of the participles *akatagogontes* and *aphentes* and the verb *ēkoluthēsan* refers to Simon, James, and John, and that unnamed person or, probably, those unnamed persons who were with Simon. Note the use of the plural in vv. 5-6.

[12] Cf. Mark 2:13-14; Matt 9:9-11; Luke 5:27-28.

[13] Mark calls him "Levi son of Alphaeus" but Luke drops the patronymic. Matthew calls him "Matthew," perhaps under a literary demand that the name of the tax collector appear on the list of the twelve disciples/apostles that Matthew has taken over from Mark (cf. Matt 10:3-4; Mark 6:16-19).

[14] Mark's words (Mark 2:14) are taken over verbatim in Matthew 9:9 and Luke 5:28.

[15] Luke 5:28; cf. Luke 5:11. Bovon describes this as "Lukan radicalism" and references Luke 9:2; 12:33; 14:26, 33. Cf. François Bovon, *Luke 1: A Commentary on the Gospel of Luke 1:1–9:50*, Hermeneia (Minneapolis: Fortress, 2002), 171, n. 24.

[16] Cf. Matt 9:11-13; Mark 2:15-17; Luke 5:29-32.

"Look, we[17] have left everything [*hēmeis aphēkamen*[18] *panta*] and have followed you" (Mark 10:28; cf. Matt 19:27). In the Markan narrative, Peter's reminder to Jesus, not found in Luke, contrasts Peter and the disciples, whose spokesperson Peter is, with the rich man of Mark 10:17-20.[19] The rich man had received an invitation to discipleship; Jesus had said "follow me" (Mark 10:21; Matt 19:21; Luke 18:22)—just as he did to Peter, Andrew, James, John, and the tax collector![20]—but the rich man declined the invitation. Instead of following Jesus, he went away, for he had many possessions.[21] In contrast, Peter reminds Jesus that the group of disciples to whom he had just spoken[22] had left everything and followed him. In the Markan context, particularly in light of the contrast between the disciples and the rich man and Jesus' short instruction on riches, Peter's "everything" refers to riches and possessions. Jesus' disciples did what the rich man was unable or unwilling to do.

Jesus' Response

Whatever the particular nuances of the disciples' leaving their all (*panta*) might have been, Jesus responds to Peter's retort with:

> Truly I tell you, there is no one who has left house or brothers or sisters or mother or father or children for my sake and for the sake of the good news, who will not receive a hundredfold now in this age—houses, brothers and sisters, mothers and children, and fields,

[17] In the Greek text the "we" is emphatic. Mark applies emphasis by means of the grammatically unnecessary *hēmeis*, "we."

[18] This is the verb used by Luke in 5:11. Its aorist tense refers to a definite action in the past. The perfect tense of the next verb, "followed" (*ēkolouthēkamen*), suggests past action whose effect continues into the present. The disciples for whom Peter speaks have been with Jesus as he evangelizes.

[19] Parallel with Matthew 19:16-22; Luke 18:18-23.

[20] Cf. Mark 1:16-20; 2:13-17; 3:13-19.

[21] In the NT the command to abandon one's possessions is found only in this story. The command may reflect the influence of an ascetically and eschatologically oriented community behind these traditions. Cf. Ernst Lohmeyer, *Das Evangelium des Markus*, 17th ed., KEK 1 (Göttingen: Vandenhoeck und Ruprecht, 1997), 214–17, 219; Joachim Gnilka, *Das Evangelium nach Markus*, vol. 2, 5th ed., EKKNT 2 (Zürich/Neukirchen/Vluyn: Benizger Verlag/Neukirchener Verlag, 1998), 84–85; Francis J. Moloney, *The Gospel of Mark: A Commentary* (Peabody, MA: Hendrickson, 2002), 200. Cf. Matt 8:20; Luke 9:58.

[22] Jesus' words to the disciples were about riches and the rewards of discipleship (Matt 10:23-31; Matt 19:23-30; Luke 18:24-30). The instruction follows the departure of the rich man and immediately precedes Peter's retort.

with persecutions—and in the age to come eternal life. (Mark 10:29-30)[23]

It is noteworthy that Jesus speaks about the disciples' leaving their houses, brothers and sisters, their mothers and fathers, but he makes no mention of their wives—neither in his rehearsal of the implications of Peter's all (*panta*) nor in his exposition of what lies in store for the disciples in the future—even though they would appear to have been married since they had children. Jesus' words are addressed not only to Peter but also to the disciples on behalf of whom he spoke.

Jesus' introduces his response to Peter with a solemn introduction, "Truly I tell you" (*amen legō hymin*), with a second-person pronoun in the plural. Commentators generally agree that the words are not intended for all believers but for the group of "disciples"—that is, those who traveled around with Jesus and learned from him. These itinerant disciples constitute a literary character in Mark's narrative. In Mark, the group of disciples includes the Twelve but is not limited to the Twelve.[24] Jesus' words are not addressed to all believers,[25] only to the itinerant group who accompanied him as he proclaimed the Good News (Mark 1:14-15).

Jesus' response moves beyond the narrow scope of Peter's self-justification with an affirmation that speaks not only of leaving one's possessions but also of leaving members of one's own family, brothers and sisters, mother and father, and children. In fact, the evangelist had already noted that two of the disciples, James and John, had already left their father, Zebedee.[26] Were the abandonment of their parents to have been permanent, Jesus' disciples would have been in contravention of the fourth commandment,[27] which Jesus had approvingly quoted just a few verses earlier in the Markan narrative (Mark 10:19).[28]

---

[23] Cf. Matt 19:28-30; Luke 18:29-30.

[24] Cf. Robert H. Gundry, *Mark: A Commentary on His Apology for the Cross* (Grand Rapids, MI: Eerdmans, 1993), 566–67.

[25] Cf. Collins, *Mark*, 481; M. Eugene Boring, *Mark: A Commentary*, NTL (Louisville: Westminster John Knox, 2006), 292.

[26] Cf. Mark 1:20 (Matt 4:21).

[27] "Fourth" commandment—that is, in the traditional Roman Catholic enumeration of the precepts of the Decalogue. Marcus suggests that Mark's order of abandoned kin, which differs from that of Luke 14:26 and *G. Thom.* 55, may be due to the tension with the commandment. Cf. Joel Marcus, *Mark 8–16*, AYB 27A (New Haven/London: Yale University Press, 2009), 732.

[28] Cf. Mark 7:9-13. According to early rabbinic tradition (cf. *Deut. Rab.* 1:15; *Sifre Deut.* 336; etc.), one who honors father and mother is the beneficiary of blessings not only in this life (cf. Exod 20:12; Deut 5:16) but also in the life to come.

That would seem not to have been the case. Jesus speaks of abandoning material possessions and of splitting from one's family for his sake and the sake of the Gospel. The latter phrase, "for the sake of the gospel" (*eneken tou euangeliou*), is a reference to the work of evangelization in which the disciples, particularly but not exclusively[29] the Twelve, were involved.[30] The disciples left their homes and their families in order to preach the Gospel. Jesus' words do not imply a permanent abandonment of the family circle.

The Extended Family

In their work of evangelization, Jesus' disciples were encouraged to stay in the homes of the people who were open to their message.[31] Welcomed into these homes, where hospitality implied extended kinship, they acquired additional[32] homes, with additional brothers and sisters, mothers and children.[33] Since the Markan narrative was written a couple of generations after the original disciples evangelized on behalf of the Gospel, the situation that Jesus describes would reflect the then-extant network of early Christian communities, where familial language was used as they gathered in one another's homes.[34] The house church was a household, a real family. At that time, the age to come had not yet begun. It would be inaugurated with the coming of the Son of Man.[35] Believers lived in the penultimate age.

---

[29] Cf. Luke 10:1-12.

[30] Cf. Mark 3:14; 6:7-12; Matt 10:5-15; Luke 9:1-6.

[31] Cf. Mark 6:10; Matt 10:11; Luke 9:4; 10:5-7.

[32] Jesus' "hundredfold" (*hekatontaplasisona*) is clearly hyperbolic. It suggests that the disciples whom he coopted into his missionizing would acquire a large number of extended kin. Cf. *T. Job* 4:6–9.

[33] Jesus' reflection on the reward that his disciples receive in this age does not include a hundredfold of fathers. This is most likely due to the fact that believers have only one father, God the Father. See also Marcus, *Mark 8–16*, 739. With regard to the omission of father because of some form of radical egalitarianism in early Christianity, see Mary Ann Beavis, *Mark*, Paideia (Grand Rapids, MI: Baker Academic, 2011), 154; Collins, *Mark*, 482.

[34] Thus Collins writes (*Mark*, 481), "This saying of Jesus is significant on two levels. On one level, it concerns Peter and the other disciples who are characters in the narrative. On another level, it addresses the situation of the audiences of the Gospel." See also John R. Donahue, *The Theology and Setting of Discipleship in the Gospel of Mark: The 1983 Père Marquette Theology Lecture* (Milwaukee: Marquette University Press, 1983), 32–42.

[35] Cf. Mark 10:62; Matt 26:64; Luke 22:69.

This age is one characterized by persecution and active hostility. Jesus tells the disciples that they will not only have the resource of an extended family but also endure "persecutions." In this respect, the disciples experience hostility even from their own families. The disciples are not unlike Jesus himself. Earlier in his gospel narrative, the evangelist Mark recounts an incident in which Jesus' own family tried to restrain him:

> Then he went home; and the crowd came together again, so that they could not even eat. When his family heard about it, they were out to restrain him for people were saying, "He has gone out of his mind." (Mark 3:19b)

The story of Jesus being accused of being mad (*exestin*) was obviously an embarrassment to early Christians, so embarrassing in fact that neither Matthew nor Luke included it in their respective revisions of the Markan story about Jesus. Those who transcribed Mark's text some centuries later were equally embarrassed.[36] Instead of writing about "his family" (*hoi par'autou*)—in Koine Greek the expression connotes people who were intimately involved with a person, especially his family and relatives— some copyists in the Western manuscript tradition wrote "those who with him" (*peri autou*), thus removing the onus from Jesus' family and kin. Although Luke omits the story of the allegation that Jesus had gone mad and his family's reaction to the allegation, he does tell a story about the folks of Jesus' hometown being so angry with him that they wanted to throw him off a cliff (Luke 4:28-29).

Persecution

Jesus had spoken to his disciples on several occasions about the persecutions that they would face. Notable among Jesus' words to his disciples is the beatitude on persecution: "Blessed are you when people hate you, and when they exclude you, revile you, and defame you on account of the Son of Man" (Luke 6:22).[37] In the missionary charge to the disciples Jesus forewarned them of the persecutions that they would face (Matt 10:17-25; Luke 12:11-12). The expanded version of the Q material

[36] Cf. Bruce M. Metzger, *A Textual Commentary on the Greek New Testament*, 2nd ed. (Stuttgart: Deutsche Bibelgesellschaft / United Bible Societies, 1994), 70; Collins, *Mark*, 226–27.

[37] Cf. Matt 5:10-11.

found in Matthew 10 explicitly mentions family strife.[38] In Jerusalem, Jesus again forewarns the disciples: "For they will hand you over to councils; and you will be beaten in synagogues; and you will stand before governors and kings because of me" (Mark 13:9).[39] The warning continues with a fearsome indication that some of this persecution will come from members of one's own family: "Brother will betray brother to death, and a father his child, and children will rise against parents and have them put to death; and you will be hated by all because of my name" (Mark 13:12-13).[40]

Despite Peter's affirmation that the disciples left[41] everything (Mark 10:28), the reality to which he refers may not have been entirely volitional on the disciples' part. Sometimes, the acceptance of Jesus' Gospel estranged believers from members of their family who did not accept his message. In such cases, the departure from the family may have been not physical but, as we might call it today, psychological, insofar as strained and perhaps broken relationships would have represented a "leaving" of one's family. A saying of Jesus preserved in the Sayings Source, appears to address this issue:

> Do you think that I have come to bring peace to the earth? No, I tell you, but rather division! From now on five in one household will be divided, three against two and two against three; they will be divided:
> father against son and son against father,
> mother against daughter and daughter against mother,
> mother-in-law against her daughter-in-law
> and daughter-in-law against mother-in-law. (Luke 12:51-53)[42]

---

[38] Cf. Matt 10:21.

[39] Cf. Mark 13:9-13; Matt 24:9-12; Luke 21:12-17.

[40] Cf. Luke 21:16-17. The Matthean version of this apocalyptic warning does not mention internecine strife.

[41] The verb *aphēkamen* is in the active voice.

[42] Cf. Matt 10:34-36, which the evangelist has incorporated into the "mission discourse." Luke 12:53 (par. Matt 10:36) alludes to Mic 7:6. Another version of the logion is found in *G. Thom.* 16: "Jesus said, 'men perhaps think that I have come to cast peace upon the world, and they do not know that I have come to cast divisions upon the earth, fire, sword, war. For there will be five in a house, there will be three against two and two against three; the father against the son and the son against the father, and they will stand alone.'"

Leaving One's Wife

In Mark and Matthew's version of the dialogue between Peter and Jesus after the episode of the rich man,[43] Jesus' response to Peter did not even allude to the possibility of husbands abandoning their wives or of wives leaving their husbands. The double omission[44] is striking. Other horizontal and family relationships are included both in Jesus' spelling out the implications of Peter's "everything" (Mark 10:29) and his commentary thereon (Mark 10:30). Peter himself had made no claim that he and his fellow itinerant missionaries had left their spouses.

In Mark's seminal literary narrative, it would have been quite startling for the reader were Jesus to have talked about male disciples leaving their wives. Jesus had just issued a solemn challenge, "What God has joined together, let no one separate" (Mark 10:9). Mark adds that the disciples received additional instruction as to what this challenge meant.[45] Could, then, Peter tell Jesus that in fidelity to him, he and his fellow disciples had separated from their wives in order to follow Jesus?

In Mark 10:28 Peter was most likely speaking on behalf of both male and female disciples who accompanied Jesus. Luke says that disciples were sent out in pairs (Luke 10:1). There is no reason to doubt that some of these pairs were married couples. As early as the third century, Origen suggested that Andronicus and Junia, the apostolic couple whom Paul greets in Romans 16:7, might have been among the pairs whom Jesus sent out.[46]

Luke's condensed version of the dialogue between Peter and Jesus (Luke 18:28-29) introduces into the discussion—namely, in Jesus' response to Peter—the idea of a disciple leaving his wife. Jesus' response supposes a situation in which the disciples were married men. According to Luke, Jesus called married men to be his disciples. In Luke, Peter's

---

[43] Matthew adds that he is a "young" man (Matt 19:20, 22; cf. Mark 10:20; Luke 18:21, whose "from my youth" had been dropped from the Matthean narrative) most likely because it would have been difficult for a person to affirm that he had kept all the commandments unless he were a relatively young man.

[44] The omission certainly implies that Mark 10:28-30 is not truly pertinent to the discussion on clerical continence and celibacy. Nor should it serve as a basis for "evangelical poverty," with regard to which, see Francis J. Moloney, *A Life of Promise: Poverty—Chastity—Obedience* (Wilmington, DE: Michael Glazier, 1984), 55–65.

[45] Cf. Mark 10:10-12.

[46] Cf. *In epist. ad Romanos* 10, 18–21 (PG 14, 1279–80).

retort to Jesus spoke of the disciples' leaving their "homes" (*ta idia*[47]) rather than their leaving "everything" (*panta*), the expression that the evangelist found in his Markan source. Luke's choice of words may have been prompted by the Lukan theme of Jesus' disciples sharing their possessions, particularly exploited in Acts and expressed in Acts 5:32 as "no one claimed private ownership [*elegen idion*] of any possessions, but everything [*apanta*] they owned was held in common."[48]

Editing the Markan story that he had used as his source, Luke omits from Jesus' commentary on Peter's words the mention of "fields" (*agrous*, Mark 10:29; Matt 19:29) and with it the reference to the rural setting of the traditional logion. The omission of a reference to fields probably results from Luke's attentiveness to the audience for which he was writing, most likely, a cultured urban-centered group.

Luke also omits the Matthean-Markan reference to "sisters" (*adelphas*) but he adds a reference to leaving one's wife (*gynaika*).[49] One female relationship, "sister," has been dropped in favor of another, "wife," and Luke has changed the sequence of the female references so that Jesus' words read: "Truly I tell you, there is no one who has left house [*oikian*] or wife or brothers or parents or children, for the sake of the kingdom of God who will not get back very much [*pollaplasiona*] more in this age, and in the age to come eternal life" (Luke 18:28-29). Bockmuehl suggests that the mention of wife in Luke 18:29 "is probably inserted for the sake of completeness or possibly in keeping with a pattern of ascetic sympa-

---

[47] The Greek *ta idia*, denotes one's own things, whether possessions or interests. In references to one's possessions, the expression can specifically connote a person's home. See the exegetical discussions apropos Luke 2:49 and John 19:27.

[48] Cf. Luke Timothy Johnson, *The Literary Function of Possessions in Luke–Acts*, SBLDS 39 (Missoula, MT: Scholars Press, 1977), 144–45.

[49] I agree with most commentators—Elisabeth Schüssler Fiorenza (*In Memory of Her: A Feminist Theological Reconstruction of Christian Origins* [New York: Crossroad, 1984], 145–46), Luke Timothy Johnson (*The Gospel of Luke*, SP 3 [Collegeville, MN: Liturgical Press, 1991], 278), and April D. DeConick (*Holy Misogyny: Why the Sex and Gender Conflicts in the Early Church Still Matter* [New York: Continuum, 2011], 56) among them—that "wife" is a Lukan redactional addition but Gundry (*Mark*, 567) apparently demurs. Schüssler Fiorenza argues that Luke's addition of "wife" represents an attempt to limit the ranks of wandering charismatic preachers to men. The Markan parallel implies that originally both men and women abandoned the comfort zone of their homes, land, and family to follow Jesus. Audet observes that taking Luke's addition of "wife" as an argument for celibacy is to do violence to the rules of grammar and to neglect the context. Cf. Audet, *Mariage et célibat*, 56.

thies also found in 14:26 and 20:35."[50] It may have been that Luke was sensitive to the Stoic and Cynic ideas circulating within the Hellenistic culture in which his intended readers lived.

The *oikia* in Jesus' response—most likely echoing Peter's "homes" (*ta idia*) —should probably be rendered by "home or household" since Luke's version of Jesus' words focuses on personal relationships rather than on material possessions,[51] such as the English "house" implies. The wife of the *pater familias* would have been, after the householder himself, the most important person in the Greco-Roman household. Accordingly, leaving one's household would seem to imply the leaving of one's spouse.

By using a simple "very much" (Luke 18:29) rather than a series of things and relationships that would be multiplied,[52] Luke's version of the consolation of those who have abandoned their households avoids the difficulty that would arise were he to have written that those who left their wives were to acquire wives "a hundredfold."

Another passage in the Gospel according to Luke also contains a striking reference to one's wife—namely, Luke 14:26. After the parable of the great supper[53] Jesus turned to the crowds and said, "Whoever comes to me and does not hate [*miseō*] father and mother, wife and children, brothers and sisters, yes, and even life itself, cannot be my disciple." The saying also occurs, in slightly different form[54] and in a different literary context in Matthew 10:37, where it is one of the sayings of Jesus that Matthew has collated into his Mission Discourse, without, however, any mention of a disciple's negative attitude and corresponding negative behavior toward one's wife: "Whoever loves father or mother more than me is not worthy of me; and whoever loves son or daughter more than me is not worthy of me."

---

[50] Markus Bockmuehl, *Simon Peter in Scripture and Memory: The New Testament Apostle in the Early Church* (Grand Rapids, MI: Baker Academic, 2012), 119. Cf. Carolyn Osiek and David L. Balch, *Families in the New Testament*, Family, Religion, and Culture (Louisville: Westminster John Knox, 1997), 136; Stephen Finlan, *The Family Metaphor in Jesus' Teaching: Gospel and Ethics* (Eugene, OR: Cascade, 2009), 62.

[51] Note also Luke's omission of "fields." Cf. I. Howard Marshall, *Commentary on Luke*, NIGTC (Grand Rapids, MI: Eerdmans, 1978), 688.

[52] Cf. Mark 10:30; Matt 19:29.

[53] Luke 14:15-24; Matt 22:1-14.

[54] Notable is Matthew's mitigation of the language. Instead of speaking about a disciple's hatred for the members of his immediate family, Matthew speaks of loving them more (*agapaō hyper*) than one loves Jesus.

As an isolated saying with no narrative context, a variant of the Q logion appears in the Coptic *Gospel of Thomas*, to wit, "He who does not hate his father and his mother will not be able to be my disciple and (he who does not) hate his brothers and his sisters and (does not) bear his cross as I have, will not be worthy of me" (*G. Thom.* 55). A somewhat similar saying occurs later in the *Gospel of Thomas*, as follows: "He who does not hate his fa[ther] and his mother as I (do), will not be able to be my [disciple]. And he who does [not] love his [father and] his mother as I (do), will not be able to be my [disciple]" (*G. Thom.* 101).

These Coptic sayings concur with Matthew in not mentioning a man's wife as a person from whom a man should—psychologically, we might say—separate himself in order to be a disciple of Jesus. This sharpens the question as to whether Luke's list of family members or Matthew's list is more faithful to the Q saying.[55] Did the Q saying make mention of a man's wife or not?

It is likely that the mention of "wife" in Luke 14:26 is a Lukan redactional alteration of the earlier tradition under the influence of Luke 14:20,[56] where an invitee declines the invitation to participate in the marriage feast because he was newly married.[57] Luke's language about a husband hating his wife is clearly hyperbolic. Luke wants to insist, as he does in his account of the various responses to the invitation to the great banquet,[58] that family and economic interests should not interfere with discipleship.

The use of hyperbole is a literary technique used by Luke[59] to underscore the radical nature of discipleship, as a pair of sayings on discipleship in Luke 9:60-61 so clearly exemplifies. The first saying, derived from

---

[55] See the terse footnote in James M. Robinson, Paul Hoffmann, and John S. Kloppenborg, eds., *The Critical Edition of Q*, Hermeneia (Minneapolis: Fortress, 2000), 451, n. 10.

[56] Cf. Joseph A. Fitzmyer, *The Gospel According to Luke X–XXIV*, AB 28A (Garden City, NY: Doubleday, 1985), 1061, 1063; Marshall, *Luke*, 592.

[57] Matthew's version of the parable of the great supper does not include this excuse (cf. Matt 22:2-6); neither is it found in *G. Thom.* 64.

[58] Cf. Luke 14:18-20.

[59] In antiquity, hyperbole (*hyperbolē*) was a well-known rhetorical device, one with which Luke, a skilled author, would have been familiar. Quintilian, one of the masters of rhetoric in Hellenistic antiquity, notes that every use of hyperbole goes beyond what is credible. Cf. R. Dean Anderson Jr., *Glossary of Greek Rhetorical Terms: Connected to Methods of Argumentation, Figures and Tropes from Anaximenes to Quintilian*, CBET 24 (Leuven: Peeters, 2000), 122–24.

Luke's Q source[60] seems to contravene a basic demand of filial piety—that of burying one's dead.[61] The second saying, found only in Luke, suggests that following Jesus demands greater commitment than does allegiance to a biblical prophet.[62]

Not to be overlooked is that the evangelist Luke links these expressions of radical discipleship with the mission of evangelization. A form of radical discipleship is required while one is sent out to evangelize. Luke has added a mission statement, "Go and proclaim the kingdom of God" (Luke 9:60b) to the Q logion[63] and has placed the brace of sayings on radical discipleship immediately before the mission of the seventy disciples (Luke 10:1-12).

Does radical discipleship for the sake of a mission imply lasting hatred for one's wife and a rejection of the marital bond? Does hyperbolic language adequately correspond to reality?

The Disciples' Work and Wives

In Mark 10:28, Peter professes that the disciples have abandoned everything in order to follow Jesus. Does that mean that they permanently abandoned their means of livelihood in order to be his disciples?

Their Boats

While on mission the disciples were not able to fish and were separated from their wives and families, but the separation does not appear to have been permanent. Luke portrays Peter as continuing to own a boat after his initial encounter with Jesus. In the original Markan story, after the fishermen had left their nets (Mark 1:18), Jesus tells his disciples to get a boat ready so that he could escape the crowds (Mark 3:9).

There is, in fact, ample evidence in the gospel stories to suggest that the disciples returned to work after they were called by Jesus. On another occasion Mark says that Jesus got into a boat, presumably to address the crowds that gathered nearby (Mark 4:1-2; Matt 13:1-2). On still another

---

[60] Cf. Matt 8:21-22.

[61] Cf. Tob 4:33; 6:15.

[62] Cf. 1 Kgs 19:19-21, a story about Elisha and Elijah.

[63] The missionary command is absent from Matthew 8:22.

occasion, Jesus got into a boat with his disciples (Mark 4:35-36;[64] Matt 8:23; Luke 8:22) and later becalmed the sea when a storm arose (Mark 4:37-41; Matt 8:24-27; Luke 8:23-25). The narrative concludes with Jesus' getting out of the boat (Mark 5:1-2; cf. Luke 8:27). Later, Jesus crosses to the other side of the sea in the boat (Mark 5:21).[65] Still later the disciples were out on the sea in the boat when Jesus walked on the water to reach them (Mark 6:45, 47-52; Matt 14:22-33;[66] Luke 6:16-21).

The epilogue to the Fourth Gospel adds a story about Peter and a few other disciples fishing sometime after Jesus was raised from the dead (John 21:1-9). According to the Johannine scenario, Peter and the other fishermen disciples had returned to their old job. In the Fourth Gospel, the fact that Peter and his companions were Jesus' disciples did not include the requirement that they abandon all their possessions and forsake their secular livelihood.

Their Houses

Shortly after the call of the first disciples, Jesus went to the home of Simon and Andrew, accompanied by the two sons of Zebedee. Simon's mother-in-law was suffering from a fever. This is the first miracle story in the Markan narrative.[67] The story has been repeated, in substantially the same way, in Matthew 8:14-15[68] and in Luke 4:38-39.[69] The narrative

[64] Mark's setting of the scene of the stilling of the storm in Mark 4:25 is such that the unspecified "them" (*autois*) of v. 35 and the third-person plural of the verbs, "leaving . . . they took" (*dielthōmen . . . paralambanousin*) clearly refer to the disciples (*tois idiois mathētais*) of Mark 4:34.

[65] Some important ancient manuscripts lack a specific reference to the boat. Cf. Metzger, *A Textual Commentary*, 72–73.

[66] The Matthean narrative includes the folkloric tale of Peter getting out of the boat to walk to Jesus (vv. 28-31).

[67] The previous episode in the Markan story, Mark 1:21-28, featured an exorcism rather than a miracle story as such.

[68] I have addressed some of the differences between the Markan and Matthean accounts, particularly those pertaining to the figure of Simon, in "The Transformation of a Motif: 'They Entered the House of Simon and Andrew' (Mark 1, 29)," SNTSU 18 (1993): 5–40.

[69] Fitzmyer considers the Lukan version of the story to be paradigmatic for the Lukan stories about Galilean women who serve Jesus (Luke 8:1-3; 23:49, 55). Cf. Fitzmyer, *The Gospel According to Luke I–IX*, 549.

portrays Simon as belonging to a family that participated in the Jesus movement early on.[70]

Even after his call, Simon Peter continued to own his own home (Matt 8:14; Luke 4:38) as did Levi (Mark 2:15; Luke 5:29; cf. Matt 9:10) and the Beloved Disciple (John 19:27), along with Jesus who had a home in Capernaum (Mark 2:1[71]). Mark's references to the house in which Jesus had discussions with his disciples about the meaning of his parables (Mark 7:17) and his teaching on divorce (Mark 10:10) say nothing about the owner of these houses but this house or houses must have belonged to Jesus, one of his disciples, or perhaps one of his female patrons.

Their Wives

The story of Jesus' miraculous curing of Peter's mother-in-law implies that Peter was married at the time of the cure. John Chrysostom made what is only implicit in the gospel narratives quite explicit. He wrote, "Where there is a mother-in-law, there is a wife; where there is a wife, there is a marriage."[72] The reference to Simon's mother-in-law in the three Synoptic Gospels is a fairly explicit suggestion in the canonical gospels that one of the disciples was married. Nevertheless, it is only an incidental implication of a narrative that portrays Jesus as a charismatic worker of miracles from the outset of his public ministry. Is it not likely that other disciples were also married?

Early patristic tradition spoke of the Apostle Philip, one of the Twelve, as having had a number of daughters. The historian Eusebius of Caesarea quotes two second-century bishops to this effect—namely, Papias of Hierapolis,[73] relatively early in the second century CE, and Polycratus of Ephesus,[74] at the end of the century. The canonical gospels make no mention of the apostle Philip's family. Given the fact that both Papias and Polycratus mention only Philip's daughters, it is virtually certain

---

[70] Cf. Rudolf Pesch, *Simon Petrus: Geschichte und geschichtliche Bedeutung des erste Jüngers Jesu Christi, Päpste und Papstum* 15 (Stuttgart: *Anton Hiersemann*, 1980), 2–7.

[71] Cf. Mark 3:19b.

[72] *In illud: Vidi Dominum (Isa 6:1), homilies 1–6* 4.3 (PG 56, 123c).

[73] Cf. Eusebius, *Ecclesiastical History* 3.39.8–9.

[74] Cf. *Eccles. Hist.* 3.31.2-3; 5.24.2. Jerome also cites the letter of Polycratus to Victor, the bishop of Rome, in which the bishop of Ephesus mentions the daughters of the apostle Philip. Cf. *De viris illustribus* 45 (PL 23, 659a).

that these early writers confused[75] the apostle Philip with Philip "the evangelist, one of the seven [deacons],"[76] with whom Paul stayed in Caesarea.[77] Luke recounts that this Philip had four unmarried daughters who had the gift of prophecy. Luke makes no mention of Philip's wife; neither do Papias and Polycratus.

Respect for Jewish Law

Returning to the evidence of the New Testament itself, no matter how incidental the cure of Peter's mother-in-law may have been, the detail is important.[78] Given the interpretation of the Torah being developed by the teachers of the Law as well as the Roman *Lex Iulia*, at least nominally in effect in Palestine, it is to be expected that Peter and the other disciples would have been married.[79] Otherwise they would have been in violation of both the Jewish Law[80] and the Roman law of first-century Palestine.

The disciples' offense against the Jewish Law would have been considered a far more serious transgression of the Law than was their plucking an ear of grain on the Sabbath in order to have something to eat (Mark 2:23-24; Matt 12:1-2; Luke 6:1-2) or their not washing their hands before eating a meal (Mark 7:1-2, 5; Matt 15:1-2). Had the disciples of Jesus not been married, their failure to do so would surely have prevented the disciples' appearance in synagogue and temple, an appear-

---

[75] Similarly, Jo-Ann Ford Watson, "Philip," *ABD* 5:310–12, at 311; and John Y. H. Yieh, "Philip," *NIDB* 4, 499–500, at 500. To the contrary, Cochini, *Priestly Celibacy*, 72.

[76] Cf. Acts 6:5. On the conflation, see Christopher R. Matthews, *Philip, Apostle and Evangelist: Configurations of a Tradition*, NovTSup 105 (Leiden: Brill, 2002), 23–34. Matthews opines that the traditions about Philip recounted in Acts 8 have all the earmarks of the activities of an apostle.

[77] Cf. Acts 21:8-9.

[78] It "clearly says enough," writes Hengel. Cf. Martin Hengel, *Saint Peter: The Underestimated Apostle* (Grand Rapids, MI: Eerdmans, 2010), 104.

[79] John 17:11, 15 are not immediately apropos to the discussion at hand, but they do provide a perspective from which to reflect on the marriage of Jesus' disciples. As late as the last half of the fourth century in the West, the anonymous author known as the Ambrosiaster was able to write, "All the apostles with the exception of John and Paul were married." *In epistolam B. Pauli ad Corinthios secundam* XI, 2; cf. PL 17.3202. Eusebius and Augustine use Psalm 109:9 to affirm that Judas had children who were orphaned after his death but their midrashic scriptural commentary is not a good source of historical information. Cf. Eusebius, *Demonstration of the Gospel* 10 (PG 22, 740); Augustine, *Enarrations on the Psalms* 108.11 (CC 40, 1590).

[80] Technically the Law required multiplying, not necessarily marriage.

ance regularly attested in the New Testament. Moreover, it is all but certain that the evangelists would have made note of the disciples' bachelorhood since their social status would have been so counter-cultural. That Jesus had unmarried disciples would have been indeed noteworthy at the time when the canonical gospels were written.

It is axiomatic that the gospel narratives consistently leave secondary figures out of their stories.[81] Secondary figures would serve only to com-plicate the narrative. Though unnamed, the wives of at least some of the disciples may have been among the Galilean women who followed Jesus to Jerusalem and took care of his needs (Mark 15:40-41; Matt 27:55; Luke 8:1-3; 23:49, 55).[82]

A contemporary reader of the gospels might be disappointed not to know the names of the wives of Jesus' disciples but rabbinic literature is likewise generally silent[83] about the names of the wives of the great rabbis, even though mention is frequently made of their children.[84] Men-tion of a rabbi's children often occurs obliquely when a rabbi is identified as the son of a named individual, who was also a rabbi. Such was the case of Rabbi Judah who is identified as the son of Tema in the Mishnah's "Sayings of the Fathers."[85]

The Matthean story of the temple tax (Matt 17:24-27) is not particularly germane to the discussion of the disciples' marriage but it is an indica-tion of Jesus' respect for the Jewish Law and of the respect that Jewish Christians had for the Law even toward the end of the first century. Matthew's vision is, after all, that Jesus came to fulfill the Law: "Do not think that I have come to abolish the law or the prophets; I have come not to abolish but to fulfill. For truly I tell you, until heaven and earth pass away, not one letter, not one stroke of a letter, will pass from the law until all is accomplished" (Matt 5:17-18).

Whatever opposition to the Law on the part of Jesus that may be found in the Synoptics derives not from Jesus' opposition to the Law *per se* but rather to his rejection of an interpretation of the Law that contravenes the well-being of God's people. And, for Jesus' Jewish contemporaries,

[81] See Hengel, *Peter*, 105.

[82] See ibid., 108, 110, 130.

[83] A notable exception is Judith, the wife of Rabbi Hiyya, who is mentioned in the Bavli (*b. Yebam.* 65b).

[84] Cf. Acts 21:8-9. There is nary a mention of Philip's wife even though Luke makes mention of his four daughters.

[85] Cf. *m. ʾAbot* 5:21.

"be fruitful and multiply" was an expression of the will of God, the first commandment in the Law.

A Family Man

Some authors say that the married Simon Peter was a family man,[86] implying that his wife had borne children. This is as much based on later tradition[87] as it is on a social situation in which a man was expected to divorce his wife and remarry had she not born children within ten years of living with her husband. As a socially acceptable pious Jew, Peter would have been expected to have a family. The time in which he lived was one in which a consensus was beginning to emerge among the teachers of the Law that God's command in Genesis 1:28 was not fulfilled until a man had at least two children.[88]

In his *Ecclesiastical History*, Eusebius of Caesarea reports that one of the arguments that Clement of Alexandria advanced against the Nicolaitan heresy was that Peter had children.[89] In the West, the fourth-century Ambrosiaster, which argued for clerical continence, conceded that Peter was chosen as chief of the apostles, despite his being married and having children.[90] The apocryphal *Acts of Peter*[91] tells a story about Peter's paralyzed daughter.[92] When she was ten, a rich man named Ptolemaeus who

---

[86] Cf. Hengel, *Peter*, 106; Pheme Perkins, *Peter: Apostle for the Whole Church*, Studies on Personalities of the New Testament (Columbia: University of South Carolina Press, 1994), 28–29.

[87] Cf. Oscar Cullmann, *Peter, Disciple, Apostle, Martyr: A Historical and Theological Study* (Philadelphia: Fortress, 1953), 23.

[88] Cf. *m. Yebab.* 6:6. See above, p. 35.

[89] See Eusebius, *Ecclesiastical History* 3.30.1; cf. Clement of Alexandria, *Miscellanies* 3.52.1–2, 4, 5.

[90] See the Ambrosiaster, *Quaestiones Veteris et Novi Testamenti* 127.33 (CSEL 40, 414).

[91] Eusebius (*Ecclesiastical History* 3.3.2) says of *The Acts of Peter*, that "we know nothing" of its being handed down as a Catholic writing, "since neither among the ancient nor the ecclesiastical writers of our own day has there been one that has appealed to testimony taken from them." This and subsequent quotations from the *Ecclesiastical History* are taken from Isaac Boyle, *The Ecclesiastical History of Eusebius Pamphilus* (Grand Rapids, MI: Baker Book House, 1988).

[92] See Wilhelm Schneemelcher, "The Acts of Peter" in Schneemelcher and Wilson, *New Testament Apocrypha*, 2, 271–321, 285–86. Two pages are missing from the Coptic manuscript at this point in the story. Apparently Ptolemaeus requested Peter's daughter in marriage several times. She was eventually kidnapped by his servants and

had seen her and her mother bathing wanted to marry her. He sent messengers to ask for her but her mother, Peter's wife, refused.

1 Corinthians 9:5

During his missionary journeys Peter was accompanied by his wife.[93] Speaking of the rights of an apostle in the *apologia* of 1 Corinthians 7, Paul asks, "Do we not have the right to be accompanied by a believing wife, as do the other apostles and the brothers of the Lord and Cephas?" (1 Cor 9:5). Hengel infers from the question that the large majority of early Christian missionaries, those whom Paul calls apostles and brothers of the Lord, were married.[94] Paul's words do indeed suggest that the missionary apostles and brothers of the Lord were married.

His rhetorical question was posed about twenty-five years after Jesus had called Simon Peter to be his disciple. The climactic position in Paul's list belongs to Cephas, the Aramaic nickname meaning "crag" or "rock," by which Peter was known in early Christian circles.[95] The nickname was routinely used of Peter by Paul.[96] When Paul writes about "Cephas" in 1 Corinthians 9:5, he is reflecting early Christian tradition and early Christian usage, as he does in other places when he refers to Peter by his Aramaic nickname.

The NRSV renders the Greek expression *adelphēn gynaika* of 1 Corinthians 9:5 as "believing wife." The Greek words literally mean "sister woman."[97] The Greek *gynē*, "woman," refers to an adult female. Since the time of Homer, the term was specifically used in reference to a mar-

---

brought to him but she became paralyzed. Later, Peter and his wife brought her home. Because of the young woman, Ptolemaeus eventually became a believer.

The extant manuscript fragments mention Peter's home but they do not indicate the location of the dramatic series of events connected with the young girl's kidnapping and her later restoration to her parents.

Questions can be raised as to whether the story originally belonged to the apocryphal *Acts of Peter*. Cf. Andrea Lorenzo Molinari, *"I Never Knew the Man": The Coptic Act of Peter (Papyrus Berolinensis 8502.4), Genre and Legendary Origins*, BCNH, Sect. Ét. 5 (Quebec: Laval University Press / Leuven: Peeters, 2000), 1–116.

[93] Cf. Perkins, *Peter*, 28.

[94] See Hengel, *Peter*, 112.

[95] Cf. Matt 16:18.

[96] Cf. 1 Cor 1:12; 3:22; 9:5; 15:5; Gal 1:18; 2:9, 11, 14. Paul refers to the man as "Peter" only in Gal 2:7-8.

[97] A footnote in the NRSV renders the two Greek words as "a sister as wife."

ried woman, thus having the connotation "wife."[98] This is clearly the meaning of the term in 1 Corinthians 7 and 9, the two chapters in the letter in which Paul writes about marriage and human sexuality.[99] In fact, were the "woman" (*gynaika*) of 1 Corinthians 9:5 not to mean wife, this would be the only instance in Paul's forty-one uses of the term in 1 Corinthians in which the term *gynē*, woman, did not mean wife. A primary rule of textual interpretation, including New Testament exegesis, is that the connotation of a term is to be drawn from the literary context in which it was used. The "woman" (*gynē*) of 1 Corinthians 9:5 must therefore be understood to mean "wife."[100]

Indeed, the social and (Roman) legal situation in a provincial capital of the Roman Empire, as Corinth was, would have created a cultural situation in which the term *gynē*, "woman," would have more readily applied to a married woman, a wife, than to an unmarried adult female, for which Paul used the term *parthenos*, "virgin," in 1 Corinthians 7.[101]

That the wife[102] is qualified as a "believing" (*adelphēn*[103]) woman reflects the ancient biblical tradition that a person marry within the family of God.

---

[98] Cf. LSJ, s.v. "*gynē*."

[99] Cf. 1 Cor 7:1, 2, 3 [2x], 4 [2x], 10, 11, 12, 13, 14 [2x], 16 [2x], 27 [3x], 29, 33, 34, 39; 11:3, 5, 6 [2x], 7, 8 [2x], 9 [2x], 10, 11 [2x], 12 [2x], 13, 15. Cf. 1 Cor 5:1; 14:34, 35.

[100] Cf. Raymond F. Collins, *First Corinthians*, SP 7, 2nd. ed. (Collegeville, MN: Liturgical Press, 2006), 336; Anthony C. Thiselton, *The First Epistle to the Corinthians: A Commentary on the Greek Text* (Grand Rapids, MI: Eerdmans, 2000), 681; Roy E. Ciampa and Brian S. Rosner, *The First Letter to the Corinthians*, The Pillar New Testament Commentary (Grand Rapids, MI: Eerdmans, 2010), 401.

[101] Cf. 1 Cor 7:25, 28, 34, 36, 37, 38.

[102] Heid postulates that the apostles may have been accompanied by their wives but that they did not have sexual intercourse with them. He argues, "we can conclude from the fact that children are not mentioned that there were no children in the company of the apostles and that therefore the apostles did not have marital intercourse" (*Celibacy in the Early Church*, 32).

[103] Paul uses sibling language, *adelphos* and *adelphē*, more than one hundred times in his extant correspondence, most often in 1 Corinthians. With but one exception, Romans 16:15, this language is always used metaphorically, to denote members of the believing community. Cf. Mary K. Birge, *The Language of Belonging: A Rhetorical Analysis of Kinship Language in First Corinthians*, CBET 31 (Leuven: Peeters, 2004), 79, 86; and Reider Aasgaard, *"My Beloved Brothers and Sisters!" Christian Siblingship in Paul*, ECC 265 (London: T&T Clark International, 2005), esp. 3, 238–39, 295. In Romans 16:15 an anonymous woman is identified as Nereus's sister (*tēn adelphēn autou*). That the term *adelphē* is to be taken in a biological sense is indicated by the qualifying personal pronoun.

Stickler (*Clerical Celibacy*, 94–95), however, argues that Paul uses the word *adelphē*, which means "sister," to support the idea that Paul is speaking about a relationship

Reflective of this tradition is Paul's affirmation that a widow is free to marry anyone she wishes, "only in the Lord" (*monon en kyriō*, 1 Cor 7:40).

The Greek text of 1 Corinthians 9:5 speaks about a "believing woman," *adelphēn gynaika*, in the singular, indicating that Paul was speaking about the other apostles, the brothers of the Lord, and Cephas being each accompanied by a woman, almost certainly their wives. Some ancient authors, writing in Latin—for example, Tertullian, the Ambrosiaster, and Pelagius—and some ancient Greek manuscripts of the New Testament in the Western tradition[104] read *gynaikas*, "women," rather than *adelphēn gynaika*, "believing woman," in 1 Corinthians 9:5.

This alternate reading, with a plural and the omission of "believing," reflects a tradition current in the West during the third through fifth centuries that early Christian evangelists were accompanied by groups of women who attended to their needs, just as Jesus' needs had been attended to.[105] The plural reading is an example of what Bart Ehrman calls "the orthodox corruption of Scripture,"[106]—that is, a modification of the text to make its reading conform to the "orthodoxy" of a later age.

Although Greco-Roman society tolerated concubines and prostitutes and Jewish society theoretically allowed polygyny, the marriage of a man to more than one wife, it would certainly have been scandalous for the leaders of the early churches to go on trips, *a fortiori* missionary trips, accompanied by a woman other than their wife. In the earliest of his letters, 1 Thessalonians 2:10, and elsewhere, Paul emphasizes that upright conduct on the part of evangelists was crucial to the preaching of the Gospel.

It is conceivable—though hardly likely—that Paul wanted his readers to think that the married Cephas traveled with an unmarried female companion rather than his wife. Such conduct would have been ill suited

---

in which continence is the norm. In corroboration, he cites three sixth-century texts—Gregory the Great, the Council of Gerona, and the Second Council of Auvergne—which use the Latin *soror*, "sister," in this sense.

[104] These include a relative few "Old Latin" (*Vetus Latina*) manuscripts and the ninth-century manuscripts designated as F and G.

[105] Cf. Luke 8:1-3, etc.

[106] Cf. Bart D. Ehrman, *The Orthodox Corruption of Scripture: The Effect of Early Christological Controversies on the Text of the New Testament* (Oxford: Oxford University Press, 1993). Given the focus of his work, Ehrman does not study 1 Corinthians 9:5. Neither does Bruce Metzger in his important work, *A Textual Commentary*, a study of the important variant readings of the text of the New Testament.

to the proclamation of the Gospel. Since Cephas was accompanied by a woman, that woman was most certainly his wife.

The Tradition Continued

After Paul, the patristic tradition continued to affirm that Peter was accompanied by his wife when he traveled as an apostle. Clement of Alexandria believed that Peter's wife traveled with him as a "sister" evangelist but that they abstained from sexual relations during the course of their travels. The postulated abstinence is without any foundation in what Paul said about Cephas being accompanied by a "believing wife." Indeed, a pair of recent authors,[107] commenting on the rhetorical question raised by Paul in 1 Corinthians 9:5, note that the question touches on a key issue already raised in 1 Corinthians, namely, a person's sexual needs. The responsible satisfaction of sexual needs is the issue that Paul specifically addresses in 1 Corinthians 7. In the light of what Paul writes in chapter 7, especially in verses 1-5, it would hardly have been possible for him to think of those whom he mentions in 1 Corinthians 9:5 as leading a life of sexual continence.

According to Clement of Alexandria, Peter's wife and the other apostles' wives were instrumental in preaching the Gospel in women's circles.[108] Ciampa and Rosner observe that Paul's rhetorical question is raised within the context of 1 Corinthians 9:3-18, a passage in which Paul raises the question of material support for his mission, the kind of financial support that he foreswore in order to preach the Gospel free of charge. Were Paul to have been accompanied by a wife[109] during his missionary voyages his wife could have reduced his workload by working as a coevangelist. Alternatively, she might have worked to support him as he carried out his ministry.[110]

In addition to Clement, other early century witnesses carry on the tradition that Peter was accompanied by his wife during the course of his missionary journeys. For example, the Pseudo-Clementine *Recognitions* and *Homilies*, probably written in the third and early fourth centu-

---

[107] Cf. Ciampa and Rosner, *First Corinthians*, 401.

[108] Cf. *Miscellanies* 3.53–54; 7.63.2.

[109] On the matter of Paul having a wife, see chapter 4, below, pp. 123–32, 134–38.

[110] On the possibilities for women to work outside the home, cf. Cohick, *Women in the World*, 225–55, esp. 232–42.

ries, respectively,[111] state that Peter's wife accompanied him to Laodicaea.[112] Clement himself portrays Peter as being a witness to his wife's martyrdom:[113]

> They say, accordingly, that the blessed Peter, on seeing his wife led to death, rejoiced on account of her call and conveyance home, and called very encouragingly and comfortingly, addressing her by name, "Remember thou the Lord." Such was the marriage of the blessed, and their perfect disposition toward those dearest to them. (*Miscellanies* 7.11)[114]

The report, preserved in this form in the first years of the third century, is echoed in Eusebius' *Ecclesiastical History*.[115]

"The Apostles and Brothers of the Lord"

Cephas—Peter to most of us—is the only person mentioned by name in 1 Corinthians 9:5 when Paul compares himself and Barnabas with those "other apostles and the brothers of the Lord and Cephas" who were accompanied by their wives as they traveled about, missionizing on behalf of the Gospel. Who were those other apostles and brothers of the Lord (*hoi loipoi apostoloi kai hoi adelphoi tou kyriou*)? At this point in his apologia Paul does not tell us who they are.

Brothers of the Lord

The ascending order of the comparative group in the rhetorical question of 1 Corinthians 9:5 suggests that "brothers of the Lord" were a more important group of early Christian missionaries than were the apostles

---

[111] See the discussion by Georg Strecker in Johannes Irmscher and Georg Strecker, "The Pseudo-Clementines," in *New Testament Apocrypha*, vol. 2, ed. Wilson, 483–541, at 484–86. The existence of the pseudo-Clementines seems to have been recognized by Eusebius (*Eccl. Hist.* 3.38) who commented negatively on their orthodoxy.

[112] Cf. *Recon.* 7.25.3; 7.36.1; 9.38; *Hom.* 13.1.1; 13.11.2.

[113] See *Miscellanies* 7.63.2.

[114] On the plausibility of the account, see Andrea Lorenzo Molinari, "Women Martyrs in the Early Church: Hearing Another Side to the Story," *Priscilla Papers* 22 (2008): 5–10, 5–7.

[115] Cf. *Eccl. Hist.* 3.30.2

but Paul does not identify those whom he includes within the group. The only person whom he identifies as a brother of the Lord in the extent correspondence is James, the brother of the Lord, whom Paul met during a visit to Jerusalem.[116] The Acts of the Apostles is hardly more helpful in providing a clue as to whom the brothers of the Lord were. The brothers of the Lord appear just once in Acts, when Luke says that after the ascension the eleven were constantly in prayer "together with certain women, including Mary, the mother of Jesus, as well as his brothers" (Acts 1:14).[117]

Apostles

As for "the apostles," we know that when Paul uses this language, he is not necessarily referring to the Twelve whom Jesus called apostles (Mark 3:14; Luke 6:13[118]). In fact, Paul never uses the name "apostles" specifically in reference to the Twelve. First Corinthians 9:5 seems to distinguish Cephas from the other apostles. In Galatians 1:18-19, however, Paul cites Cephas, along with James, the brother of the Lord, as an apostle.

For Paul, the title "apostle" (*apostolos*) is functional. It applies to early Christian missionaries who were sent out to preach the Gospel in Jesus' name and in that way to lay the foundation for a church, a gathering of believers.[119] In Paul's usage, "apostle" is a title and function—though not an office, as such—that Paul could apply to himself[120] and to others. In his letters, he uses the title in reference to Barnabas (1 Cor 9:5[121]), Silvanus and Timothy (1 Thess 2:7), Andronicus and Junia (Rom 16:7[122]), and unnamed others[123] (1 Cor 4:9;[124] 12:28, 29; 15:7, 9;[125] Gal 1:17), but he never uses the term in specific reference to "the twelve apostles."

---

[116] Cf. Gal 2:19.

[117] The verse mentions "his brothers" (*tois adelphois autou*) but the reference is obviously to those who might be called "the brothers of the Lord." On the ambiguities inherent in the Greek expression, see Joseph A. Fitzmyer, *The Acts of the Apostles*, AB 32 (New York: Doubleday, 1998), 216–17.

[118] Cf. Matt 10:2, 5.

[119] Cf. 1 Cor 15:28, 29.

[120] Cf. Rom 1:1; 11:13; 1 Cor 1:1; 4:9; 9:1, 2, 5; 15:9 [2x]; 2 Cor 1:1; Gal 1:1.

[121] Cf. Acts 14:4, 14.

[122] Cf. Eldon John Epp, *Junia: The First Woman Apostle* (Minneapolis: Fortress, 2005).

[123] That is, other than Paul and Barnabas.

[124] The "apostles" of 1 Corinthians 4:9 certainly included Paul and Apollos, probably Sosthenes (cf. 1 Cor 1:1), and likely others as well.

[125] In 1 Corinthians 15:7 the "apostles" are clearly distinct from the Twelve mentioned in 1 Corinthians 15:5, the only reference to the Twelve within the entire New Testament Pauline corpus.

An Apostolic Couple

In the lengthy list of third-person greetings in Romans 16 that is so revealing about the nature of the community of God's beloved and holy people in Rome, Paul writes, "Greet Andronicus and Junia [*Andonikon kai Iounian*], my relatives who were imprisoned with me; they are prominent among the apostles, and they were in Christ before I was" (Rom 16:7).

Junia is a Latin feminine name often given to female slaves by members of the Junia family. Some of these slaves became freedwomen. Junia was such a common name for a woman that it appears on more than 250 Greek and Latin inscriptions found in Rome alone.[126] Early New Testament manuscripts, going back to the first-accented Greek manuscripts, accented the name *Iounian* as if it were the name of a woman, Junia. This was the way that the name was understood by the Fathers of the Church, many of whom considered Junia to have been the wife of Andronicus.

A number of later manuscripts, beginning with some ninth-century minuscules, accented the Greek *Iounian* as if it were the name of a man, Junias. Giles of Rome (1243–1316) is a milestone in the break from the patristic tradition. After him, editors of the Greek manuscripts regularly accented the name as if it were masculine. Translators used Junias, a man's name, in their respective versions. The reason for this masculinization of the name seems to be a prejudicial notion that rejected the possibility of a woman being an apostle.[127]

There is, however, no evidence that Junias was ever used as a man's name in the New Testament era. Hence, it is virtually certain that Junia is a woman's name. Indeed, the famed eleventh-century commentator on Romans, Theophylact of Ohrid (1055–1107), seems to have been surprised that Paul describes her as prominent among the apostles, "especially since Junia is a woman."[128] Junia is considered as a woman's name in the modern editions of the New Testament in Greek[129] and in the vast majority of recent translations of Romans.

---

[126] Roman evidence yields twenty-nine references to a man named Andronicus.

[127] Jewett writes, "the name 'Junias' is a figment of chauvinistic imagination." See Robert Jewett, *Romans: A Commentary*, Hermeneia (Minneapolis: Fortress, 2007), 962.

[128] Cf. *Expositio in epist. ad Romanos* 114 (PG 124, 551–52).

[129] On the text-critical issue, cf. Metzger, *A Textual Commentary*, 475–76; Joseph A. Fitzmyer, *Romans*, AB 33 (New York: Doubleday, 1993), 737–38; and Jewett, *Romans*, 961–62.

Among text critics there is virtually no support for a variant reading in the manuscript tradition that gives the woman's name as Julia (*Ioulian*), probably under the influence of Romans 16:15, whose manuscript tradition includes the variant reading "Junia." The tradition attests to some confusion between the two names.

Some authors identify Junia with the Joanna who was among Jesus' female patrons.[130] She was almost certainly the wife of Andronicus.[131] Not only would this be the natural reading of Paul's text but it is also a reading supported by Eastern and Western patristic traditions. In the East, Origen and Theodoret of Cyrus speak of Junia as the wife of Andronicus.[132] Among the Latin Fathers, both the Ambrosiaster and Jerome wrote of her in similar fashion.[133] None, however, could be clearer than Hatto, archbishop of Mainz in the early tenth century, who wrote in his commentary on Romans that "we must consider them to be man and wife."[134] In the East, the tenth-century calendar of saints attributed to the Emperor Basil Porphyrogenitus describes Andronicus as "having with him as consort and helper in godly preaching the admirable woman Junia."[135] Tradition clearly considered Andronicus and Junia to have been a married couple, as is suggested by an unbiased reading of Paul's text.

Paul says that the married couple, probably a Jewish couple,[136] "are prominent among the apostles" (*epistēmoi en tois apostolois*). John Chrysostom, the most important of the Eastern patristic commentators on Paul's letters, praises the wife, saying, "How great the wisdom of this woman that she was even deemed worthy of the apostles' title."[137] To be an apostle is great; to be prominent among them is greater still.[138]

Why Andronicus and Junia merited Paul's laudatory description is not entirely clear. It is likely that they missionized in Rome itself and

---

[130] Cf. Luke 8:3; 24:10. So, for example, Richard Bauckham, *Gospel Women: Studies of the Named Women in the Gospels* (Grand Rapids, MI: Eerdmans, 2002), 165–69, 181–86; and, following Bauckham, Ben Witherington III, *What Have They Done with Jesus? Beyond Strange Theories and Bad History—Why We Can Trust the Bible* (Grand Rapids, MI: Eerdmans, 2004), 15–25; Ben Witherington III, *Paul's Letter to the Romans: A Socio-Rhetorical Commentary* (Grand Rapids, MI: Eerdmans, 2004), 387–90.

[131] Cf. Craig S. Keener, *Paul, Women and Wives: Marriage and Women's Ministry in the Letters of Paul* (Peabody, MA: Hendrickson, 1992), 241–42.

[132] Cf. Origen, *In epist. ad Romanos* 10.21 (PG 14, 1280); Theodoret, *Interpretatio epist. ad Romanos* 16.7 (PG 82, 219–20).

[133] Cf. Ambrosiaster, *Commentarius in epist. ad Romanos* 16.7 (CSEL 81, 480); Jerome, *Liber interpretationis hebraicorum nominum* 72.15 (CC 72, 150).

[134] Hatto, *In epist. ad Romanos* 16 (PL 134, 282).

[135] Cf. *Acta Sanctorum, Maii 4*, edited by the Bollandists (Rome/Paris: V. Palmé, 1886). The feast of Saints Andronicus and Junia was celebrated on May 17.

[136] Cf. Witherington, *Romans*, 387, 389.

[137] *In epist. ad Romanos* 31.2 (PG 60, 669–70).

[138] Cf. Epp, *Junia*, 33; Veronica Koperski, "Women in Romans," in *The Letter to the Romans*, ed. Udo Schnelle, BETL 226 (Leuven: Peeters, 2009), 441–51, esp. 449–51.

were instrumental in founding one of the house churches in the imperial capital. It may be that they were among the visitors from Rome in Jerusalem at the time of Pentecost (Acts 2:10, 41)[139] or they may have been part of the group of Hellenists about whom Luke writes in Acts 6.[140] Perhaps they are to be included within the group whom Paul identifies as "all the apostles" (*tois apostolois pasin*) of 1 Corinthians 15:7.[141]

Romans was written after 1 Corinthians. Paul knew Andronicus and Junia prior to his writing to Roman believers. At one point the couple had been imprisoned with him.[142] Hence, he might well have included Andronicus among the married male evangelists who traveled with their wives.

Might Paul have also been thinking of Aquila and Prisca who hosted a house church and on whose behalf Paul greeted the Corinthians[143] as apostles? Paul does not use the "apostle" epithet in reference to them but he does describe the pair as his coworkers in Christ (*tous synergous mou en Christō Iēsou*, Rom 16:3), language that he typically uses of his fellow evangelists.[144] Aquila and Prisca were a married couple who traveled—sometimes with Paul (Acts 18:18), sometimes on their own (Acts 18:2)—and who evangelized (Acts 18:26).[145] They are not called apostles, although they might well have been.

Were it possible to conclude decisively that Apphia was the wife of Philemon (Phlm 1–2), the two might be another couple that Paul could have had in mind as he formulated the rhetorical question of 1 Corinthians 9:5. There is, however, no evidence that this possibly married couple ever traveled as evangelists and would therefore merit the de-

---

[139] Cf. Fitzmyer, *Romans*, 29; Jewett, *Romans*, 964. Origen, *In epist. ad Romanos* 10, 18–21 (PG 14, 1279–80), mentioned the possibility of the pair being included among the "seventy-two" disciples that Jesus sent out (cf. Luke 10:1).

[140] This possibility is offered by Cranfield. Cf. C. E. B. Cranfield, *The Epistle to the Romans*, 2, ICC (Edinburgh: T&T Clark, 1979), 790.

[141] Cf. James D. G. Dunn, *Romans*, 2, WBC 38 (Dallas: Word Books, 1988), 895; Brendan Byrne, *Romans*, SP 6 (Collegeville, MN: Liturgical Press, 1996), 453.

[142] Cf. Rom 16:7.

[143] Cf. 1 Cor 16:19.

[144] Cf. Marie Noël Keller, *Priscilla and Aquila: Paul's Coworkers in Christ Jesus*, Paul's Social Network: Brothers and Sisters in Christ (Collegeville, MN: Liturgical Press, 2010), 50–52.

[145] Cf. Mario Barbero, "A First-Century Couple, Priscilla and Aquila: Their House Churches and Missionary Activity" (PhD thesis; The Catholic University of America, Washington, DC, 2001).

scription of apostles. Paul's question reveals, nonetheless, that Cephas-Peter traveled with his wife as he evangelized and that in the first Christian generation he was not alone in doing so.

"And There Are Eunuchs Who Have Made Themselves Eunuchs for the Sake of the Kingdom of Heaven"

If the first generation of Jesus' disciples were not only married but after Jesus' death and resurrection were accompanied by their wives as they evangelized, what can be made of Jesus' instruction to his disciples about those "who have made themselves eunuchs for the sake of the kingdom" (Matt 19:12)?[146]

Eunuchs

In the ancient world, the majority of eunuchs were despised and scorned. Lucian, the second-century CE satirist and rhetorician, wrote that a eunuch is "neither man, nor woman but something . . . monstrous, alien to human nature [*exō tēn anthrōpeias physeōs*]."[147] Most eunuchs were castrated slaves. Some eunuchs were enslaved and castrated prisoners of war. Some men became eunuchs as a result of a war injury. Some priests ritualizing in the worship of Artemis, Cybele, or some other Near Eastern fertility cult castrated themselves as a token of ritual purification and a sign of lifelong dedication to the deity. These, too, were despised, except by the devotees of the cults within which these priests performed.

Within Judaism, eunuchs were deprived of the rights pertaining to men in general or to the male members of their tribe. For example, eunuchs were excluded from the worshiping assembly (Deut 23:1)[148] and the priesthood (Lev 21:17-21). They were not allowed to be members of the Sanhedrin and they were not allowed to serve as judges in criminal cases. Eunuchs symbolized futility and frustrated desire.[149] In his *Special*

---

[146] Stefan Heid states, "The famous saying of Jesus about eunuchs stands at the beginning of any further reflection on the prehistory of clerical continence" (*Celibacy in the Early Church*, 20).

[147] Lucian, *Eunuch.* 6–11; cf. Herodotus, *Hist.* 8:106; Josephus, *Ant.* 4.290–91.

[148] Cf. *m. Yebam.* 6:6; 8:4–6; *b. Yebam.* 63b.

[149] Cf. Sir 29:4; 30:20. Some texts are, however, less negative in their judgment of eunuchs. See, for example, Isaiah 56:3-8 and Wisdom 3:14-15. The trito-Isaiah offers eschatological assurance to eunuchs who fulfill three conditions, namely, Sabbath

Laws, Philo describes the group of worthless persons (*hoi mochthēroi*). "It begins," he writes, "with the men who belie their sex and are affected with effemination. . . . For it expels those whose generative organs are fractured or mutilated" (*Spec. Laws* 1.325). At Qumran, men who had been castrated were excluded from the holy assembly.[150]

Notwithstanding societal disdain for eunuchs, some eunuchs, both in the East and in Rome, rose to high and important positions in family, the court, and government. The classic *Greek-English Lexicon* of Liddell and Scott defines a eunuch (*eunouchos*) "as a castrated person employed to take charge of the women and employed as a chamberlain,"[151] indeed, overseeing a harem was a duty entrusted to eunuchs[152] but the term eunuch also served to describe royal officials with other duties, like the financial officer of the Ethiopian queen, Candace, whose evangelization by Philip is recounted by Luke in Acts 8:26-40.

Luke's identification of the treasury official is one of the two places in the New Testament in which eunuchs are mentioned. The other is the set of statements about eunuchs that appears as an appendix to Matthew's account of Jesus' being tested by a group of Pharisees with regard to divorce (Matt 19:3-9).[153] The account represents a substantial reworking of the text found in Matthew's source at Mark 10:2-9. According to Mark, the disciples were uncertain as to the nature of Jesus' response and so questioned Jesus about it (Mark 10:10). Answering them, Jesus pronounced a two-part logion that relates divorce to adultery (Mark 10:11-12). Matthew's revision of the text includes a version of the first logion in the discussion with the Pharisees, making it the climax of Jesus' response to the Pharisees' question (Matt 19:9).

In a world in which it was relatively[154] easy for a man to divorce his wife—the disciples of the great rabbi Hillel are quoted as saying that divorce was permitted if a woman spoiled a meal and the early second-century martyred rabbi, Aqiva, is quoted as saying that a man may

---

observance, choosing what pleases the Lord, and holding fast to the covenant. Cf. Joseph Blenkinsopp, *Isaiah 46–66*, AB 19B (New York: Doubleday, 2003), 139–40.

[150] Cf. 4QMMT 42.

[151] LSJ, s.v. "*eunouchos*."

[152] Cf. Esth 2:14-15.

[153] Cf. Raymond F. Collins, *Divorce in the New Testament*, GNS 38 (Collegeville, MN: Liturgical Press, 1992), 104–45.

[154] In many instances, the payment of the *ketubah* would serve as a deterrent to divorce.

divorce his wife if he finds someone more beautiful to marry[155]—Jesus' forceful saying describing divorce as a violation of the sixth commandment took Jesus disciples' aback. For them Jesus' words changed the nature of the marital commitment with which they had been familiar, the commitment that they had made themselves. Perplexed, they say to Jesus, "If such is the case of a man with his wife, it is better not to marry" (Matt 19:10). They find it difficult to think about marriage without the possibility of divorce. The evangelist's formulation of their words evinces ample evidence of his own hand and suggests that it is he who has created a narrative context that warrants appending the eunuch sayings to the debate about divorce.[156]

Jesus' Logion

In what Jeannine Brown calls a "debriefing moment,"[157] Jesus, recognizing that the logion on divorce is hard to accept, says that the only ones who can accept it are those whom God enables to do so. Not all are open to Jesus' teaching on divorce[158]—a countercultural challenge—but only those who have received God's enabling gift to receive it in their hearts and live accordingly.

By way of explanation,[159] the Matthean Jesus adds: "For there are eunuchs who have been so from birth,[160] and there are eunuchs who have been made eunuchs by others, and there are eunuchs who have made themselves eunuchs for the sake of the kingdom of heaven. Let anyone accept this who can" (Matt 19:12). A little more than a half century later, Justin Martyr paraphrased this saying as follows: "There are eunuchs

---

[155] Cf. *m. Git.* 9:10.

[156] Cf. Collins, *Divorce*, 120.

[157] Cf. Jeannine K. Brown, *The Disciples in Narrative Perspective: The Portrayal and Function of the Matthean Disciples* (Atlanta: Society of Biblical Literature, 2002), 48.

[158] "This teaching" (*ton logon touton*), v. 11, refers back to Jesus teaching on divorce (v. 9), not ahead, to the eunuch statement of v. 12c. In Matthew the formulaic expression always refers to something that has preceded (cf. Matt 7:24, 26, 28; 19:1, 22; 26:1; 28:15). See the discussions in Metzger, *A Textual Commentary*, 30; Collins, *Divorce*, 120–22; Ulrich Luz, *Matthew 8–20*, Hermeneia (Minneapolis: Fortress, 2001), 499–500, 502. Those who suggest, as did much older exegesis, that the phrase looks ahead to verse 12c overlook the fact that 12c is embedded in an explanation; it is not part of an independent affirmation.

[159] Note the explanatory *gar* in v. 12.

[160] Literally, "from the mother's womb" (*ek koilias mētros*).

who were born so; and there are eunuchs who were made so by men; and there are eunuchs who have made themselves so for the kingdom of heaven's sake; not all however can receive this saying."[161]

Although this threesome of eunuch sayings appears only in Matthew, it is all but certain that it is not a Matthean creation. Not only do the words "eunuch" (*eunouchos*) and "make a eunuch" (*eunouchizō*)[162] appear nowhere else in Matthew, nor for that matter anywhere else in the New Testament apart from the Lukan story of the treasurer in the court of Queen Candace, but the idea of voluntary castration would have been inherently abhorrent to Matthew's Jewish-Christian audience. Not even Josephus and Philo who were generally laudatory of the celibacy of some Essenes (and Therapeutae) used the metaphor of voluntary castration as a way to describe those celibates.

If the odd triad, somewhat awkwardly placed between the debate on divorce and Jesus' blessing of the children,[163] albeit introduced by a redactional objection on the part of the disciples,[164] did not originate with Matthew himself, it is most likely a bit of oral tradition[165] that Matthew has appropriated. Indeed, there is a strong likelihood that the three sayings go back to Jesus himself. John Meier sums up his discussion of the matter by writing, "On the whole, then, the criteria of embarrassment, discontinuity, and coherence argue impressively for the position that the

---

[161] Cf. *1 Apol.*, 15 (PG 6, 349). Blinzler's study of Justin's version of the saying revealed ten differences between it and the version found in Matthew. Cf. Josef Blinzler, "Zur Ehe unfaähig . . .—Auslegung von Mt 19, 12," in idem, *Aus der Welt und Umwelt des Neuen Testaments, Gesammelte Aufsätze* (Stuttgart: KBW, 1969), 20–40; "Justinus Apol. I 15,4 und Matthäus 19, 11–12," in *Mélanges bibliques en hommage au R. P. Béda Rigaux*, ed. Albert M. Descamps and André de Halleux (Gembloux: Duculot, 1970), 45–55.

[162] The noun occurs three times in Matthew 19:12 and five times in the story about the royal official (Acts 8:27, 34, 36, 38, 39). The verb *eunouchizō* appears nowhere in the NT apart from its two uses in Matthew 19:12, in the second and third sayings.

[163] In Mark 10:1-16, the blessing of the children immediately follows the disciples' request for clarification.

[164] The disciples' intervention reflects Mark 10:10 but its content is clearly different from that of Matthew 19:10. On the redactional nature of vv. 10-11, cf. Alexander Sand, *Reich Gottes und Eheverzicht imn Evangelium nach Matthäeus*, SBS 109 (Stuttgart: KBW, 1983), 51–55; Stephenson H. Brooks, *Matthew's Community: The Evidence of His Special Sayings Material*, JSNTSup 16 (Sheffield: JSOT, 1987), 107–9.

[165] The three-part formulation of the saying would have facilitated its retention and transmission.

eunuch saying, in some form or another, derives ultimately from Jesus himself."[166]

Jesus' Apologia Pro Vita Sua

Most probably the three-part saying originated as a kind of apology by Jesus in response to those who accused him of being a eunuch because he was not married. We have no clear evidence that this was the case but there is ample evidence of the fact that slurs were directed against Jesus throughout his life.[167] We have already mentioned the accusation that Jesus was out of his mind, that he had gone mad (Mark 3:19b). He was accused of being a glutton and a drunkard (Luke 7:34; Matt 11:19). He was accused of socializing with tax collectors and sinners (Mark 2:16; Matt 9:10) and of being their friend. He was thought to be a sinner (John 9:16). Some leaders of the Jews accused him of being a Samaritan and a demonic (John 8:47). He was called a blasphemer (Mark 14:64; Matt 26:65). Jesus was a victim of vicious name-calling. The five principal strands of the canonical gospel tradition, Mark, Q, Matthew, Luke, and John, portray Jesus as someone who was taunted with derogatory names and hurtful one-liners. For many Jews, Jesus was a strange and scandalous figure, no better than a pagan or heathen courtier; hence, the barbs.

The accusation that Jesus was a eunuch is one item among others in the negative litany. The gospels repeatedly portray Jesus as responding to such unseemly accusations. The three-part eunuch saying was probably Jesus' response to the accusation that he was a eunuch. That the New Testament makes so little mention of eunuchs is not surprising.

---

[166] John P. Meier, *A Marginal Jew: Rethinking the Historical Jesus*, vol. 1: *The Roots of the Problem and the Person*, ABRL (New York: Doubleday, 1991), 344–45; cf. Francisco Marín, "Un ricurso obligado a la tradición presinóptica," *EstBib.* 36 (1977): 205–16; Sand, *Reich Gottes*, 50, 74, Francis J. Moloney, "Matthew 19:3-12 and Celibacy: A Redactional and Form Critical Study," *JSNT* 2 (1979): 42–60; *Disciples and Prophets: A Biblical Model for the Religious Life* (London: Darton, Longman and Todd, 1980), 105–14; *A Life of Promise*, 88–108. Sand references Walter Grundmann and Herbert Braun as supporting this view.

[167] Cf. John P. Meier, *A Marginal Jew: Rethinking the Historical Jesus*, vol. 3: *Companions and Competitors*, ABRL (New York: Doubleday, 2001), 505. Jerome Kodell has suggested that the slur had been directed against Jesus' unmarried disciples, but it was much more likely a slur directed against Jesus himself, the object of many a slur during his public ministry. Cf. Jerome Kodell, "The Celibacy Logion in Matthew 19:12," *BTB* 8 (1978): 19–23, 19.

Hobnobbing with "the religious low life of Palestine,"[168] Jesus would have few opportunities to meet court figures such as Philip did when he met a eunuch who belonged to Candace's entourage. Accordingly, Jesus would have had little need to have spoken about eunuchs were it not for the likelihood that he appropriated the language of his detractors in defending himself.

Before he delivers his apologetic punch line, Jesus mentions two categories of eunuchs well-known in Jewish literature. Rabbis distinguished between "the eunuch of the sun" (*seris hammah*), the eunuch by nature, the male child born with damaged testicles, and the "eunuch of man" (*seris ʿadam*), the male who had been made a eunuch by another human being, a castrated person.[169] These two categories of eunuchs, the first two cited in Jesus' logion refer to a physical reality. They refer to persons who were born with damaged testicles and to those who had been castrated by some other human being, most likely as a form of punishment or of domination by a military conqueror or an affronted slave-owner.

Commenting on the ritual of *haltitzah*, the ceremonial removal of a sandal by a widow spurned by her deceased husband's brother who refused to accept his obligation to marry her and beget children for his brother's house (Deut 25:5-10), the aforementioned Aqiva made a judicial decision based on the distinction. He said that if the defiant brother "was a man-made eunuch he submits to *haltitzah* and his brothers submit to *haltitzah* from his wife . . . but if he was a eunuch by nature he does not submit to *haltitzah* nor do his brothers submit to *haltitzah* from his wife" (*m. Yebam.* 8:4).

Luz observes that the first two groups of eunuchs were particularly despised and ridiculed within Judaism.[170] The first group was unable to fulfill God's command to beget children; they were impotent. Josephus urges that these eunuchs should be avoided, especially because they could not fulfill the command found in Genesis 1:28.[171] Moreover, said Josephus, they had feminine souls and bodies. Men who were castrated by others had a bad reputation because castrated priests were a feature of pagan worship, for example, the cults of Cybele and Dea Syria.

---

[168] The phrasing comes from Meier, *A Marginal Jew*, vol. 1, 344.
[169] Cf. *m. Yebam.* 8:4–6; *m. Zabim* 2:1.
[170] Cf. Luz, *Matthew 8–20*, 501.
[171] Cf. Josephus, *Ant.* 4.290–91.

Given the traditional abhorrence of Jews for physical castration, it is hardly likely that Jesus' third saying refers to men who have physically castrated themselves or had themselves castrated by someone else. Reprising the language of his taunters, Jesus most likely used the term in a figurative sense, even though such usage of the term was rare, if not unprecedented, at the time.[172] The strange image—Meier describes it as a "shocking symbol"[173]—may even have contributed to the Matthean tradition's retention of the saying. It was, in fact, a logion *sui generis*. The figurative meaning of eunuch in the third logion would mean that some people, eunuchs, in a figurative sense—Heid describes what Jesus was talking about as "spiritual castration"[174]—did not marry and procreate although they were capable of doing so.

In the saying, the verb form "made themselves eunuchs" (*hoitines eunouchisan heautous*) is the aorist tense. As such, the logion is in reference to the past, to an action that took place at some previous point in time. The logion is not a gnomic[175] saying pertinent to the present and the future. Jesus is speaking about people in the past who had made themselves eunuchs for the sake of the kingdom of heaven. He himself was one such individual. Such is the nature of his self-defense, handed down to the evangelist within an oral tradition to which Matthew alone among the evangelists—so it would appear—was privy.

The plural form of the saying suggests that Jesus' *apologia* was not only about himself. Most likely, Jesus was also speaking about and defending John the Baptist.[176] Like Jesus, John the Baptist was also the object of derogatory remarks.[177] The canonical gospels often reflect the interaction between Jesus and the desert prophet.[178] Matthew even portrays them as proclaiming the same message about the coming of the kingdom:

---

[172] LSJ offer no examples of a metaphorical use of the term; BAGD cites only Matthew 19:12c. A figurative use of "eunuch" appears in Clement of Alexandria (*Miscellanies* 3.7.59) in dependence on Matthew. In secular writings, the third-century CE sophist, Philostratus, is known to have used the term in a metaphorical sense. Cf. *Vita Apollonii* 6.42.

[173] See Meier, *A Marginal Jew*, 3, 64, 622.

[174] Cf. Heid, *Celibacy in the Early Church*, 27.

[175] The so-called gnomic aorist is rare in the NT, where it is found mostly in parables; cf. Matt 13:4, 46, 48; Jas 1:11, 24; 1 Pet 1:24. Cf. BDF 333.1.

[176] Cf. Donald A. Hagner, *Matthew 14–18*, WBC 33B (Dallas: Word, 1995), 550; Meier, *A Marginal Jew*, 3, 505; Audet, *Mariage et célibat*, 57–58.

[177] See the Q saying in Luke 7:33; cf. Matt 11.18.

[178] Cf. Mark 1:9-11; Matt 11:16-19; Luke 7:18-23; John 1:29-36; etc.

"Repent, for the kingdom of heaven has come near" (Matt 3:2, 17). Jesus and John the Baptist were prophetic figures who proclaimed the imminence of the kingdom, the idea that life as usual was soon coming to an end. The eschatological urgency of their message affected their lives. One and the other, Jesus and John, embraced celibacy for the sake of the kingdom that was about to come.[179] That the enigmatic saying of Matthew 19:12c is in the past tense and refers particularly to Jesus and John the Baptist, with perhaps the figure of the prophet Jeremiah on the horizon,[180] is most important for the purposes of the present study.

The Logion in Matthew's Narrative

Yet to be explored is the function of the saying within the literary context of Matthew 19:1-12. When he wrote his gospel, the evangelist was not so much reflecting on the situation of the historical Jesus as he was on the situation of his late first-century Jewish-Christian community and the implications of Jesus' teaching on divorce for them.[181] What was the meaning of Jesus' logion for Matthew's generation of Jewish Christians?

Within the small literary unit created by the evangelist, the punch line of the three-part *mashal*, a figurative saying, responds to the objection that in the light of the seriousness of divorcing one's spouse without the warranted reason it would be better not to marry (v.10).[182] The Matthean Jesus responds to that objection by saying that it is not up to humans to make a decision not to marry. Rather, only those whom God has called and whom God has enabled to remain unmarried—*in casu*, Jesus and John

---

[179] Launderville notes that it is a social or political crisis that gives rise to a practice of celibacy. Cf. Dale Launderville, *Celibacy in the Ancient World: Its Ideal and Practice in Pre-Hellenistic Israel, Mesopotamia, and Greece* (Collegeville, MN: Liturgical Press, 2010), xx. The imminent inbreaking of the Kingdom of God, the focus of the common message of John and Jesus constituted such a crisis.

[180] Cf. Jer 16:2.

[181] Matthew's addition of "for any cause" (v. 3) and his deletion of the reference to a wife divorcing her husband provide evidence of Matthew's accommodation of the Markan story to a Jewish(-Christian) audience.

[182] Quentin Quesnell rightly observes that the function of the disciple's word in the gospel narrative "is to ask questions, to misunderstand or object, or simply to advance the action dramatically. They do not enunciate the Christian ideal for life." Cf. Quesnell, "Made Themselves Eunuchs for the Kingdom of Heaven (Mt 19, 12)," *CBQ* 30 (1968): 335–58, 343.

the Baptist—should remain unmarried. Within the context of fidelity to the *mitzvah* of Genesis 1:28,[183] Matthew's Jesus does not present celibacy as an alternate lifestyle available to those who would choose it.

What about John?

The late fourth-century Ambrosiaster admitted that Peter was married with children.[184] Indeed this writer held that, "All the apostles, with the exception of John and Paul, were married."[185] We will examine Paul's marital status in another chapter, but what about John?

The Ambrosiaster reflected the common opinion that John was not married,[186] one that he shared with commentators, such as Epiphanius of Salamis, Jerome, Augustine, Paulinus of Nola, and Proclus of Constantinople.[187] The tradition that John was not married, as this selection of patristic authors indicates, is found in the East as well as the West. The tradition is attested relatively late in the history of the patristic church. Epiphanius wrote his most famous work, the *Panarion*, in the late fourth century; the witness of the other Fathers comes from the fifth century.

In the late second century the *Acts of John* describes a prayer offered by John, just prior to his death, which includes the following:

> Thou who has kept me also till this present hour pure for thyself
> and untouched by union with a woman; who when I wished to
> marry in my youth didst appear to me and say: "John, I need thee";
> who when I was about to marry didst prepare for me a bodily sick-
> ness; who, though disobeyed, on the third occasion when I wished
> to marry didst prevent me, and then at the third hour of the day

---

[183] According to Matthew 19:4, Jesus cited Genesis 1:27 in his argument with the group of Pharisees.

[184] Cf. The Ambrosiaster, *Quaestiones Veteris et Novi Testament* 127.33 (CSEL 50, 414).

[185] *In epist. B. Paul. Ad Corinthios II* 11.2 (PL 17.320a; CSEL 81, 2).

[186] See also the Ambrosiaster, *Quaestiones Veteris et Novi Testamentum* 127.33 (CSEL 50, 414).

[187] Cf. Epiphanius, *Refutation of All Heresies* 58.4; 78.13 (PG 41, 1016a; 42, 720a); Jerome, *Against Jovinian* 1.26, 34 (PL 23, 246b–c, 270a); Augustine, *Tractates on the Gospel of John* 124.7 (CC 36, 687); *The Good of Marriage* 21 (CSEL 41, 221); *Against Faustus the Manichaean* 30.4 (CSEL 25, 751); Paulinus of Nola, *Epist.* 50 (PL 61, 416a; CSEL 29, 421); Proclus of Constantinople, *Homily 4: Praise of Holy Mary, Mother of God* 5 (PG 65, 730b; Nicholas Constas, *Proclus of Constantinople and the Cult of the Virgin: Homilies 1–5 Texts and Translations*, VCSup 66 [Leiden: Brill, 2003]).

didst say to me upon the sea, "John, if thou were not mine, I should have allowed thee to marry." (*Acts of John* 113)[188]

The misogynism of the text is clearly apparent in what follows. Having been cured of a two-year period of blindness, the apostle speaks of "the repugnance even of looking closely at a woman."[189] Fortunately, the fifth session of the Council of Nicea of 787 said of this apocryphal text, "No one is to copy [it]; not only so, but we consider that it deserves to be consigned to the fire."[190]

The Arguments

The reasons why some Fathers of the Church alleged that John the apostle was not married are worth pursuing. Proclus, writing toward the middle of the fifth century, interpreted the Markan phrase "Boanerges, that is, sons of thunder"[191] to mean that John and his brother James had received a most eminent gift from God—that is, the gift of virginity. Restricting the gift to the two, Proclus seems to imply that the other apostles were married.[192]

In approximately the same era, Augustine opined that Christ loved John with a special love because he had practiced chastity from childhood. Jerome argued along similar lines but Augustine admitted that there were "no conclusive proofs in canonical Scripture."[193] Augustine equated the apostle John, son of Zebedee, with the Beloved Disciple of the Fourth Gospel, as did Jerome who referenced John reclining next to Jesus.[194]

Epiphanius and Paulinus, as well as Jerome somewhat later in his refutation of Jovinian,[195] referenced the Johannine scene at the foot of the cross, in which Jesus entrusted his mother to the disciple whom he loved

---

[188] Cf. Kurt Schäferdiek, "The Acts of John" in Schneemelcher and Wilson, *New Testament Apocrypha*, 2, 152–209, 203.

[189] Ibid., 203.

[190] Ibid., 156.

[191] Cf. Mark 3:37. The descriptive epithet does not appear in Matthew and Luke.

[192] Cf. Cochini, *Priestly Celibacy*, 79.

[193] *Tractates on the Gospel of John* 124.7 (CC 36, 687).

[194] Cf. John 13:23, *en tō kolpō tou Iēsou*, literally, "on Jesus' bosom."

[195] Cf. *Against Jovinian* 1.34 (PL 23, 270a).

(John 19:25b-27).[196] It was fitting, these authors thought, that Jesus' virgin mother should be entrusted to a virgin disciple. Epiphanius, for example, writes: "Why did he [Jesus] not entrust her rather to Peter, or Andrew, or Matthew, or Bartholomew? It is undoubtedly because of his virginity that John was granted [this privilege]."[197] From his conviction that John was a virgin Epiphanius inferred that James, the brother of John, had embraced the same kind of life.

Despite basing his views on the virginity of John on the opinions of earlier commentators on Scripture, whom he did not name, Augustine admitted that there really was no scriptural proof of the apostle's virginity.[198] John's virginity, argued Augustine, was fitting since he was a figure of the heavenly life. In the absence of any conclusive scriptural proof, the Fathers' most potent argument for the view that the apostle John was not married appears to be that it was fitting for him to have been a virgin.

The Beloved Disciple

Any argument from appropriateness is weak but that is the very linchpin of the patristic argument that the Apostle John was not married. The fittingness of the argument is based on the identification of John, the Synoptic tradition's son of Zebedee, with the Beloved Disciple of the Johannine tradition. Only in the Fourth Gospel is it said that the Beloved Disciple lay on Jesus' chest as they reclined at supper. It is only in the Fourth Gospel that the mother of Jesus appears at the foot of the cross in the company of the Beloved Disciple.

Few contemporary scholars equate the Fourth Gospel's Beloved Disciple with John, one of the Twelve.[199] The assumption that John, the son of Zebedee, is none other than the one called the Beloved Disciple cannot be maintained. Pursuing the issue, R. Alan Culpepper writes by way of conclusion that "it is clear that the Gospel of John does not identify the Beloved Disciple as John the son of Zebedee and that there are other

---

[196] John 19:25b-27.
[197] *All Heresies* 78.10 (PG 42, 714c).
[198] *Tractates on the Gospel of John* 124.7 (CC 36, 687).
[199] Cf. Colleen M. Conway, "Beloved Disciple," *NIDB* 1, 422–423, esp. 423.

aspects of the characterization of the Beloved Disciple which are difficult to square with the traditional identification."[200]

Once the link between John, the son of Zebedee, and the Beloved Disciple has been broken, the patristic argument for the celibate state of John—and his brother, in the case of Epiphanius and Proclus—falls to pieces. John's virginity is only a dream, wrote Audet.[201] Audet may have overstated the matter but, as Augustine said many centuries ago, there is no scriptural proof that John was not married, even less so—if that is possible—in our day than in his.

Although some demur, holding that the Beloved Disciple was only a literary character, a symbol of the Church, it is likely that the Johannine characterization of the Beloved Disciple is based on an historical figure. The Fourth Gospel offers no real suggestion that this figure was an unmarried virgin.

Conclusion

If there is no conclusive proof that the son of Zebedee was not married, neither is there conclusive proof that any of the other apostles were unmarried. In fact, there is incontrovertible evidence that Peter was married at the time of his call and that he continued to be united to his wife after the death and resurrection of Jesus. The canonical gospels' narrative segments give no indication that the disciples of Jesus were not married. The social and religious conditions of their time and place would have dictated that they be married—can it not be assumed that they were observant Jews?—the gospels provide no evidence to the contrary.

There are, to be sure, a few logia that taken out of context, both in centuries past and at the present, suggest that the disciples of Jesus abandoned their wives. Read within their narrative contexts, the logia

---

[200] R. Alan Culpepper, *John the Son of Zebedee: The Life of a Legend*, Studies on Personalities of the New Testament (Columbia: University of South Carolina Press, 1994), 76. See also James H. Charlesworth, *The Beloved Disciple: Whose Witness Validates the Gospel of John?* (Valley Forge, PA: Trinity Press International, 1995), 197–213. As the years went on, the great Johannine scholar Raymond Brown also became skeptical about the identification of the Son of Zebedee with the Beloved Disciple. See *The Community of the Beloved Disciple* (New York: Paulist, 1979), 31–34; *An Introduction to the Gospel of John*, ed. Francis J. Moloney, ABRL (New York: Doubleday, 2003), 191.

[201] Cf. Audet, *Mariage et célibat*, 71.

do not substantiate this suggestion. Rather, they suggest that the logia are to be interpreted within an eschatological setting, in which the kingdom of God was expected to be near. Eschatological urgency led the apostles to forsake their homes in order to preach the Gospel. The proximity of the kingdom urged them to preach about it and anticipate it in the exorcisms that they performed.[202] Temporary absence from their wives,[203] and the continence that it necessarily entailed, was a condition that they embraced for the sake of the mission of evangelization[204] but the gospels in no way suggest that leaving one's wife, family, and home permanently was a condition of discipleship.

As an eschatological prophet, Jesus appears to have been celibate but, as Meier repeatedly states,[205] our canonical gospels offer only a single part of a verse—namely, Matthew 19:12c—that points positively to Jesus' unmarried status. The plural form of the verb in the logion suggests that John the Baptist was quite likely unmarried as well, but the evidence is even less clear in the case of John the Baptist than it is in the case of Jesus. Jesus' logion on eunuchs does not warrant the suggestion that his disciples should chose to forgo marriage or that they abandoned sexual intercourse with their spouses once they had become followers of Jesus.

---

[202] Cf. Mark 6:13; cf. Mark 6:7; Matt 10:8; Luke 9:1.

[203] Cf. Ulrich Luz who writes, "Jesus' married disciples did not live permanently without their wives" (*Matthew 8–20*, 501).

[204] The gospels are, of course, totally silent about the sexual intimacy between the apostles and their wives. It is anachronistic and probably farfetched to portray the apostles of the canonical gospels as leading a life of sexual continence within marriage. There is no first-century evidence which points in this direction.

[205] Cf. Meier, *A Marginal Jew*, vol. 1, 322; vol. 3, 624.

The Apostle Paul

Commenting on a number of issues pertaining to the interpretation of biblical texts, the fourth-century writer known as the Ambrosiaster expressed the conviction that "all the apostles, with the exception of John and Paul, were married."[1] The Ambrosiaster was not alone in writing that Paul was not married. From patristic times to the present, many writers and even more believers assume that Paul was not married. Typical is the opinion of Ugo Schnelle who writes, "Paul did not marry; he obviously lived alone out of conviction."[2]

Remain Unmarried as I Am

To justify their opinion that Paul was not married, many Fathers of the Church[3] cite a passage from Paul's First (extant) Letter to the Corinthians. Some twenty years after becoming a believer in Jesus, Paul wrote: "I wish that all were as I myself am.[4] But each has a particular gift from

---

[1] *In epist. B. Paul. ad Corinthios II* 11.2 (PL 17, 320a).

[2] Udo Schnelle, *Apostle Paul: His Life and Theology* (Grand Rapids, MI: Baker Academic, 2005), 58. Schnelle cites 1 Corinthians 7:1, 8 and 9:5 as references for this otherwise unexamined assertion.

[3] Cf. Crouzel, "Celibacy," 462.

[4] Jerome quotes only this passage from Paul's when writing about the apostle's celibacy. See Jerome, *Against Jovinian* 1.34 (PL 23, 270a). In an annotation on the verse in *The Jewish Annotated New Testament* (p. 297), Shira Lander writes, "Paul is celibate. There is no evidence that Paul married."

God, one having one kind and another a different kind" (1 Cor 7:7). A few verses later in the missive, Paul wrote, "To the unmarried and the widows I say that it is well for them to remain unmarried as I am" (1 Cor 7:8).

Translation

"*Traduttore, traditore,*" literally, "translator, traitor," is a well-known Italian adage. Affirming that a translator is a traitor to the text being translated, the adage succinctly captures the reality of the fact that every translation is an interpretation. Never does a translation perfectly render the meaning of the text at hand. There are many reasons for this but two stand out. The first of these is that each and every language has its own particular linguistic structures. The structures of one language are not easily shifted into the structures of another language. The other important reason is that translation is not simply a matter of words. Words and expressions reflect a culture and cultures differ from one another. Translation is an effort to express thoughts expressed in one culture in the idiom of another culture.

1 Corinthians 7:7, 8

Reading 1 Corinthians 7:7 and 8 in the NRSV and several other modern translations,[5] which say that Paul was "unmarried" (v. 8), the uncritical reader assumes that Paul was not married and that he was never married. Webster's offers "not now or previously married" as a first definition of "unmarried." With further precision, the Revised Standard Version, predecessor of the NRSV, had translated the final words in verse 8 as "remain single as I am."

The problem is that the Greek equivalent of "unmarried" (NRSV) or "single" (RSV) is not found in the Greek text. The translators have supplied "unmarried" and "single" to interpret the text for their readers. Other translators have not been as aggressive in their interpretation of the text. Thus, the King James Version renders the final words of verse

---

[5] For example, the New International Version renders the Pauline dictum of v. 7 as "It is good for them to stay unmarried as I am," while the Common English Bible reads, "I am telling those who are single and widows that it's good for them to stay single like me."

8 as "if they abide as I am," leaving the reader to grapple with the ambiguity of Paul's "even as I myself" in verse 7 (KJV).

In the two verses under discussion, Paul's Greek is exceptionally succinct. The Greek translated as "were as I myself am" in verse 7 (NRSV) is *einai hōs kai emauton*, literally, "be as I myself." The Greek of verse 8's "remain unmarried as I am" is *meinōsin hōs kagō*, literally, "stay as I too." Paul's terse language includes the contraction *kagō*, which results from the elision of *kai*, "and," and *egō*, "I," a handy "me too" in most of its uses.

Paul's Greek lacks the "am" found in the NRSV translation of both verse 7 and verse 8 as well as the "unmarried" in the translation of verse 8. What did Paul really mean by these seven words, *einai hōs kai emauton* and *meinōsin hōs kagō*, which have served as the foundation for the assumption that the apostle never married?

1 Corinthians 7

Peter Brown wrote of the seventh chapter in Paul's First Letter to the Corinthians in which the two concise clauses are found that it is the one chapter "that was to determine all Christian thought on marriage and celibacy for well over a millennium."[6] Will Deming, saying that this chapter is "one of the most influential discussions of marriage and celibacy in the entire Christian tradition," concurs with Brown's judgment of the importance of the chapter.[7] Stefan Heid describes the chapter as "the notorious seventh chapter of his [Paul's] First Letter to the Corinthians."[8]

A Problem

Paul wrote 1 Corinthians 7 in response to a letter that he had received from the Corinthians, as he himself explicitly states in 1 Corinthians 7:1: "Now concerning the matters about which you wrote: 'It is well for a man not to touch a woman.'" The interpretation of this verse, especially

[6] Peter Brown, *The Body and Society: Men, Women and Sexual Renunciation in Early Christianity*, Lectures on the History of Religions, N.S. 13 (New York: Columbia University Press, 1988), 54.

[7] Cf. Will Deming, *Paul on Marriage and Celibacy: The Hellenistic Background of 1 Corinthians 7*, 2nd ed. (Grand Rapids, MI: Eerdmans, 2004), xix.

[8] Heid, *Celibacy in the Early Church*, 33.

its second part (1 Cor 7:1b), is key to understanding the entire chapter. Ancient manuscripts lacked punctuation. As a result, there is some disagreement as to whether the words "It is well for a man not to touch a woman" (1) express Paul's view, (2) are a quotation from the letter that Paul received, or (3) a summary of the views that so concerned some of the Corinthians that they wrote to Paul about them.

These opinions are reflected in the punctuation of the text in the different English translations. For centuries, the common view was that "It is well for a man not to touch a woman" expressed the core of Paul's ideas about the physical expression of human sexuality. Reflecting this approach, the KJV offered "Now concerning the things whereof ye wrote unto me: It is good for a man not to touch a woman" as a translation of the opening verse of chapter 7. According to this interpretation, reflected in the punctuation of the verse, the words "It is good for a man not to touch a woman" express an ideal of sexual asceticism, one that Paul accepted, promoted, and explained in the remainder of chapter 7.

The NRSV punctuates the verse rather differently from the way that the KJV did. In the NRSV's translation, the words "it is well for a man not to touch a woman" are placed within quotation marks. A similar punctuation is found in other recent translations of the texts, for example, in the New American Bible, which translates 1 Corinthians 7:1 in this way: "Now in regard to the matters about which you wrote: 'It is a good thing for a man not to touch a woman.'" The use of quotation marks to encompass the words "it is well for a man not to touch a woman" suggests that these words do not express Paul's own view; rather, they are an expression of the problem about which the Corinthians wrote to Paul.

Reading 1 Corinthians 7:1 in this fashion casts a different light on the entire seventh chapter. Rather than the opening words of the chapter being Paul's statement in favor of sexual asceticism and our reading the chapter from this perspective, the entire chapter is Paul's response to an exaggerated asceticism espoused by some Corinthians. Today most commentators[9] and translations, for example, the NRSV and the NAB, regard

---

[9] Cf. Gordon D. Fee, *The First Epistle to the Corinthians*, NICNT (Grand Rapids, MI: Eerdmans, 1987), 275–76; Roy E. Ciampa and Brian S. Rosner, *The First Letter to the Corinthians*, The Pillar New Testament Commentary (Grand Rapids, MI: Eerdmans, 2010), 272; Raymond F. Collins, *First Corinthians*, SP 7, 2nd ed. (Collegeville, MN: Liturgical Press, 2006), 252–54; Judith M. Gundry-Volk, "Controlling the Bodies: A Theological Profile of the Corinthian Sexual Ascetics (1 Cor 7)," in *The Corinthian Correspondence*, ed. Reimund Bieringer, BETL 125 (Leuven: University Press/Peeters, 1996), 519–41. On p. 529, n. 1, Gundry-Volk offers a sampling of some of the early

the words in 1 Corinthians 7:1b as a pithy summary, if not a direct citation, of the problem mentioned in the Corinthians' correspondence with Paul.[10] The words might have been a kind of slogan bandied about in some Corinthian circles.

The idea that the words of 1 Corinthians 7:1b represent the point of view of some Corinthians is not a new one. The idea was expressed by Origen in the early third century[11] and is found in two ninth-century Arabic versions of the text,[12] but the idea faded from currency under the influence of encratist tendencies within the Church, only to be revived in recent years.

That Paul was influenced by his Jewish heritage and that he took his Judaism seriously[13] is increasingly evident in recent studies on Paul, especially those studies that represent what is sometimes called the New Perspective in Pauline studies.[14] Since Paul was a Jew whose anthropology was shaped by the Genesis creation stories, it would have been out of character for him to teach that it is not good for a man to touch a woman.[15] Should sexual intercourse be morally evil, then marriage itself

---

twentieth-century proponents of this view. Chrys Caragounis, however, demurs from the current consensus. See Chrys C. Caragounis, " 'Fornication' and 'Concession'? Interpreting 1 Cor 7, 1-7," in Bieringer, *Corinthian Correspondence*, 543–60, 546, 559.

[10] Kenneth Bailey, for example, writes: "The Corinthians *wrote to him* about such things as: Is it well for a man not to touch a woman? . . ." (his emphasis). See Kenneth E. Bailey, *Paul through Mediterranean Eyes: Cultural Studies in 1 Corinthians* (Downers Grove, IL: IVP Academic, 2011), 198.

[11] Cf. Claude Jenkins, "Origen on I Corinthians. III," *JTS* 9 (1908): 500–514, 500.

[12] Cf. Bailey, *Paul through Mediterranean Eyes*, 200.

[13] Cf. 2 Cor 11:22; Phil 3:4-6; etc. In addition to these passages there must be added Romans 9–11, which begins with Paul's anguished plea on behalf of his own people (Rom 9:1-5). That he continued to be involved with Jewish communities during the course of his ministry to Gentiles is confirmed by his own reference to the lashings that he received at the behest of Jewish leaders, not once but five times (2 Cor 11:24, 26). Cf. Raymond F. Collins, *Second Corinthians*, Paideia (Grand Rapids, MI: Baker Academic, 2013), 231–32. See also Cf. J. Brian Tucker, *"Remain in Your Calling": Paul and the Continuation of Social Identities in 1 Corinthians* (Eugene, OR: Pickwick Publications, 2011), 92–105.

[14] Unfortunately, Wil Deming's otherwise excellent study, *Paul on Marriage and Celibacy*, does not sufficiently take into account the role that Paul's Judaism played in the apostle's understanding of celibacy. Cf. Calvin J. Roetzel, *Paul: The Man and the Myth*, Studies on the Personalities of the New Testament (Minneapolis: Fortress, 1999), 137.

[15] The expression "to touch a woman" is a euphemism meaning to have sexual relations with a woman.

is sinful and evil, a view that Paul explicitly rejects in 1 Corinthians 7:28, 36.

Epistolary criticism has also had its part to play in the current consensus that 1 Corinthians 7:1b represents the Corinthians' point of view, not that of Paul. It is now widely recognized that "now concerning" (*peri de*[16]) is an epistolary formula. The two words are used in letters to introduce topics raised in a letter that a letter writer has received—topics to which he or she is about to respond. The formula requires that the topic to be discussed is identified, as it is when Paul uses the formula later in the letter. Had the words "it is well for a man not to touch a woman" not been the topic about which the Corinthians had asked in their letter to the apostle, Paul would not have specified the topic about which the Corinthians had written to him, something an accomplished letter writer like him would not have done.

Recent studies have shown that, in writing 1 Corinthians, Paul cites and takes issue with a number of slogans used at Corinth.[17] Prior to responding to the letter that he had received, Paul had dealt with two other Corinthian slogans, "All things are lawful for me" (1 Cor 6:12)[18] and "Food is meant for the stomach and the stomach for food" (1 Cor 6:13). Now, in 1 Corinthians 7:1b, he takes up another slogan that he wants to discuss, a troublesome slogan about which the Corinthians had written, "It is well for a man not to touch a woman." Later in this letter Paul will address other popular slogans.[19] He deals with all of them in more or less the same systematic matter.

That 1 Corinthians 7:1b is a slogan, albeit possibly one formulated by Paul or his correspondents to describe the issue at hand, is almost self-evident. "It is good/well for a man" (*kalon anthrōpō*[20]), the first clause of

---

[16] Cf. 1 Cor 7:1, 25; 8:1, 4; 12:1; 16:1, 12.

[17] Cf. Jerome Murphy-O'Connor, "Corinthian Slogans in 1 Corinthians 6:12-20," in idem., *Keys to First Corinthians: Revisiting the Major Issues* (Oxford: Oxford University Press, 2009), 20–31; Collins, *First Corinthians*, 252–54. Murphy-O'Connor identifies 1 Corinthians 7:1b as a slogan on page 31 of his study.

[18] Cf. 1 Cor 10:23.

[19] Cf. 1 Cor 8:1, 4, 8; 10:23; 13:2; 15:13.

[20] Paul uses the construction, the substantivized *kalos*, "good/well," followed by a dative and an infinitive only in 1 Corinthians—namely, in 7:1, 26; 9:15; cf. 7:8. The formula *kalon anthrōpō*, with its generic *anthrōpos*, appears in the extant correspondence only in 7:1, 8.

7:1b, is a formulaic expression,[21] one used in sayings and slogans. More-over, the euphemism for sexual intercourse used by Paul, "to touch a woman" (*gynaikos haptesthai*) is for the most part alien to Paul. The only other time that it appears in his correspondence is in 2 Corinthians 6:17, where it is found in another quotation—namely, a citation of Isaiah 52:11 (LXX). These features of 7:1b suggest that Paul is not expressing his own opinion in the verse. Rather, he is referring to an issue raised in the Co-rinthians' letter to him, an issue that he expresses a need to address. Perhaps he does so because as a Jew he considers the sexual mores of Gentiles to be suspect.[22] Gentile Christians seem to have constituted the majority of Christians in the capital of the Roman province of Achaia.

Paul's Response

To address the issue that concerned the Corinthians who wrote to him, Paul—accomplished rhetorician that he was—divides the question. After affirming that as a matter of principle every man should have his own wife and every wife her own husband, Paul writes about those who are married (vv. 2-7). Then he addresses himself to "the unmarried and the widows" (vv. 8-9). The third group that he addresses consists of those who might be considering divorce (vv. 10-11). The fourth group is made up of "the rest," those who are married to non-believers (vv. 12-16). Fi-nally he addresses himself to those who have not yet married, "virgins" (*tōn parthenōn*), in his parlance (vv. 25-38). The chapter concludes with a brief exhortation to a Christian woman who has lost her husband and Paul's autobiographical affirmation that he has the Spirit of God (vv. 39-40).

In the final words of the chapter, "And I think that I too have the Spirit of God" (1 Cor 7:40b), Paul's "I too" (*kagō*[23]) is emphatic. The emphasis may suggest that Paul is implicitly comparing himself with those who had urged sexual asceticism.[24] His Spirit-inspired teaching on human

---

[21] Cf. Collins, *First Corinthians*, 257, which cites Paul's contemporary, the Stoic Musonius Rufus, as using the formula (frag. 8.60.6–10). Cf. Homer, *Iliad* 9.615; Sopho-cles, *Antigone* 72; etc.

[22] Cf. Rom 1:24-27; 1 Thess 4:5. Satlow observes that "attacks on the 'other's' sexual laxity is a common form of self-definition in rabbinic sources" (*Jewish Marriage*, 168).

[23] The contraction is also used in 1 Corinthians 7:8.

[24] Cf. C. K. Barrett, *The First Epistle to the Corinthians*, BNTC (Peabody, MA: Hen-drickson, 1993), 186.

sexuality counters theirs. They may have considered that they were above such physical realities as sex because they were endowed with the Spirit.[25] Paul will address one of the relevant issues with regard to the Spirit in 1 Corinthians 12–14 where he specifically takes up the issue of "spiritual gifts" (*peri de tōn pneumatichōn*, 1 Cor 12:1).

1 Corinthians 7:17-24

To understand the specifics of Paul's exhortations to each of the five groups of sexual relation situations that he addresses in chapter 7, it might be well to begin with verses 17-24, a section of the chapter that might be passed over as a digression or an aside in Paul's discourse on human sexuality. One of the characteristic features of the literary style of 1 Corinthians is Paul's use of a chiastic structure (A-B-A').[26] He begins with a topic (A), then seemingly digresses to another topic, which in fact, provides a basic perspective from which to reflect on the topic (B), and then returns to the topic at hand, often addressing specific aspects of the topic (A').

The apostle uses this rhetorical technique to good advantage in dealing with food offered to idols in chapters 8–10 and with spiritual gifts in chapters 12–14. Within these units, Paul's reflection on his willingness to forgo his rights (1 Corinthians 9) and his excursus on love (1 Corinthians 13) provide the perspectives from which he wants his audience to consider the topics under discussion.

So it is with chapter 7. Rather than verses 17-24 of chapter 7 being a section to skip over, the verses must be seriously pondered because they provide the key to the entire seventh chapter of 1 Corinthians. As a matter of principle Paul writes, "Let each of you lead the life that the Lord has assigned, to which God called you. This is my rule in all the churches"[27] (v. 17). Almost like a refrain, this same thought recurs in verses 20 and 24. The refrain sets off verses 1 Corinthians 7:17-24 as a

---

[25] The matter of the identity and nature of the pneumatics at Corinth is far too complex to be treated in the present study.

[26] See John J. Collins, "Chiasmus, the 'ABA' Pattern and the Text of Paul," in *Studiorum paulinorum congressus internationalis catholicus*, 2, AnBib 19 (Rome: Pontifical Biblical Institute, 1961), 575–84. Since then, it has become commonplace for commentators to take note of Paul's use of the rhetorical technique.

[27] The two sentences of the translation are a single sentence in Greek. The two notions are joined by *kai houtōs*, "and so," thus, more literally, "and so I have ordered in all the churches/assemblies."

discrete literary unit within chapter 7. Paul's third use of the refrain embedded within the unit at verse 21 divides the unit into two component parts. The refrain identifies the key notions of the unit—namely, God's call, the verb "call" (*kaleō*) appears in all three of the marking verses, as well as in verses 18 [2x], 21, and 22 [2x], and the appropriate human response to God's call, remaining in the social condition in which people have been called. The verb "remain" (*menō*) likewise appears in the three marking verses.

The first part of the "digression" deals with one's ethnic status, being Jew or Gentile, of which circumcision or lack thereof is the physical sign. To those Jews who would seek to have indications of their circumcision physically removed[28] and to those Gentiles who would seek circumcision, Paul says, "Let each of you remain in the condition in which you were called" (v. 20).

The second part of the apparent aside deals with a person's social status. In Paul's social world, there were people who were free[29] and others who were slaves. A good part of the population of a cosmopolitan city like Corinth belonged to the latter class. Probably more than a third of the total number of inhabitants were slaves.[30] Addressing himself to people in both social situations, the free and the enslaved, Paul says, "In whatever condition you were called, brothers and sisters, there remain with God" (v. 24).

The thrice-repeated "Remain as you are" (vv. 17, 20, 24) is what J. Brian Tucker calls Paul's "primary ideological perspective" with regard to a believer's social and cultural condition.[31] God's call is paramount. There is no need for people to attempt to change their ethnicity or their social status because of God's call. God has called them as members of a race

---

[28] Cf. 1 Macc 1:15; Josephus, *Ant.* 12.241; *T. Mos.* 8 3. The procedure is called epispasm.

[29] Those who were free would include those who were born free as well as those who had been freed.

[30] Wall and Steele observe that, "As many as half of those who lived in the Roman cities of Paul's world were slaves, and a sizeable percentage of the others were former slaves." Cf. Robert W. Wall and Richard B. Steele, *1 & 2 Timothy and Titus*, The Two Horizons New Testament Commentary (Grand Rapids, MI: Eerdmans, 2012), 341. As far as Corinth is concerned, Scott Bartchy estimates that one-third of the population was in slavery, one-third consisted of freedmen and freedwomen, and one-third was free. Cf. S. Scott Bartchy, ΜΑΛΛΟΝ ΧΡΗΣΑΙ: *First-Century Slavery and the Interpretation of 1 Corinthians 7:21*, SBLDS 11 (Missoula, MT: Scholars Press, 1971), 58–59.

[31] Cf. Tucker, *"Remain in Your Calling,"* 227.

and as members of a class. Believers should be content to remain in the condition in which they were called.

Ethnicity and social class are two factors that distinguish humans from one another. Paul's sociological analysis—simplistic by contemporary standards—was dualistic. All of humanity could be divided into two, from several different points of view. There were two ethnicities, Jews and Gentiles. There were two social classes, the free and the enslaved. The third divisor of humanity is gender. In an oft-quoted verse of Galatians, Paul notes that all three social dividers are transcended in Christ. He writes, "There is no longer Jew or Greek, there is no longer slave or free, there is no longer male and female; for all of you are one in Christ Jesus" (Gal 3:28). In 1 Corinthians 7:17-24, Paul speaks of the social division between Jew and Gentile, slave and free, telling all of them to remain as they are, in the social condition in which they were called, in order to teach a lesson about the male-female relationship. The apostle challenges men and women to remain in the situation they were in when they were called to accept Christ as their Lord.

If people are married, they should continue to live like married folks (vv. 2-7). If a spouse has died and a person has not remarried, he or she should accept their solitary state (vv. 8-9). If some are thinking about abandoning their spouse, they should not do so (vv. 10-11). If they are married to a nonbeliever, they should not forsake their marriage (vv. 12-16). If they are "single," they shouldn't seek to get married (vv. 25-38). To people in all five of these sexual situations, Paul says "remain as you are in God."

With regard to the relationships between men and women, Paul is a realist. Hence, he has practical advice for people in all five categories, including the group of married people about whom he writes in verses 2-7. Most probably he writes about this group first of all, not only because they were in the numerical majority in the church of God in Corinth,[32] but also because their marital unions were threatened by those who might have taunted them with, "It is well for a man not to touch a woman."

1 Corinthians 7:25-38

The context in which Paul urges social stability is the imminence of the Parousia. Paul defers mention of this situation until he deals at some

---

[32] Cf. 1 Cor 1:2.

length with the never married in verses 25-38. Urging those people not to marry, Paul pointedly writes, "In view of the impending crisis [*dia tēn enestōsan*[33] *anankēn*], it is well for you to remain as you are" (*hoti kalon anthrōpō to houtōs einai*, v. 26). The reader cannot help but notice the gnomic character of the opening words, *kalon anthrōpō*, "It is well for a man," "It's a good thing for someone to . . ." The words repeat the formula that Paul had used in verse 1.

The apostle offers his advice because of the crisis. What is the crisis at hand? The Greek word translated as "crisis" in 1 Corinthians 7:26 (NRSV), *anankē*, has a wide variety of meanings, the most common of which are "constraint," "compulsion," and "obligation."[34] Paul uses the term *anankē* with a connotation of obligation in 1 Corinthians 7:37; 9:26; 2 Corinthians 9:7; and Philemon 14. In hardship catalogues, he uses the term to mean "affliction" or "hardship."[35] In 1 Corinthians 7:26, the "crisis" consists of the forthcoming eschatological woes,[36] albeit not to the exclusion of a variety of distressful circumstances that can be seen as harbingers of the impending crisis.

The eschatological connotation of Paul's "impending crisis" is confirmed by what he writes just three verses later. Explaining his remarks on why the not yet married should not marry, he says, "I mean, brothers and sisters, the appointed time has grown short" (*ho kairos synestalmenos*

---

[33] The qualifying *enestōsan* can mean "present" or "impending."

[34] The related verb *anankazō* means "compel someone to do something."

[35] Cf. 2 Cor 6:4; 12:10. All told Paul uses the noun nine times: Rom 13:5; 1 Cor 7:26, 37; 9:16; 2 Cor 6:4; 9:7; 12:10; 1 Thess 3:7; Phlm 14.

[36] Thus, writing about the use of the word group in the New Testament, August Strobel ("*anankē*," EDNT 1:77–79) observes, "1 Cor 7:26 gives pointed expression to belief in the *present* (eschatological) time of distress." See the extensive discussion in Anthony C. Thiselton, *The First Epistle to the Corinthians: A Commentary on the Greek Text*, NIGTC (Grand Rapids, MI: Eerdmans, 2000), 572–76. Cf. F. F. Bruce, *1 and 2 Corinthians*, NCB (London: Oliphants, 1971), 74; Collins, *First Corinthians*, 293; Craig S. Keener, *1–2 Corinthians*, New Cambridge Bible Commentary (Cambridge: Cambridge University Press, 2005), 68–69; Joseph A. Fitzmyer, *First Corinthians*, AYB 32 (New Haven, CT: Yale University Press, 2008), 314. Fitzmyer references Zephaniah 1:15 for a similar meaning. Winter and Blue refer specifically to the midcentury famine in Corinth. Cf. Bruce W. Winter, "Secular and Christian Responses to Corinthian Famines," TynBul 40 (1989): 86–106; Bradley B. Blue, "The House Church at Corinth and the Lord's Supper: Famine, Food Supply and the *Present Distress*," CTR 5 (1991): 221–39. I find O. Larry Yarbrough's contention that the term refers to an inability to control sexual desire unconvincing. Cf. O. Larry Yarbrough, *Not Like the Gentiles: Marriage Rules in the Letters of Paul*, SBLDS 80 (Atlanta: Scholars, 1985), 103.

estin, 1 Cor 7:29). The passage concludes with a climactic "For the present form of this world is passing away" (*paragei gar to schēma tou kosmou toutou*, 1 Cor 7:31b). The explanatory *gar* ("for") clearly indicates that Paul is explaining what he has just written.

What Paul writes in verse 29 is a formal declaration. His epistolary "I mean [*phēmi*]," followed by the vocative form of address, is declarative rather than interpretive. What Paul is about to say is something that he wants his readers to understand, something about which he wants them to be absolutely clear. Paul wants his audience to know that the appointed time (*kairos*) has grown short. The time to which he refers is significant time, decision-making time, not chronological time (*chronos*). The perfect passive participle used by Paul suggests that someone/thing is responsible for the shortening of the time and that the process has already begun. The passive voice suggests that it is God who is shortening the time. Early Christian eschatological expectations considered that God was totally in control of the passage of days prior to the Parousia. Mark 13:20 mentions the Lord cutting short those days; Matthew's rephrasing of the Markan verse uses a passive—a divine or theological passive—to express the same idea. The thought expressed by Paul in verse 29 expresses a similar idea.

Paul does not mention the Parousia as such in either verse 29 or verse 31 but he began his letter by reminding the Corinthians that they were waiting for the revelation (*apokalypsis*) of our Lord Jesus Christ (1 Cor 1:7). Immediately thereafter he mentioned the Day of our Lord Jesus Christ (1 Cor 1:8). This coming revelation of the Lord Jesus Christ impinges on the existence and behavior of the Corinthians.[37] The eschatological end time has already begun but it will reach a definitive phase with the Parousia. The Parousia means that the world as we know and experience it is coming to an end. Paul states this explicitly in verse 31b when he writes about the form of this world (*to schēma tou kosmou toutou*) passing away. His words recall what is written in *4 Ezra* 4:26, "the age is hurrying swiftly to its end."[38]

This eschatological perspective colors everything that Paul writes in 1 Corinthians 7. It is particularly important for understanding Paul's counsel when he writes about the unmarried, widows (v. 7), and virgins (v. 25). Remaining as they are implies that they should not marry. Mar-

[37] Cf. Rom 13:11-14; 1 Thess 5:1-8.
[38] Cf. *4 Ezra* 2:34.

riage is a social institution. In both Jewish and Greco-Roman society, marriage was beneficial insofar as people married to produce heirs, particularly male heirs. If the time in which readers were living were to be as short as Paul apparently suggests in 1 Corinthians 7:29-31, marriage would not be able to produce its expected result. Why marry to have a family, when there is not enough time to do so?

Paul's emphasis on the coming eschaton may have been influenced, at least in part, by the problem at Corinth. The excessive sexual asceticism of some Corinthians may have been due to an erroneous understanding of eschatological existence,[39] existence in light of the coming of the Parousia.[40] They may have thought that the final times were already fully present,[41] the final times in which people neither marry nor are given in marriage.[42] Paul responds that that time has not yet come. The time may be short but the time of decision still exists; within this time the holiness of God's people must be preserved.

Paul's expectation of the imminent Parousia[43] led him to urge the Corinthians to remain as they were, particularly with regard to their sexual situation since that was the problem that was mentioned in the letter he had received—a problem so serious that Paul felt constrained to respond at some length and in detail.

Paul

Paul offers himself as an example of someone who was willing to remain as he was, but what was his marital status? There is no single text in the apostle's extant correspondence that answers this question straight out and with full clarity.

[39] See Gundry-Volk, "Controlling the Bodies," 529–30, 540.

[40] Paul treats another eschatological issue in chapter 15. Occasionally it has been suggested that the issue to which Paul responds is not an absolute denial of future resurrection as much as it is an assertion that the future is already present because believers already possess life in the Spirit.

[41] In 1 Corinthians 15, Paul speaks to those who denied a future resurrection from the dead, convinced, perhaps, that the end times were already present.

[42] Cf. Luke 20:35.

[43] 1 Thessalonians 4:15, 17 express Paul's expectation that he would be alive at the Parousia. Since he considered himself to be already an old man in the decade in which he wrote his extant letters (Phlm 9), he would have expected the Parousia to occur in the not too distant future.

The Charism of Marriage

By reading Paul's text too quickly, some have taken Paul's reference to a gift from God (*charisma ek theou*) in 1 Corinthians 7:7, the last verse in the first section of his disquisition on undue sexual asceticism, as a reference to his own celibacy. In context, however, the gift from God to which he was referring is clearly marriage,[44] as even the early Fathers of the Church acknowledged.[45] Unlike the sloganeers of Corinth who disparaged marriage and its sexuality, Paul affirms that marriage with its mutual sexual expressions is a gift from God, a charism.

Paul's reference to the gift of marriage is clearly distinguished from his own situation. As he is writing to the Corinthians, Paul professes marriage to be a gift from God. A strong "but" expresses the view that the situation that he describes as a gift from God is different from his own: "I wish that all were as I myself am. But [*alla*] each one has a particular gift from God, one having one kind and another a different kind [*ho men houtōs, ho de houtōs*]" (1Cor 7:7). This first mention of a charism in the letter—this is, in fact, the first time that Paul uses the word in his extant correspondence—is consistent with what Paul writes about other charisms (*charismata*) later in the letter.

"To each his own" is the way that Ernst Käsemann summed up what Paul writes in 1 Corinthians 12:7-11.[46] The Spirit apportions the gift of God, just as the Spirit chooses. God gives a particular gift, but not others, to every person who has received the Spirit in baptism. For Paul to marry

[44] Cf. Fitzmyer, *First Corinthians*, 282. Fitzmyer explicitly rejects the view of Conzelmann who opined that marriage is not "here described as a charisma." Cf. Hans Conzelmann, *1 Corinthians: A Commentary on the First Epistle to the Corinthians*, Hermeneia (Philadelphia: Fortress, 1975), 118. For views similar to Conzelmann's, see Kurt Niederwimmer, *Askese und Mysterium: Über Ehe, Ehescheidung und Eheversicht des christlichen Glaubens*, FRLANT 113 (Göttingen: Vandenhoeck & Ruprecht, 1975), 96, n. 70; Peter Brown, *The Body and Society: Men, Women, and Sexual Renunciation in Early Christianity* (New York: Columbia University Press, 1988), 56–57; Gundry-Volk, "Controlling the Bodies," 533; Deming, *Marriage and Celibacy*, 124.

[45] Cf. Origen, *Commentary on 1 Corinthians* 3.34.42–45 in Jenkins, "Origen on I Corinthians. III," 503; Theodoret of Chyrrus, *Commentary on the First Epistle to the Corinthians* 202 (PG 82, 274).

[46] Ernst Käsemann, "The Theological Problem Presented by the Motif of the Body of Christ," in idem, *Perspectives on Paul*, NTL (Philadelphia; Fortress, 1971), 102–21. The sense of Käsemann's "to each his own" is vastly different from the dismissive fashion in which these words are used in contemporary parlance. Käsemann wanted to affirm that each Spirit-endowed believer has at least one charism but not others.

at this point in his life would have been for him to change what he considered to be his God-given social status at that time.[47]

Unmarried

If Paul was not married at the time when he was writing to the Corinthians, what was his situation? The apostle provides an answer in the second part of his response to the Corinthians: "To the unmarried and the widows I say[48] that it is well for them to remain unmarried as I am" (1 Cor 7:8). I have already noted that the "unmarried" in the NRSV's translation of Paul's self-comparison is not found in the Greek text, which employs a pithy phrase to make the comparison. In order to understand the comparison, we must begin by looking at the group with which the apostle compares himself. Paul addresses himself "to the unmarried and the widows" (*tois agamois kai tais chērais*). These are the people with whose situation Paul's own condition is comparable. Who are they?

Who are the unmarried, the *agamoi*, to whom Paul is offering advice about marriage? Many readers assume that Paul's "unmarried" means "single" or "never married," but that interpretation is not quite what the term means. The privative alpha (*a*) with which the adjective, used as a substantive in verse 8, begins indicates that *agamoi* describes people who are simply "not married." The category includes both the single—that is, those who have not yet married and perhaps never will be—as well as those who were once married but are no longer married. The no longer married group includes the divorced as well as those who have lost their spouses through death.

The word *agamos*, "unmarried," is rarely used by Paul. In fact, it occurs only in 1 Corinthians 7, which contains the longest reflection on marriage and sexual relationships in the apostle's extant correspondence. The first occurrence of the word, in the plural, is found here in verse 8. It occurs a second time—this time in the singular—in verse 11 where it has reference to a woman who has separated from her husband through divorce. The third occurrence is in verse 32 where *agamos*, contrasted with the

---

[47] Cf. Bruce W. Winter, "1 Corinthians 7:6-7: A Caveat and a Framework for 'The Sayings' in 7:8-24," *TynBul* 48 (1997): 57–65, 64.

[48] "I say" (*legō*) may be emphatic. Cf. Christoph Senft, *La première épître de Saint Paul aux Corinthiens*, CNT 2/7, 2nd ed. (Geneva: Labor et Fides, 1990), 91; Fitzmyer, *First Corinthians*, 283.

married man (*ho de gamēsas*) of verse 33, is used in reference to an unmarried man who may be contemplating marriage. The fourth time that Paul uses the adjective—again in the singular and in substantivized form—is in verse 34 where it describes a woman, apparently not yet married, who is contrasted with a married woman (*he gamesasa*[49]). In sum, the adjective can be used as a noun and, in a masculine form, can refer to a woman. In fact, in two of Paul's three uses of the singular masculine form of the adjective, he has a woman in mind.

Lexically, therefore, the *agamoi* of verse 8 may include any or all of six groups of people, the single, the divorced, and those whose spouses have died, whether they be men or women. In context, however, the possible connotations of the term are fewer. Throughout the entire passage, Paul juxtaposes men and women. This is clearly the case in the first, third, and fourth subunits of his rhetorical argument. There is no reason to doubt that he juxtaposes men and women in verse 8, the third subunit, in which he speaks of the unmarried and widows.[50] The *agamoi* are men who are not married.

There are, however, three categories of unmarried men: the single, the divorced, and those who are widowers. Although "not previously married" falls within the range of possibilities for the meaning of *agamoi*, given the rhetoric of Paul's argument in 1 Corinthians 7, that would not be a reasonable connotation of the term in verse 8. First of all, Paul's line of thought is consistent in chapter 7. The argument is balanced throughout the chapter. The apostle contrasts men and women in similar situations. In verse 8, Paul speaks about women who have lost their husbands. It is hardly likely that he would compare them with men who were not yet married.[51] In Paul's social situation and given the Jewish matrix that

---

[49] The participle is also found in v. 34. A similar contrast is found in Xenophon, *Symp.* 9.7.

[50] Fitzmyer offers "widowers" as a possible meaning of the *tais chērais* of v. 8 but offers no examples of the term being used of men. The noun is in the feminine form. An analogous male form (*chēros*, "widower") existed but came into common use only later. Given Paul's consistency in juxtaposing men and women and the common understanding of *chēra*, it is all but impossible to understand *tais chērais* other than as a term describing women who have lost their husbands through death, "widows" in the proper sense of the term.

[51] Commenting on a passage in the Tosefta, *t. Ketub.* 1:1, Satlow writes about the Babylonian Talmud's important assumption, to wit, "*a woman who had previously married would not ordinarily be married to a man who had never been married. Both Talmuds deal explicitly with this issue in their discussion of the marriage blessing.*" Cf. Satlow, *Jewish Marriage*, 184 [his emphasis].

colors the expression of his thought in the chapter, the not yet married person would probably have been no older than thirty.[52] Men normally married women younger than themselves. Is Paul, in verse 8, talking about young men and widows? Lexically that is possible. In the context of Paul's argumentation, it is highly unlikely.

A second reason for excluding the never married as a connotation of the *agamoi* of verse 8 is that Paul will talk about not yet married men in the fifth subunit of his argument, 1 Corinthians 7:25-38, a subunit in which Paul explicitly addresses the unmarried, *parthenoi*, "virgins," in his idiom. Dividing the question as he does, Paul first addresses himself to men who are not yet married (vv. 27-28a). Later in the subunit, in verses 32 and 36-38, he directs his *paraenesis* to men who are not yet married. The *parthenoi* of verses 25-38 are distinct from the *agamoi* of verses 8-9. The *agamoi* of this pair of verses are like widows, people who no longer have a spouse. The gender balance of Paul's phrase suggests that in this context, *agamoi* is Paul's way of speaking about widowers.[53]

In the first half of the third century, one of the greatest of early Christianity's commentators on Scripture, Origen of Alexandria, noted that Paul compared himself with the *agamoi* rather than with the *parthenoi*.[54] Rather than comparing himself with men who have never been married, the apostle compares himself with men and women who had previously been married. Comparing himself with the *agamoi*, as he does in verse 8, Paul seems to suggest that at the time that he was writing 1 Corinthians he was no longer married,[55] though he once had been.

Roger Gryson has suggested that at the time 1 Corinthians was being written, Paul was separated from his wife.[56] Expressing this view, Gryson seems to be in agreement with Clement of Alexandria that Paul was married but that he was not accompanied by his wife during his missionary travels.[57] The implied reference is, of course, to 1 Corinthians 9:5.

---

[52] Cf. Sarah B. Pomeroy, *Families in Classical and Hellenistic Greece: Representations and Realities* (Oxford: Clarendon, 1997), 6, 23, 59; and *passim*, *Xenophon Oecumenicus: A Social and Historical Commentary* (Oxford: Clarendon, 1994), 268–69.

[53] Cf. Collins, *First Corinthians*, 268; William F. Orr and James A. Walther, *I Corinthians*, AB 32 (New York: Doubleday, 1976), 209–10; Fee, *First Corinthians*, 287–88; Bailey, *Paul through Mediterranean Eyes*, 203–4.

[54] Cf. Fragment on 1 Cor, 35, in Jenkins, "Origen on 1 Corinthians. III," 504. Cf. Gryson, *Origines*, 2, 18.

[55] Eduardo Arens, "Was Paul Married?," *TBT* 66 (1973): 1188–91, esp. 1189.

[56] Cf. Gryson, *Origines*, 18, n. 6.

[57] See *Miscellanies* III, 6 (GCS 52, 220); Cf. Eusebius, *Eccl. Hist.* III, 30, 2.

However, temporary separation from one's wife, even for as long as the period of one of Paul's missionary trips, does not appear to have been among the connotations of the term *agamos* in antiquity.

A Widower?

Does this mean that Paul was a widower? The thought that the apostle Paul was a widower was already expressed by some patristic authors, such as Methodius, a third-century bishop of Olympus and opponent of Origen, and Ambrose, the fourth-century bishop of Milan, who was Augustine's father in faith.[58] Theodoret of Cyrrhus argued otherwise, claiming that Paul was too young to have been a widower at the time.[59] Early in the twentieth century the question of Paul's being a widower was raised in a pair of articles by Joachim Jeremias, who explicitly asked "Was Paul a Widower?"[60] Exploiting the narrative contexts of the three accounts of Paul's "conversion" in Acts[61] and the invitation by an official of the Jewish synagogue in Antioch in Pisidia,[62] Jeremias argued that Paul was an ordained wise man, a *hākām*, and a member of the Sanhedrin with the power to make legal decisions. This would have meant that he was at least forty years old[63] at the time of his Damascus experience.

Jeremias inferred more than he should have from the Lukan accounts. Moreover, his reference to Paul's ordination and his citations of the Bavli are anachronistic with regard to the time of Paul and so would have been irrelevant as far as the apostle was concerned. Nonetheless, Jeremias

[58] Cf. Methodius, *Symposium* XII, 82–83 (PG 18, 80); Ambrose, *Virginity* 18 (PL 16, 315).

[59] Cf. *Comm. In 1 Cor 7:7-8* (PG 82, 273cd). Gryson (*Origines*, 74) opines that Theodoret may have read Acts 7:58 too rapidly and thus have misinterpreted Luke's reference to Paul's age. When he wrote 1 Corinthians, Paul would have been in his mid- to late forties.

[60] Cf. Joachim Jeremias, "War Paulus Witwer?," *ZNW* 25 (1926): 310–12; and "Nochmals: War Paulus Witwer?," *ZNW* 28 (1929): 321–23. The second article was written as a response to Erich Fascher, "Zur Witwerschaft des Paulus und der Auslegung von 1 Cor 7," *ZNW* 28 (1929): 62–65. Albrecht Oepke continued the discussion a few years later with "Probleme der vorchristlichen Zeit des Paulus," *TSK* 105 (1933): 387–424.

[61] Especially Acts 9:1-2; 22:5; 26:12. On the Damascus experience, see Raymond F. Collins, "Paul's Damascus Experience: Reflections on the Lukan Account," *LS* 11 (1986): 99–118.

[62] Cf. Acts 13:15.

[63] Cf. *b. Sotah* 22b.

may have been on to something with regard to Paul's marital status when he raised the possibility of Paul being a widower.

Luke incorporates a brief account of Paul's life as a Jew in his account of Paul's apology to the Jews (Acts 22:3-21). He tells us that although Paul was born in Tarsus, he was reared in Jerusalem[64] where he was a student of the great rabbi Gamaliel, the grandson of Hillel.[65] The historicity of the account has been called into question.[66] The account is clearly a Lukan composition[67] and Luke has a decided interest in Jerusalem. Among other things, the evangelist has an interest in establishing a Jerusalem connection for Paul.

The Lukan introduction to Paul's defense before Agrippa generally echoes what is described in Acts 22. In Acts 26, Paul is said to have said to King Agrippa: "All the Jews know my way of life from my youth, a life spent from the beginning among my own people and in Jerusalem. They have known for a long time . . . that I have belonged to the strictest sect of our religion and lived as a Pharisee" (Acts 26:4-5).

In itself, there is nothing implausible about an intelligent and zealous Jew seeking out a prominent teacher in order to learn more about his heritage.[68] That Paul was intelligent is obvious from his writings; that he was a zealous Jew is something to which he attests in his own words. In his letters, the apostle does not offer very much by way of biographical detail about his education but the letters show that Paul was well versed in the Jewish Scriptures and that he interpreted them, using hermeneutical principles similar to those employed within the school of Hillel. About his education, he says only that, "I advanced in Judaism beyond many among my people of the same age, for I was far more zealous for the traditions of my ancestors" (Gal 1:14).

---

[64] Acts 7:58 and 23:16 corroborate the detail about Paul's spending early years in Jerusalem.

[65] Cf. Bruce D. Chilton and Jacob Neusner, "Paul and Gamaliel," in *In Quest of the Historical Pharisees*, ed. Jacob Neusner and Bruce D. Chilton (Waco, TX: Baylor University Press, 2007).

[66] Notably by Ernst Haenchen. Cf. Ernst Haenchen, *The Acts of the Apostles: A Commentary* (Philadelphia: Westminster / Oxford: Blackwell, 1971), 625.

[67] Hans Conzelmann, *Acts of the Apostles*, Hermeneia (Philadelphia: Fortress, 1987), 186; Joseph A. Fitzmyer, *The Acts of the Apostles*, AB 32 (New York: Doubleday, 1998), 703; etc.

[68] Cf. Helen K. Bond, "Gamaliel," *NIDB* 2 (Nashville: Abingdon Press, 2007), 520.

With regard to his life as a Jew and comparing himself with his contemporaries, Jews like himself, Paul states that his moral, spiritual, and intellectual formation in Judaism exceeded theirs.[69] His comparison is based on his zeal for the Torah-based teachings that had been handed down within the Pharisaic[70] schools of Judaism. His credentials as a pious and zealous Jew were impeccable.[71] Proof positive of his concern for the fulfillment of his ancestral traditions was his willingness to persecute violently the Church of God in Jerusalem, to the point of attempting to wipe it out completely.[72]

Commenting on what he calls the "complacently competitive tone" of Galatians 1:14, Jerome Murphy-O'Connor opines that the passage "betrays the stranger who has successfully integrated into Jewish Jerusalem through perfect conformity to the norm" and concludes that it is probable "that Paul cheerfully bowed to the expectations that young men should marry in their early twenties."[73] Had Paul been married, not only would he have been readily integrated into the company of young Jewish men in Jerusalem, he would also have enjoyed easy access into Jewish synagogues, similar to the kind of entry that Luke repeatedly describes in his accounts of Paul's missionary voyages.[74]

In his Letter to the Philippians, Paul reiterates that it was his zeal for the Law and the Pharisaic interpretation of the Law that led him to persecute the Church.[75] In this letter, the apostle describes the ancestral heritage which was his before he forsook its advantages because of his experience of Christ. He writes:

> If anyone else has reason to be more confident in the flesh, I have
> more: circumcised on the eighth day, a member of the people of
> Israel, of the tribe of Benjamin, a Hebrew born of the Hebrews; as

[69] The imperfect tense of "advanced" (*prooekopton*) indicates that this was a continuing process, as was his violent persecution of the Church. Compare with the imperfect *ediōkon*, "was persecuting," in verse 13.

[70] Cf. Phil 3:5.

[71] Cf. Richard N. Longenecker, *Galatians*, WBC 41 (Dallas: Word, 1990), 30.

[72] Cf. Gal 1:13.

[73] Cf. Murphy-O'Connor, *Paul*, 63.

[74] Cf. Acts 13:5, 14; 14:1; 17:10, 17; 18:4; 19:8; 24:12; cf. 16:13; 22:19; 26:11.

[75] Cf. Phil 3:6. Paul speaks of his persecution of the Church in a third passage—namely, 1 Corinthians 15:9, without providing any motivation for his actions. In this verse, his activity demonstrates his unpreparedness to receive a vision of the Lord and be called to the apostolate.

to the law, a Pharisee; as to zeal, a persecutor of the church, as to righteousness under the law, blameless. (Phil 3:4b-6)

As was the case with the description of his birth and rearing in Galatians 1:14, he compares himself favorably with his coreligionists. Paul was an Israelite, a Benjaminite, and a Hebrew,[76] as was confirmed by his ritual circumcision on the appointed day, the eighth after his birth. The circumstances of his birth gave him reason to be proud, but they were beyond his control.

What was under his control was the lived expression of his Jewish heritage. He chose to adhere to the Law according to the way it was expounded by the Pharisees.[77] He manifested his zeal for the Law as he understood it by his active persecution of the Church,[78] the assembly of believers in Jesus. As for his relationship with God and his fellow Jews, he considered himself to be blameless. His was a track record of which he could be proud although he fully rejected it once Christ entered his life.

The Law for which Paul was zealous was that expounded within the Pharisaic tradition, the tradition that included not only the precepts of the Torah but also the oral tradition that interpreted the Torah. The Pharisaic tradition with which Paul was familiar—whether or not he actually studied under Gamaliel is incidental to what he writes in Philippians—included the formative traditions from which the later rabbinic tradition on marriage examined in chapter 2 of this study emerged.[79] With regard to that interpretation of the Law, Paul says that he is blameless. He affirms his personal rectitude. He fulfilled the oral and written Law entirely.

---

[76] Cf. 2 Cor 11:22.

[77] Philippians 3:5 is Paul's only explicit reference to his belonging to the Pharisees. On the self-portrait of Paul in Phil 3:4b-6, his *cursus honorum*, see Yara Matta, *À cause du Christ. Le retournement de Paul le Juif*, LD 256 (Paris: Cerf, 2013), 113–69.

[78] Cf. Gal 1:14; 1 Cor 15:5. Luke's threefold account of Paul's conversion (Acts 9:1-9; 22:3-21; 26:2-23) describes Paul's persecution of the Church, adding narrative details that are not found in Paul's extant letters. Among those details are the letters of credence that Paul is said to have obtained from the Jerusalem authorities (Acts 9:2; 22:5; 26:10), a detail that betrays the Lukan sentiment to link Paul with Jerusalem.

[79] The rabbinic tradition found in the *Mishnah* and both Talmuds basically derives from the School of Hillel. Paul's exposition of the Scriptures is similar to that of the Hillelites. Luke's reference to the apostle's education at the feet of Gamaliel would confirm Paul's association with that branch of Pharisaism. Cf. Chilton and Neusner, "Paul and Gamaliel," 217.

According to the righteousness (*kata dikaiosynēn*) called for by the Law, he was without any fault.[80] Were Paul not to have been married, it would have been impossible for him to affirm his personal rectitude, within the parameters of Judaism, in such unqualified fashion. In sum, it is most probable that Paul once had a wife and at the time of the composition of 1 Corinthians, he was a widower.[81]

"Do We Not Have the Right to Be Accompanied by a Believing Wife?"

Paul poses this rhetorical question later in the letter, as we have already seen.[82] The question is asked and not answered[83] in Paul's self-styled "defense" (*apologia*)[84] in chapter 9 of 1 Corinthians. The chapter is a key element in Paul's discussion of food offered to idols (1 Corinthians 8–10). One of the features of Paul's rhetorical argument, especially in 1 Corinthians, is his use of a chiastic A-B-A' structure in advancing his position.[85] The A element raises the question and gives an initial response. The B element offers what appears to be a rhetorical aside, although, in fact, it states a matter of principle that undergirds the initial response. Having

---

[80] Paul's understanding of righteousness evolved considerably from that which was his at the time when he persecuted Christians but that issue is beyond the scope of the present study. Cf. *The Biblical Foundations of the Doctrine of Justification: An Ecumenical Follow-Up to* The Joint Declaration on the Doctrine of Justification (Mahwah, NJ: Paulist, 2012), 58–85; Gerald F. Hawthorne and Ralph P. Martin, *Philippians*, WBC 43, rev. ed. (Nashville: Thomas Nelson, 2004), 187–88.

[81] Murphy-O'Connor notes that whereas older commentators thought that Paul was never married, modern scholars tend to the opinion that he was indeed a widower. As examples of the tendency, Murphy-O'Connor cites Fee and Légasse. Cf. Murphy-O'Connor, *Paul*, 62; Fee, *First Corinthians*, 288, n. 7; Simon Légasse, *Paul Apôtre: Essai de biographie critique* (Paris: Cerf/Fides, 1991), 45. See also Josephine Massingbird Ford, *A Trilogy on Wisdom and Celibacy*, Cardinal O'Hara Series 4 (Notre Dame, IN: University of Notre Dame Press, 1967), 70–71, and various other authors.

[82] See above, pp. 89–92; 1 Cor 9:5

[83] Rhetorical questions, a major feature in Hellenistic and contemporary rhetoric, are typically not answered by those who pose them. Paul, however, often provides his readers with the answer to his questions. A competent reader of Paul's letters would have paused after a rhetorical question in the public reading of the text before moving on to the answer provided by Paul. This would have enabled the reader/hearer to formulate his or her own response before hearing Paul's response to the question.

[84] Cf. 1 Cor 9:3.

[85] See above, p. 118.

stated the principle, Paul returns to the topic at hand (A') in more detail and frequently with pointed specifics.

Paul's overall argument is that "knowledgeable" Corinthians should be willing to forgo their "right"[86] to eat food that had once been offered to idols so as not to scandalize—in the sense of leading astray[87]—those whose faith was not as sophisticated as theirs is. To make his point, Paul offers himself as an example of someone who willingly forgoes the eating of meat so as not to cause other Christians to fall (1 Cor 8:13). The use of example was considered to be an important argument by Hellenistic rhetoricians. Paul was familiar with the technique and so expounds on his use of freedom and the exercise of his rights immediately after he has cited himself as an example in 8:13. Stephen Langton's division of the chapter at this point should not deter the reader—as it did not deter those who first listened to the reading of Paul's letter—from realizing that Paul's *apologia* follows immediately after Paul had offered himself as an example for the Corinthians to follow in the matter of eating food.

The subject of the *apologia* is Paul's freedom and the exercise of his rights in pursuit of his apostolic mission. Paul begins his defense with the rhetorical question, "Do we not have the right [*exousia*[88]] to our food and drink?" (1 Cor 9:4). The issue of Paul's financial support seems to have been a bone of contention between himself and some Corinthians. It is an issue to which the apostle returns in the extant Second Letter to the Corinthians, pointedly and poignantly so in 2 Corinthians 11:7-11. Paul is adamant about his self-support even at the price of sometimes going hungry because he did not earn enough wages as someone who was occasionally engaged in leather work.[89]

Paul wanted to preach the Gospel free of charge; some within the Corinthian community felt that they should support his apostolic endeavors. The social context of the tension between Paul and these believers is that of the support of teachers.[90] Teachers were typically supported in one of four ways. Some had wealthy patrons while others were paid for their efforts. Some teachers pursued their own occupation in order to

---

[86] *Exousia* in 1 Cor 8:9. Cf. 1 Cor 9:5.

[87] Cf. 1 Cor 8:11-12.

[88] Cf. 1 Cor 8:9; 9:5.

[89] Cf. 2 Cor 11:27; Collins, *Second Corinthians*, 232.

[90] Cf. Raymond F. Collins, *The Birth of the New Testament: The Origin and Development of the First Christian Generation* (New York: Crossroad, 1993), 11–15, 218–20 and the literature, ancient and modern, cited therein.

support themselves while others resorted to begging in order to obtain the basic necessities of life. Rather than being beholden to the family of one wealthy individual or receiving donations for his proclamation of the Gospel, Paul preferred to preach the Gospel without burdening those to whom he preached[91]—that is, he refused to receive financial support from them. Paul did not want to be a client of those to whom he preached. For him, the freedom of the Gospel was at stake; it could not be purchased.

Given the situation, it is little wonder that Paul's defense of his right to forgo financial support is the burden of his defense (1 Cor 9:3-18). The rhetorical question apropos his willingness to forgo the right to be accompanied by a wife in 1 Corinthians 9:5 is virtually a rhetorical aside. It could, however, be argued that the verse functions as the B element in a chiastic structure whose contents are a series of rhetorical questions (1 Cor 9:4-14). All but one of the questions pertain to Paul's right to earn his living by preaching the Gospel. The one exception is the question that pertains to his and Barnabas's right to be accompanied by their wives while they traveled about preaching the Gospel.

Rhetorically, the question, with its unstated response, undergirds the rest of Paul's argument. It was to be taken for granted that Christian missionaries were married and that they would be accompanied by their wives.[92] It was their right to do so and they exercised that right. The right was so self-evident and the practice a matter of such general experience that Paul could use his unmarried state—he was after all, *agamos*, unmarried (1 Cor 7:8)—as a forceful argument in support of his willingness to forgo financial support from the Corinthians. Just as he was willing to forgo marriage and apparently committed to do so, so he was committed to a refusal to accept financial support for preaching the Gospel. Both actions on the part of Paul were largely countercultural and would have surprised most Corinthians, with the exception of that ascetic group whose position is summarized by Paul in 1 Corinthians 7:1b.

That Paul was most likely a widower when he wrote 1 Corinthians is sufficient for our study. The curious would, however, like to know more

---

[91] Cf. 1 Thess 2:9; etc. By way of an apparent exception to his general practice, Paul did receive support from believers at Philippi. He received the financial support after he had departed from the city and was therefore no longer beholden to its inhabitants. Cf. Phil 4:15-16.

[92] Heid remarks, "Having a woman in one's company seems to have been the mark of a genuine apostle" (*Celibacy in the Early Church*, 30).

about Paul's marriage—for example, the name of his wife and the circumstances of her death. That he does not mention his wife is, at this time, not surprising. In the culture of the times and given the social status of women, wives are rarely mentioned in Jewish literature. It has already been noted that the New Testament does not provide modern readers with the name of Simon Peter's wife nor does it mention her existence,[93] yet the fact that Peter had a wife is implied by the fact that he had a mother-in-law, as is attested in the Synoptic Gospels. We have also noted that rabbinic literature rarely mentions the wives of prominent rabbis and even less often does it cite the name of a prominent rabbi's wife. Paul himself mentions no member of his family, neither his family of origin nor a family that he might have founded. That Paul had at least one sibling, a sister, is noted in Acts 23:16 when Luke mentions that Paul's nephew warned the apostle about an ambush that was being set for him in Jerusalem.

Notwithstanding the fact that it is inherently unlikely that Paul would have mentioned the name of his wife except if she would have been one of his principal fellow missionaries as were Silvanus, Sosthenes, and Timothy, whose names are cited as greeting the communities to which Paul wrote,[94] there have been times in the course of Church history when Lydia has been proposed as the person to whom Paul was married.

The suggestion is based on the idea that "Lydia" (*Lydia*) etymologically means a woman from Lydia in Asia Minor. In the case of the woman who, according to Luke, hosted Paul during his visit to Philippi,[95] "Lydia" may have the nickname of a woman whose given name was Euodia or Syntyche[96] or the anonymous person whom Paul calls his "loyal companion" (*gnēsie syzyge*) in Philippians 4:3. In Philippians 4:2, Paul urges Euodia and Syntyche to reconcile their differences.[97]

---

[93] That is, with the exception of 1 Corinthians 9:5. See the discussion of this passage, above, pp. 89, 91–93.

[94] Silvanus in 1 Thess 1:1; Sosthenes in 1 Cor 1:1; Timothy in 2 Cor 1:1; Phil 1:1; 1 Thess 1:1; Phlm 1. Another named coevangelist is Titus who figures prominently in 2 Corinthians.

[95] Cf. Acts 16:14, 40.

[96] Cf. Colin J. Hemer, *The Book of Acts in the Setting of Hellenistic History*, ed. Conrad H. Gempf, WUNT 49 (Tübingen: J. C. B. Mohr / Paul Siebeck, 1989), 114, 231.

[97] The various possibilities as to the cause of their estrangement are surveyed by John Reumann in *Philippians*, AYB 33B (New Haven/London: Yale University Press, 2008), 628.

Theodore of Mopsuestia once exploited a rumor to suggest that Syntyche was a man, Syntyches by name, Euodia's husband and sometime jailer at Philippi.[98] In light of the fact that Paul's text has the name in the feminine, supported by the feminine pronouns of verse 2, as well as the fact that epigraphical evidence attests to "Syntyche" as a woman's name—as well as the meager evidence on which Theodore based his opinion—modern scholars believe that Euodia and Syntche were a pair of female leaders within the Christian community in the Roman colony at Philippi.[99]

Paul asks his loyal companion to help the women reconcile their differences. Who is this loyal companion? Modern commentators generally suggest that the loyal companion is a man but the list of possibilities as to who it might be is endless. Timothy, Silas, Luke, Epaphroditus, and even Peter or Christ himself have been proposed as possibilities.[100] Epaphroditus may well be the most likely candidate since he was the one who carried the letter[101] to Philippi.

In Greek, "companion" (*syzyge*) is the vocative substantivized form of the adjective *syzygos*,[102] which means "yoked together." The lexical group, to which the adjective belongs, was often used of animals yoked together for plowing. Used of humans, the adjective means "united," especially by marriage.[103] In substantivized female form, the adjective means "wife;"[104] in the masculine, it means "companion." The problem in interpreting the meaning of *gnēsie syzyge* in Philippians 4:3 is that there

---

[98] Cf. Acts 16:16-39.

[99] See Florence Morgan Gillman, *Women Who Knew Paul*, Zacchaeus Studies (Collegeville, MN: Liturgical Press, 1992), 43–49; "Syntyche," *ABD* 6, p. 270.

[100] Cf. Hawthorne-Martin, *Philippians*, 242; Peter T. O'Brien, *Commentary on Philippians*, NIGTC (Grand Rapids, MI: Eerdmans, 1991), 480–81; Reumann, *Philippians*, 628–29.

[101] Whether extant Philippians is a single letter or a composite text is currently a matter of scholarly debate. The issue lies beyond the scope of the present study. See the discussion in Reumann, *Philippians*, 7–15.

[102] Footnotes *ad locum* in the NAB and the NRSV offer the possibility that Syzygos is a proper name. The name appears in the NAB at Philippians 4:3. Nonetheless, and notwithstanding the opinion of some older commentators, there is no evidence that "Syzygos" was ever used as a personal name. CF. BAGD, s.v. "*syzygos*."

[103] Cf. Aeschylus, *Libation-Bearers*, 599. A related adjective *syzygios*, in an active sense, "uniting," was used of the goddess Hera, the wife of Zeus and goddess of marriage. Cf. LSJ, s.v. "*syzygios*."

[104] Thus, Euripides in *Alcestis* 314, 342; *T. Reub.* 4:1; and others.

is no difference between the masculine and feminine forms of the adjective in the vocative singular. Thus, the expression *gnēsie syzyge* could refer to a loyal wife or a devoted male companion.

Around the turn of the third Christian century, Origen's teacher Clement of Alexandria thought that Paul was asking his wife,[105] his devoted companion, for help in resolving the issues between Euodia and Syntyche. Clement believed that Paul's wife was not with him at the time of Paul's writing the letter because he did not take her along during his missionary travels. More than a millennium later, as a historical-critical approach to Paul's letters was beginning to develop, some scholars—most notably Erasmus and Renan[106]—took the "loyal companion" of Philippians 4:3 to be a reference to Paul's wife, whom they identified with the woman of Philippi, named Lydia.

The suggestion that Lydia might possibly have been Paul's wife possesses a scintilla of textual evidence, albeit not enough to be convincing. On the other hand, there is no textual evidence whatsoever as to the fate of Paul's wife, had Paul been a widower, as the available evidence seems to suggest. Murphy-O'Connor opines that Paul's wife and family may have succumbed to an earthquake or a plague.[107] If that were the case, Paul, an angry but devout Pharisee, may have focused his anger against Christians, a group whom he considered to be a divisive and disloyal group within the Judaism of his day. Even if displaced anger is not the reason for Paul's fierce persecution of Christians, we know the outcome of the story.

Murphy-O'Connor opines that the displaced anger theory is plausible but the "evidence" is all too meager. Psychologizing interpretations of Scripture are generally to be avoided. In fact, we know less about the death of Paul's wife than about her life. From what he wrote to the Corinthians in 1 Corinthians 9:5, we know that Paul was not accompanied by his wife during his missionary travels. Being with a wife during his travels was something that Paul forsook for the sake of the Gospel. What he forsook was not remarrying after the death of his wife and being ac-

---

[105] Cf. *Miscellanies* III, 6 (GCS 52, 220). See also Eusebius who references Clement in *Eccl. Hist.* III, 30, 2, Origen followed the opinion of his teacher in taking "loyal companion" as a reference to Paul's wife. Cf. Origen, *Comm. on Rom* 1, 1 (PG 14, 839bcd).

[106] Cf. Ernest Renan, *Saint Paul* (New York: Carleton, 1869), 148.

[107] Cf. Murphy-O'Connor, *Paul*, 64–65.

companied by a new wife. Had he not been able to remain continent, he would have undoubtedly followed his own advice and remarried[108] for he would have been free to marry.[109] As he awaited the Parousia, Paul was content to remain as he was, so content, in fact, that he offered himself as an example of someone who remained as they were in their situation of eschatological proximity.

The expectation of an imminent Parousia created the conditions in which Paul willing forsook his right to have a believing wife accompany him in his missionary voyages. That same expectation colored not only his personal attitude toward marriage but also the exhortations on human sexuality that he addressed to faithful believers in Corinth.

[108] Cf. 1 Cor 7:9.
[109] Cf. 1 Cor 7:40.

5

The Apostle's Advice

If all indications point toward Paul being a widower at the time of the composition of 1 Corinthians, one bit of advice that he offered to married couples is often overlooked. That is the concession about which he writes in 1 Corinthians 7:5-6a. Had he been married at the time of the letter's composition, the allowed concession would not have permitted him to travel as he did without his wife.

"Do Not Deprive One Another Except for a Set Time"

With the possible exception of the words about bishops being married only once (1 Tim 3:2; Titus 1:6), there is no New Testament passage referenced more often in the patristic literature and precanonical texts with regard to clerical celibacy and clerical continence than 1 Corinthians 7:5,[1] "Do not deprive one another except perhaps by agreement for a set time, to devote yourselves to prayer, and then come together again, so that Satan may not tempt you because of your lack of self-control."

---

[1] According to the scriptural indices found in their respective works, Roger Gryson's *Origines* (*Les Origines du célibat ecclésiastique du premier au septième siècle*, Recherches et syntheses, Section d'histoire 2 [Gembloux: Duculot, 1970]) cites the use of the verse on eighteen pages of his book while Stefan Heid's *Celibacy in the Early Church: The Beginning of Obligatory Continence for Clerics in East and West* (San Francisco: Ignatius Press, 2000) treats the verse on fourteen pages of his historical study.

The Argument a Minore ad Maius

As often as not, Paul's words were introduced into the historical discussion on clerical celibacy and continence in the form of an argument *a minore ad maius*. A good example of the phenomenon is the decretal "*Dominus inter*," which reported on the Roman Synod of 385. The papal decretal has been preserved in a document, "*Canones synodi Romanorum ad Gallos episcopos*," often cited as the tenth letter of Pope Siricius (384–99).[2] The recent critical edition of the text attributes "*Dominus inter*" to Siricius' predecessor in the see of Rome, Damasus, who was assisted in the composition of the document by Jerome, the biblical scholar.[3] In part,[4] the decretal stated:

> For if it said to laymen, "Abstain from one another so as to be free for prayer" (1 Cor 7:5), and those clerics still serve the creature by begetting, then they may have the name of priests, but they cannot have the merit.[5]

Alluding to the scriptural text as it does, the Synod argued in a kind of *a fortiori* fashion. If even laymen were obliged to forgo sexual relations with their wives in order to pray, how much more were clerics similarly constrained! Were they to enjoy fruitful sex with their wives, they may be priests but they are not allowed to engage in priestly functions. "Continence," says Heid, who bases himself on Clement of Alexandria and 1 Corinthians 7:5, "was necessary for prayer."[6]

In his work on 1 Corinthians, Origen, the most influential of Clement's students, expounded the view that sexual abstinence creates a climate conducive to prayer.[7] Preaching on Numbers, he offered a more radical

---

[2] Cf. PL 13, 1181–1194.

[3] Cf.. Yves-Marie Duval, *La décrétale Ad Gallos Episcopos: son texte et son auteur*, VCSup 73 (Leiden: Brill, 2005).

[4] Although it is not the oldest of the Roman decretals, "*Dominus inter*" is the oldest decretal whose text has been preserved in its entirety, thanks to Siricius' letter to Himerius. The decretal, which prohibited clerical cohabitation, is the oldest Roman decree on clerical continence. It was said that Siricius left his wife and children when he was elected bishop of Rome.

[5] Cf. Siricius, *Epist.* 10, 7 (PL 13, 1186; cf. Duval, *Ad Gallos Episcopos*, 95).

[6] See Heid, *Celibacy in the Early Church*, 67; Clement, *Miscellanies* 3.12.79.1; 3.18.107.5 (GCS Clem. Alex. 2, p. 231, lines 16–21; p. 264, lines 5–9).

[7] See Origen, Frg., 34, in Claude Jenkins, "Origen on I Corinthians. III," *JTS* 9 (1908): 501–2.

view on 1 Corinthians 7:5. The apostle tells married people, Origen explains, " 'Do not refuse yourselves to each other, unless through mutual agreement for a given occasion, so as to free yourselves for prayer, and then come together again,' it is therefore certain that perpetual sacrifice is impossible for those who are subject to the obligations of marriage."[8] Elsewhere, alluding to 1 Corinthians 9:5, Origen opines that it is not wise to try to pray in a place where sexual relationships take place.[9]

In the West, the *a fortiori* argument drawn from 1 Corinthians 7:5 was clearly expressed in the decretal *"Etsi tibi"* that Innocent I sent to Victricius, the archbishop of Rouen on February 15, 404:

> If Paul writing to the Corinthians, says: "Abstain from one another so as to be free for prayer" (1 Cor 7:5) and thus instructs the lay people, how much more shall the priests, whose constant duty it is to pray and to offer sacrifice, be obliged to abstain from this sort of intercourse.[10]

Within the space of a single generation, two ancient documents of Roman provenance—the decretals *"Dominus inter"* and *"Etsi tibi"*—cited what Paul wrote to the Corinthians in 1 Corinthians 7:5, "Abstain from one another so as to be free for prayer," as a principal, if not perhaps *the* principal argument for clerical continence and ultimately for clerical celibacy.

Taken out of Context

Divided into our present chapters in the thirteenth century, the Bible was divided into verses in the sixteenth century.[11] The words, "Abstain from one another so as to be free for prayer," are part of a single sentence in Greek, as follows, "Do not deprive one another except perhaps by agreement for a set time to devote yourselves to prayer, and then come

---

[8] Cf. Origen, *Hom. 23.3 in Num.* (GCS Orig 7, p. 215, lines 11–16; SCh 441–42). Cf. Christian Cochini, *Priestly Celibacy*, 155–58; Heid, *Celibacy in the Early Church*, 101–3.

[9] Cf. *De oratione* 31.4 (PG 11, 553).

[10] *Epist* 2.9.12 *ad Victricium* (PL 20, 475c–477a).

[11] The division of the New Testament into its customary verses first appears in a diglot 1550 edition of the New Testament in Latin and Greek by Robert Estienne (1503–59), generally known as "Stephanus."

together again, so that Satan may not tempt you because of your lack of self-control" (1 Cor 7:5). Jerome's Vulgate translation of the passage renders the verse in this fashion: *Nolite fraudare invicem, nisi forte ex consensu ad tempus, ut vacetis orationi et iterum revertimini in idipsum, ne tentat vos satanas propter incontinentiam vestram.*

In comparison with the use made of the text by Origen, much more adept in the interpretation of the Scriptures than were the Roman authorities,[12] the decretals' interpretation of the cited passage was faulty in many respects. First of all, the citation's eleven words in the English translation—only seven words in the original Greek[13] and five words in the Latin Vulgate—have been lifted from the single sentence to which they belong. They are no longer part of the sense unit to which the words taken from Paul's text belong in his letter. They have been removed from the context in which Paul wrote them, with the result that their meaning has been skewed.

Moreover, both decretals state that the exhortation to "abstain from one another so as to be free for prayer" are words addressed to lay people. In a radical sense that is true. The Church of God at Corinth was comprised of God's people (*laos*). Paul, however, does not use this terminology to describe the Corinthian congregation except in the appropriated use of Isaiah 28:8 in 1 Corinthians 14:21: "In the law it is written, 'By people of strange tongues and by the lips of foreigners I will speak to this people [*tō laō toutō*]; yet even then they will not listen to me.'"[14]

The language of the Roman documents implies that within the people of God a distinction is to be made between lay people and clerics. Otherwise, an *a fortiori* argument could not have been developed. Paul does

---

[12] Arguably Rome's introduction to the Eastern understanding of the Scriptures began with the Roman Synod of 382 to which Pope Damasus I (366–84) had invited Jerome, the noted biblical scholar, as a kind of *peritus*. That synod issued the first canon of the books of the Bible in the West. The 385 synod took place after Damasus had died. Siricius was elected pope in December 384. The fact that Siricius was complicit in the expulsion of Jerome from Rome is an indication of the bad blood that existed between the bishop of Rome and the biblical scholar.

[13] In some Greek manuscripts, most of which came from Christianity's second millennium, the phrase contains an additional three words so that the text reads "to devote yourselves to *fasting and* (*nēsteia kai tē*) prayer." See below, p. 151. John Chrysostom was familiar with the longer form of the text but his interpretive comments are based on the shorter form found in N-A[28].

[14] Cf. 1 Cor 10:7 with its citation of Exod 32:6 and 2 Cor 6:16 with a quotation of Lev 26:12.

not entertain any such distinction, neither in 1 Corinthians nor in any other letter of his extant correspondence. The introduction of the distinction into the interpretation of the text implies that any interpretation based on the distinction is necessarily anachronistic from an historical point of view. In 1 Corinthians 7:5, Paul was addressing married Corinthian believers, the majority of the adult members of the Church of God at Corinth, not a group of lay people as distinct from clergy.

Far more serious than the introduction of an anachronistic distinction into the use of Paul's text is the grammatical violence wreaked on Paul's words by taking them out of context. The principal verb in Paul's sentence is "abstain" (*apostereite*).[15] In Paul's text the verb "abstain" is qualified by a negative, "not" (*mē*). Rather than "instructing" people to abstain from sexual intercourse, as *"Etsi tibi"* implies, Paul tells his addressees not to abstain from sexual intercourse. There was, however, an exception. Paul writes: "Do not deprive one another *except [ei mēti an*[16]] . . . *to devote yourselves to prayer."* There is a vast difference between the decretals' reading of Paul, *"Deprive one another* for the sake of prayer" and what Paul actually said, *"Do not deprive one another except* for the sake of prayer."

That sexual abstinence is a departure from the norm is already implied by the verb that the apostle uses to speak about it. "Abstain" (*apostereite*) is a verb with negative connotations.[17] It generally means to rob, despoil, or defraud. It suggests depriving another or withholding from another person what is their due. The Greek word appears in the Greek text of an important piece of Jewish marriage regulation, Exodus 21:10, "If he takes another wife to himself, he shall not diminish [*ouch aposterēsei*[18]] the food, clothing, or marital rights of the first wife." Abstinence within marriage is depriving one's spouse of what is her or his due.[19]

---

[15] The rules of Latin syntax are such that "abstain" is no longer the principal verb. In the Vulgate "do not" (*nolite*) is the principal verb; abstain is an infinitive (*fraudare*).

[16] The Greek particle *an* intensives the exceptive *ei mēti*. The intensifying particle is absent from 𝔓[46] and a few other ancient manuscripts. In Latin, the exceptive particles (cf. BDF 346) are rendered as *nisi forte*, "except perhaps."

[17] Cf. LSJ and BAGD, s.v. "*apostereō*"; MM 650; Mal 3:5; Sir 4:1; 34:21-22; Mark 10:19; 1 Tim 6:5. *EDNT* 1:142 offers "rob, steal" as the principal meanings of the verb.

[18] Pietersma and Wright's *New English Translation of the Septuagint* (New York: Oxford, 2007) renders the expression as "he shall not withhold." In this edition Larry J. Perkins was responsible for the translation of Exodus.

[19] Cf. 1 Cor 7:3.

Paul qualifies the use of the exception as a concession, not a command as the appearance of the unqualified imperative "abstain" in the decretals' citation of the verse implies. The apostle writes, "This I say by way of concession, not of command" (*touto de legō kata syngnōmēn ou kat' epitagēn*[20]), in verse 6. The decretals' and subsequent legislative use of 1 Corinthians 7:5 consistently fail to take note of the concessive and exceptional nature of Paul's words about sexual abstinence for the sake of prayer.

A fourth fault in the decretals' use of the Pauline phrase is their omission of two of the conditions that the apostle imposes on the use of his concession—namely, "by agreement" (*ek symphōnou*) and "for a set time" (*pros kairon*[21]). The pair of decretals that we have cited omits both of these conditions. The condition of the requisite mutual agreement of the spouses is nonetheless sometimes found in later texts.

Some Considerations

In order to understand what Paul meant in 1 Corinthians 7:5, it is necessary to look more closely at Paul's response to the problematic sexual asceticism succinctly described in the slogan, "It is well for a man not to touch a woman" (1 Cor 7:1). Paul begins with a matter-of-fact recognition of the power of human sexuality. He speaks of the power of the sexual drive in the language of his times, writing, "because of cases of sexual immorality" (*dia de tas porneias*).[22] These are the first words that Paul uses in his response to the challenge of radical sexual asceticism. His words are a call to "get real." In dealing with human sexuality it is necessary to recognize the powerful reality of sex. Chrys Caragounis, a Greek New Testament scholar, using Tobit 8:7 as an argument, says that *porneia* can be used metonymically of the *sexual urge* or the *desire for sex*

---

[20] *Hoc autem dico secundum indulgentiam, non secundum imperium* in the Vulgate.

[21] In the Vulgate's Latin, the respective prepositional phrases are *ex consensu* and *ad tempus*.

[22] The Greek *porneia*, often translated as fornication, is a comprehensive term that applies to any form of sexual immorality. *Porneia* is the single vice that appears most often on the New Testament's vice lists. Cf. Raymond F. Collins, *Sexual Ethics and the New Testament: Behavior and Belief* (Companions to the New Testament. New York: Crossroad, 2000), 80–88, 96–98.

and translates 1 Corinthians 7:2 as "on account of the sexual urges, let each man have his own wife."[23]

Throughout his letter, Paul appeals to the community of believers at Corinth to live as God's holy people.[24] Doing so includes an ethical dimension. The members of God's holy people must relate to one another as befits their situation as people called to be holy. Their relationships include their sexual relationships. Paul was astounded that evidence of sexual immorality (*porneia*), of a kind that even nonbelievers, *pagans*, would not tolerate was found within the Church of God at Corinth, a community that was called to be holy. The apostle was shocked that the community tolerated a form of sexual immorality, adultery and incest[25]—a kind of sexual immorality that not even nonbelievers would abide (1 Cor 5:1-8). Citing the Scriptures,[26] Paul urged the congregation to expel the person engaged in that kind of sexually immoral conduct.

In the apostle's view of the Church and in his understanding of anthropology, there was simply no place for sexual immorality within God's holy people. Turning his attention to what we would today call the human person, Paul wrote, "The body [*sōma*[27]] is not meant for fornication [*porneia*] but for the Lord" (1 Cor 6:13). Sexual immorality and the Lord are incompatible with one another. In no uncertain terms, the apostle to the Corinthians told the community at Corinth to flee from sexual immorality (*pheugete tēn porneia*, 1 Cor 6:18), a challenge that he had addressed to the believers at Thessalonica in the very first of his extant letters (1 Thess 4:3). Avoidance of sexual immorality was Paul's rule with regard to human sexuality.

To those who advocated sexual abstinence, Paul responded with a reminder that sexual immorality exists, the kind of sexual immorality

[23] His emphasis. Cf. Chrys C. Caragounis, " 'Fornication' and 'Concession?' " in Bieringer, *Corinthian Correspondence*, 550–51.

[24] Cf. 1 Cor 1:2.

[25] Cf. 1 Cor 5:1c.

[26] Deut 17:7 in 1 Cor 5:13. Cf. John Paul Heil, *The Rhetorical Role of Scripture in 1 Corinthians*, Studies in Biblical Literature (Atlanta: Society of Biblical Literature, 2005), 89–101.

[27] In Paul's anthropology the "body" (*sōma*) encompasses more than the merely physical aspects of the human being. It may be the most comprehensive term in Paul's holistic anthropology, approximating what we might call the human person. Paul, of course, was not familiar with the insights into the human person provided by psychology and the behavioral sciences developed within the past hundred or so years.

that they were to avoid if they were to live as God's holy people. How to do that was then the issue. Avoiding marriage, as the slogan "it is well for a man not to touch a woman" suggests, would not only create the danger of immorality existing within the community but also fly in the face of Roman mores and the Julian law. Paul "wants," as Thurston suggests,[28] "to diminish the risks of sexual immorality within the community and to reduce the chance of criticism from without."

Throughout the letter Paul is concerned with social disruption in the community. Irresponsible avoidance of marriage and sexual abstinence could not but lead to further disruption within the community. Given the importance of heirs in both Greco-Roman society and Jewish tradition, it is remarkable that Paul does not introduce children into his rejoinder to the slogan until, well into his argument, he discusses the children of a mixed-marriage (1 Cor 7:14).

Paul categorically rejects celibacy as a way to avoid sexual immorality. To avoid sexual immorality, says Paul, "each man should have his own wife and each woman her own husband" (1 Cor 7:2). His instruction echoes what he had said to the people of Thessalonica in 1 Thessalonians 4:4.[29] What he has to say is deeply rooted within the Jewish tradition.[30] Not only do the creation stories announce the God-given mandate to procreate (Gen 1:28), they also proclaim that men and women are meant for each other in marriage (2:20-28). Paul's view that marriage helps to avoid sexual immorality echoes ideas expressed in such Jewish literature as Tobit 4:12 and *T. Levi* 9:9-10.[31]

Sex within Marriage

Paul's view on marriage continues to reflect the insights of his Jewish tradition as he continues with, "The husband should give to his wife her conjugal rights, and likewise the wife to her husband" (1 Cor 7:3). Paul continues with an argument in support of this statement—namely, that

---

[28] Bonnie Bowman Thurston, *Women in the New Testament: Questions and Commentary*, Companions to the New Testament (New York: Crossroad, 1998), 42.

[29] Cf. *JANT* at 1 Thess 4:4 and Raymond F. Collins, "The Unity of Paul's Paraenesis in 1 Thess. 4.3-8: 1 Cor. 7.1-7, A Significant Parallel," *NTS* 29 (1983): 420–29.

[30] For a Jewish view on 1 Cor 7:1-7, cf. *JANT*, 297.

[31] This approach to marriage led to a traditional Roman Catholic view that *remedium concupiscentiae* is one of the ends of marriage. Urged excessively, the idea leads to an extremely negative view of the human relationship that is marriage.

"the wife does not have authority over her own body, but the husband does; likewise the husband does not have authority over his own body, but the wife does" (1 Cor 7:4). For Paul, marriage is not platonic. It is a relationship that is expressed in frequent sexual intercourse by the spouses. Paul's views in this regard are consistent with his Jewish understanding of marriage. The *Jewish Annotated New Testament* correctly observes: "Jewish tradition mandates a certain frequency of sexual intercourse according to a man's profession; it also discusses limited periods of voluntary abstinence."[32] In support of this observation, its author, Shira Lander, cites *m. Ketub.* 5:6 and *t. Ned.* 5:6.[33] Reporting on a dispute between the disciples of Hillel and those of Shammai, the Mishnah says:

> If a man vowed to have no intercourse with his wife, the School of Shammai say; [She may consent] for two weeks. And the School of Hillel say: For one week [only]. Disciples [of the Sages] may continue absent for thirty days against the will [of their wives] while they occupy themselves in the study of the Law; and laborers for one week. (*m. Ketub.* 5:6)

Not only does this passage of the Mishnah speak about the length of a time that a couple may refrain from sexual intercourse but it also introduces the idea that the wife must consent to whatever ideas her husband might have about avoiding sexual intercourse for a while. Commenting on this Mishnaic passage and referencing Exodus 21:10, "If he takes another wife to himself, he shall not diminish the food, clothing, or marital rights of the first wife," the Babylonian Talmud says:

> The times for conjugal duty prescribed in the Torah are: for men of independence, every day; for laborers, twice a week; for ass-driver, once a week; for camel-drivers, once in thirty days; for sailors, once in six months. These are the rulings of Rabbi Eliezer. (*b. Ketub.* 61b)

The Bavli reflects the common Jewish tradition, found in Paul as well, that sexual intercourse is a normal part of marriage. Only serious reasons are allowed to interrupt an active conjugal life. Thus, men of leisure are

---

[32] Cf. *JANT* at 1 Cor 7:3.

[33] See also the discussion in Raymond F. Collins, *First Corinthians*, SP 7, 2nd ed. (Collegeville, MN: Liturgical Press, 2006), 256–57.

expected to participate in the conjugal embrace every day and workers every two days. Some occupations require a man's physical absence from his wife but Eliezer ruled that these periods should be limited. The man who took goods from the village to the central market was permitted a week's absence. Required to travel greater distances, camel-drivers were allowed a month's absence and sea-farers a half a year.

The Talmud also commented on the Mishnah's special provision for those engaged in the study of the Law. Asking, "For how long [may they go away] with the permission [of their wives]?" the Bavli responds "For as long as they desire" (*b. Ketub.* 61b). This vague answer was far from practical. So the Talmud immediately asks another question, "What should be the usual periods?" The rabbinic authorities, Rab and Rabbi Johanan, offered different responses to the question:

> Rab said: One month at the college and one month at home; for it is said in the Scriptures, in any matter of the courses which came in and went out month by month throughout all the months of the year. Rabbi Johanan, however, said: One month at the college and two months at home; for it is said in the Scriptures, A month they were in Lebanon and two months at home. (*b. Ketub.* 62a)

Rab based himself on the "month after month" of 1 Chronicles 27:1 while Johanan cited Solomon's allowing workers a home leave of two months after a month's work in Lebanon as a precedent (1 Kgs 8:14).

The rabbinic texts were composed after Paul's letter to the Corinthians. They are, however, indicative of an ongoing concern within Judaism that husbands not be separated from their wives for an undue period of time. That a discussion of the matter is attested as going back to the time of the disciples of Hillel and Shammai suggests that the concern was present among Jews in Paul's day. Hillel and Shammai preceded Paul in the study of the Torah. Luke tells us that Paul was a student in the School of Hillel, specifically, that he studied under Rabbi Gamaliel, the student and grandson of Hillel.[34]

The apostle's instruction, allowing, by way of exception, married couples to forgo sexual intercourse on the conditions of mutual agreement and for a set time, belongs to the aforementioned Jewish tradition, attested from the time of the schools of the great rabbis Hillel and Shammai until the time of the Babylonian Talmud, roughly half a millennium.

---

[34] Cf. Acts 22:3.

Paul's statement that sexual abstinence is acceptable for the sake of prayer (*hina scholasēte tē proseuchē*) also belongs to that tradition.

Jewish tradition also admits the possibility of sexual abstinence for the sake of prayer.[35] A classic expression of this tradition is found in the *Testament of Naftali*: "There is a time for having intercourse with one's wife (*kairos gar synousias gynaikos autou*), and a time to abstain for the purpose of prayer (*kairos enkrateias eis proseuchēn autou*)" (*T. Naf.* 8:8). This text dates to the second century BCE, antedating Paul by some two hundred years or so. Echoing Ecclesiastes 3:5b, "a time to embrace, and a time to refrain from embracing," the *Testament of Naftali* text indicates that there is a time for sexual abstinence (*enkrateia*) for the sake of prayer, a thought that resonates well with the apostle's instruction in 1 Corinthians 7:5.

In sum, the three conditions for sexual abstinence that Paul sets down in 1 Corinthians 7:5 bear witness to his Jewish tradition. Of the three, the temporary nature of sexual abstinence is the one that merits Paul's greatest concern. To indicate that the period of sexual abstinence should be limited, the apostle uses a classic adverbial expression, *pros kairon*,[36] "for a set time." The expression connotes a period of time, not a long period of time but rather a short or limited period of time.[37] The phrase appears in the Latin Vulgate as *ad tempus*, a phrase taken over in the contemporary legal lexicon with the meaning of temporary.

Come Together Again

Paul notes that the period of sexual abstinence has a *terminus ad quem*, a time of closure. Unlike the ancient rabbis, Paul does not specify the length of time during which spouses may forgo sexual union but he clearly says that the couple who refrain from sex for the sake of prayer should come together again. In fact, the mutually agreed and limited period of time during which a couple abstains from sexual intercourse has a clear purpose: "to devote yourselves [*scholasēte*] to prayer and then come together again [*palin epi to auto ēte*]."

[35] Cf. Exod 19:15; Philo, *Moses* 2, 68–69; *Sifre Num.* on Num 12:1 [99]; *Exod. Rab.* 19; 46:3; *'Abot de Rabbi Nathan* 9.39; *Tanh.* 8.8; *b. Pesah.* 87b; *b. Sabb.* 87a. See also 1QSa 1:25-26 which mandates three days of abstinence in preparation for the eschatological holy war.

[36] Cf. Sophocles, *Ajax* 38; *Trachiniae* 59; etc.

[37] Cf. BDF 239 (4). See also Luke 8:13.

The two verbs in the purpose clause, *scholasēte* ("devote") and *ēte* ("be" [together] are in the subjunctive. They are correlative with one another. Unfortunately modern English translations of the Greek text introduce a punctuation mark[38] before Paul's correlating *kai*, "and," leading the unsuspecting reader to think that Paul links "come together" with "separate." In fact, he does not do so. Paul links "devote" and "come together." Coming together so as not to be tempted by Satan is linked with devotion to prayer. Paul says that couples may refrain from sexual intercourse for the sake of prayer and returning to one another.

Is Paul suggesting, as some modern rabbis do, that temporary sexual abstinence for religious reasons enhances the quality of the sexual relationship? Paul does not answer the question, although it would be interesting to know the answer that he might offer. What he does say is that a return to an active sexual life after a short span of temporary continence for the sake of prayer is necessary "so that Satan may not tempt you because of your lack of self-control" (*hina mē peirazē hymas ho satanas dia tēn akrasian hymōn*). Paul consistently portrays Satan as the enemy of God and God's holy people.[39] Those who subject themselves to prolonged sexual abstinence are liable to fall victim to Satan's clutches and thus imperil the holiness of the community. With his reference to Satan, the tempter, Paul returns to the theme of his primary maxim on sexual morality—namely, that members of the believing community are to avoid sexual immorality.

Within this context, Paul can abide sexual continence within marriage but only if three conditions are fulfilled: (1) that the abstinence be mutually agreed on by husband and wife; (2) that it be limited to a relatively short period of time; and (3) that its purpose be prayer.[40] Paul's insistence on the mutual agreement of the spouses is consistent not only with the general Jewish tradition that a wife has a recognized right to have sexual intercourse with her husband and that her consent is required should there be a period of temporal abstinence but also with the mutuality of the marital relationship that Paul repeatedly emphasizes in 1 Corinthians

[38] A semicolon in the KJV; a comma in NJB, REB, NAB, and NRSV; a period in the NIV. The Vulgate's *revertimini* is an imperative form of the deponent verb *revertor*.

[39] Cf. Rom 16:20; 2 Cor 2:11; 11:14; 12:7; 1 Thess 2:18. Cf. 1 Tim 1:20. See further T. J. Wray and Gregory Mobley, *The Birth of Satan: Tracing the Devil's Biblical Roots* (New York: Palgrave Macmillan, 2005), 129–36; Raymond F. Collins, *Second Corinthians*, Paideia (Grand Rapids, MI: Baker Academic, 2013), 58–60.

[40] See Collins, *First Corinthians*, 257.

7:2-3. Of the three conditions, Paul lays the most stress on the limited time period during which sexual abstinence may be tolerated.

Despite what Paul clearly wrote, Heid comments: "Occasional marital continence 'for the sake of prayer' was from the very beginning an undisputed practice in both the East and West, based on the clear instruction of Paul (1 Cor 7:5).[41] This is not to be understood as a few days but rather in terms of weeks and months that accompanied prolonged fasting."[42]

A lengthy period of sexual abstinence accompanied by prolonged fasting may have been the practice of Eastern and Western churches but such a practice ought not to be considered to have been based on 1 Corinthians 7:5. First of all, the reference to fasting (*nēsteia kai tē* is a post-apostolic interpolation into Paul's text.[43] It is found in a "correction" of the ancient Codex Sinaiticus, most of the second-millennium Greek manuscripts and the Renaissance's *Textus Receptus*.[44] Introduced into the text in the interest of asceticism, the reference to prayer and fasting is another instance of the orthodox corruption of Sacred Scripture,[45] in this case, a modification of the scriptural text in the light of the orthopraxis of a later period of time.

Secondly, and significantly, there is no way that Paul's "for a set time," his *pros kairon* and the Vulgate's *ad tempus* can be construed as a reference to a lengthy period of time, one lasting several weeks and even months or a lifetime. Such an interpretation of the text is simply *contra mentem apostoli*.

"Let Even Those Who Have Wives Be as Though They Had None"

What was Paul's mentality? It has already been noted that everything that Paul writes in 1 Corinthians 7 is colored by his apocalyptic worldview and his eschatological expectation of an imminent Parousia. It is necessary to return to that apocalyptic worldview because, as he ad-

---

[41] For this statement, Heid references Cholij in *Clerical Celibacy*, 144–47.

[42] Heid, *Clerical Celibacy*, 322.

[43] Cf. Bruce M. Metzger, *A Textual Commentary on the Greek New Testament*, 2nd ed. (Stuttgart: Deutsche Bibelgesellschaft/United Bible Societies, 1994), 488.

[44] The sixteenth-century *Textus Receptus* was based on a handful of second-millennium manuscripts. Cf. Raymond F. Collins, *Introduction to the New Testament* (New York: Doubleday / London: SCM, 1983), 105–6.

[45] See above, p. 91, n. 106.

dresses himself to those contemplating marriage—and, it would seem, marriage in the relatively near future—Paul writes, "Let even those who have wives be though they had none" (1 Cor 7:29c).[46]

Pope Leo I cited these words when he wrote to Anastasius, the bishop of Thessaloniki, toward the middle of the fifth century. He wrote, "Indeed, if those who do not belong to the order of clerics are free to enjoy conjugal relations and to beget children, we must, in order to manifest [what is] the purity of a perfect continence, not permit carnal relations even to subdeacons: 'so that those who have [a wife] be as if they did not have one' and those who do not have one remain single."[47] A few years later, the first canon of the First Council of Tours (461) cited 1 Corinthians 7:29c in much the same fashion, to wit, "If the faithful are advised to observe chastity, according to the doctrine of the Apostle, 'so that these who have a wife be as if they did not have one,' how much more the priests and deacons, attached to the service of the divine altar, must practice it."[48] The *a fortiori* use of Paul's words in these two passages receives explicit expression in the canonical text's "how much more."

Without reference to the source of the words, "Let even those who have wives be though they had none," and not exploiting them as the premise of an *a fortiori* argument, Aurelius of Carthage cited 1 Corinthians 7:29b in the twenty-fifth canon formulated in the African Synod of 419:

> As we have dealt with certain clerics, especially lectors, as regards continence with their wives, I would add, very dear brothers, what was confirmed in many synods, that the subdeacons who touch the sacred mysteries and also the deacons, priests and bishops, in conformity with the ordinances concerning them, will abstain from their wives "as if they did not have one": if they do not do so, they will be rejected from any ecclesiastical function.[49]

---

[46] Meier notes that there are three passages in the New Testament that deal with the voluntary renunciation of marriage—Matthew 19:12; 1 Corinthians 7:7-8; and 1 Corinthians 7:25-30, adding Revelation 14:4 as a fourth possibility. Cf. Meier, *Marginal Jew*, vol. 1, 344. Revelation 14:4 is not treated in my study since it has not been regularly used in the discussion of clerical celibacy and clerical continence.

[47] *Epist. ad Anastasium Thessalonicensem episcopum*, 4 (PL 54, 672b–73a).

[48] CC 148, 43–144.

[49] Cf. CC 149, 133–34.

What did Paul intend when he wrote "Let even those who have wives be though they had none" to the members of the believing community at Corinth some four centuries before Leo wrote to Athanasius and Tours and four centuries before the leaders of the African churches[50] legislated as they did? Paul clearly states that he wants his addressees to understand the eschatological situation in which they were living:

> I mean, brothers and sisters, the appointed time has grown short; from now on, let even those who have wives be as though they had none, and those who mourn as though they were not mourning, and those who rejoice as though they were not rejoicing, and those who buy as though they had no possessions, and those who deal with the world as though they had no dealings with it. For the present form of this world is passing away. (1 Cor 7:29-31)

A Literary Inclusion

Although there are no linguistic links between verses 29b and 31c, the similarity of thought between Paul's two expressions is sufficient to qualify the passage (1 Cor 7:29-31) as a discreet unity constituted by a literary inclusion and highlighted by a formal introduction.

The encompassing phrases speak of the coordinates of human existence, time and space. Each of these realities is designated by a term that, as it were, humanizes them. Time (*kairos*, v. 29b) is a time for opportunity, a time for decision, a critical time. This time is limited; that the eschaton is impinging changes the character and quality of the shortened time in which the Corinthians are living.[51] This world (*tou kosmou toutou*, v. 31a) is the ordered and inhabited world. Using a classic phrase,[52] Paul writes specifically of this world in its present form,[53] the world as his contemporaries knew and experienced it. The world as the Corinthians knew it was passing away. To cite Thiselton, "the external structures of this

---

[50] Augustine of Hippo was among the 240 African bishops present at the synod.

[51] Cf. Roy E. Ciampa and Brian S. Rosner, *The First Letter to the Corinthians*, The Pillar New Testament Commentary (Grand Rapids, MI: Eerdmans, 2010), 344.

[52] "The form of this world" (*to schēma tou kosmou*); cf. Euripides, *Bacchanals*, 882; Philostratus, *Life of Appolonius* 8.7; etc.

[53] Cf. BAGD, s.v. "*schēma*"; Wolfgang Pöhlmann, *EDNT* 3:138, s.v. "*schēma*."

world are slipping away."[54] The two verb forms "has grown short" (*syn-estalmenos estin*) and "is passing away" (*paragei*) indicate that the process has begun. The end-times have already begun to dawn but they are not yet, hence the time is indeed critical; decisions need to be made and soon.[55] There is no time to waste.

The short pericope has two additional features that merit consideration. The four-word introduction, "I mean, brothers and sisters" (*touto de phēmi, adelphoi*), not only breaks the flow of Paul's thought but does so with a certain amount of formality. Paul often indicates some change of thought by appealing directly, calling on his addressees as "brothers and sisters" (*adelphoi*). The formula of direct address indicates that what Paul has to say has relevance for the entire community, not just for those contemplating marriage, even though what he has to say is embedded within that section of chapter 7, the fifth section as Paul divides the question, that gives his response to the query of the Corinthians' letter insofar as it pertains to the not-yet-married who expect to marry and are expected to marry.

A Declaration and an Explanation

Paul's "I mean" (*phēmi*) does not mean that Paul needs to clarify something that he has just said. Rather it means something like "I affirm" or "I want to make this point." The verb is one that Paul rarely uses. The *touto* "this," which serves as the direct object of the verb in verse 29a, looks forward to what is to come. Thus, Thiselton translates the four-word introduction as "I affirm this point,"[56] somewhat less Victorian

---

[54] Anthony C. Thiselton, *The First Epistle to the Corinthians: A Commentary on the Greek Text*, NIGTC (Grand Rapids, MI: Eerdmans, 2000), 585.

[55] With reference to the earlier studies of Wimbush and Caird, Thiselton makes an important distinction between a theology of eschatological imminence and a chronology of eschatological imminence, a theological stance and a temporal estimate. Cf. Thiselton, *First Corinthians*, 578; G. B. Caird, *The Language and Imagery of the Bible* (London: Duckworth, 1980), 269–71; Vincent L. Wimbush, *Paul, the Worldly Ascetic: Response to the Lord According to 1 Corinthians 7* (Macon, GA: Mercer, 1987), 23–48.

[56] Thiselton, *First Corinthians*, 579. Neither Thiselton nor the NRSV translate the Greek *de*, a weak connective linking the declaration with what Paul has written thus far.

than Robertson and Plummer's "This I do declare."[57] The apostle clearly wants his readers to understand what he is about to say to them. His words almost have the character of a formal declaration, whose significance is not to be overlooked if the readers are really to understand what Paul is writing, what they have just heard read to them.

The Greek phrase *touto de phēmi, adelphoi,* translated as "I mean, brothers and sisters" that Paul uses as an introduction to 1 Corinthians 7:29b-31a appears only one other time in Paul's extant correspondence—namely, in 1 Corinthians 15:50, where the phrase serves a function similar to that of its use in 1 Corinthians 7:29b. The words begin a new pericope and underscore the importance of the principle that is about to be enunciated. Paul writes: "What I am saying, brothers and sisters, is this: flesh and blood cannot inherit the kingdom of God, nor does the perishable inherit the imperishable" (1 Cor 15:50). Exegesis of this passage lies beyond the scope of the present study but it surely is more than a curiosity to note that Paul uses these formal introductory words to introduce an eschatological statement in both instances. Moreover, each of Paul's statements of principle are introduced into a fairly long passage in which Paul responds to a question/objection coming from the Corinthians and that in each instance he divides the question in responding.

A second feature of Paul's construction that warrants further consideration is his use of the postpositive *gar* to introduce the final seven words (in Greek) of the short pericope: "For the present form of this world is passing away" (*paragei gar to schēma tou kosmou toutou,* 1 Corinthians 7:31b). These words constitute the second element in his ring construction. They hearken back to 7:28b, and with it constitute 7:28b-31b as a literary unit. Both statements refer to the coordinates of human existence and are in the indicative. With his use of the positive and explanatory *gar,* Paul states that the actual situation—read, that of the dawning eschaton—in which they live is the reason why his addressees should heed the exhortation(s) in the subjunctive mood that is placed within the encompassing end pieces of the ring construction. It is the eschatological condition of the Corinthians that should motivate them to heed Paul's counsel. Should this situation not be real, then the exhortation is virtually meaningless for it has lost its *raison d' être.*

---

[57] Archibald Robertson and Alfred Plummer, *A Critical and Exegetical Commentary on the First Epistle of St. Paul to the Corinthians,* ICC, 2nd ed. (Edinburgh: T&T Clark, 1914), 154.

The context in which Paul writes, "Let even those who have wives be as though they had none," is so very important if the apostolic exhortation is to be understood. This phrase is the first of five parallel statements:

> v. 29 b: from now on [*to loipon*],
>   let [*hina*]
>   even those who have wives be as though they had none
>   [*kai hoi echontes gynaikas hōs mē echontes ōsin*],
> v. 30 a: and those who mourn as though they were not mourning
>   [*kai hoi klaiontes hōs mē klaiontes*],
> v. 30 b: and those who rejoice as though they were not rejoicing
>   [*kai hoi chairontes hōs mē chairontes*],
> v. 30c: and those who buy as though they had no possessions
>   [*kai hoi agorazontes hōs mē katechontes*],
> v. 31a: and those who deal with the world as though they had no
>   dealings with it
>   [*kai hoi chrōmenoi ton kosmon hōs mē katachrōmenoi*].

The context within which these five exhortations are enclosed indicates that they are counsel for the penultimate times. The penultimate times have already begun with the death and resurrection of Jesus but the eschaton is not yet fulfilled. Hence, I use the language of penultimate times, language that speaks of the already but not yet of Christian existence. The reality that the five bits of advice are counsel for the penultimate times is suggested not only by the framework within which they are located but also by the initial "from now on" (*to loipon*), which introduces and pertains to the entire series.

The initial "let" (*hina*) likewise pertains to the entire series. In this case, "let" followed by a verb in the subjunctive possesses the rhetorical force of an imperative even if it could be argued that the thrust of Paul's remarks is hortatory or permissive rather than mandatory.[58] The subjunctive is reflected in the "be" (*ōsin*[59]) of Paul's first bit of advice. As "from now on" so "let be" (*hina ōsin*) pertains to all five exhortations. The verb, found in the first exhortation, is to be supplied in the other four. Otherwise the parallelism among the five exhortations is readily apparent. In the first three exhortations, the negated participle is identical to the af-

---

[58] Cf. BDF 387 (3).
[59] The third-person-plural present subjunctive of the verb "to be" (*eimi*).

firmative participle. In the fifth exhortation the negated participle is a compound form of the affirmative principle. The fourth exhortation is a relatively minor exception to the otherwise strict pattern of Paul's exhortations. In this fourth exhortation "having" is negated, while "buying" is affirmed.

At first glance Paul's exhortations resonate with advice given by Stoic and Cynic moralists. For the philosophic moralists it was important that a person distance himself or herself from the world in order to gain internal sovereignty, full control over the self, in order to live in freedom and harmony with the universal Logos. Given the material similarity between Paul's exhortations and theirs, the apostle's hortatory remarks are at home within the Hellenistic world and could be understood by his largely Gentile audience. But the apostle has a reason for speaking as he does that is different from that of the contemporous moralists. He made that quite clear to the Corinthians in his opening remarks. For him the matter of principle is that the appointed time has grown short not that people should subject themselves to the *Logos*.

Apocalyptic Judaism often used the language of the inversion of normal human relationships to speak about the age to come.[60] Paul's "as though not" (*hōs mē*) is language found in apocalyptic Judaism.[61] The apostle's eschatological perspective is the real context of his exhortations and he has made clear to the Corinthians that it is from that perspective that he writes. Not only has he expressed that as a matter of principle in v. 29a-b but he has also stated that the dawning eschaton is the reason why the Corinthians should live in accord with his exhortations.[62]

The eschaton is characterized by an "eschatological reversal." The eschatological reversal is part of the Christian legacy. The core of the beatitudes enjoys every claim to originate in the teaching of Jesus himself. The beatitudes in both their Matthean and Lukan versions (Luke 6:20-23; Matt 5:1-12), as well as the Lukan woes (Luke 6:24-26), proclaim that things will be different when the kingdom of God arrives in its fullness. The Magnificat, echoing Hannah's prayer and celebrating the fulfillment of Israel's eschatological hope, proclaims: "He has brought down the powerful from their thrones, and lifted up the lowly; he has filled the

---

[60] Cf. *2 Bar.* 10:13-15; *m. Soṭah* 9:15.

[61] Cf. *4 Ezra* 16:42-45; etc.

[62] Roetzel draws attention to the link between Paul's eschatological expectations and holiness in *Paul*, 37–38.

hungry with good things, and sent the rich away empty" (Luke 1:52-53).

The coming eschaton lays claim upon those who already participate in it by reason of their baptismal participation in Christ's death and resurrection. Hence Paul can exhort the Corinthians to act as he did. That the first of his exhortations pertains to marriage is understandable. Not only is the entire seventh chapter of his letter devoted to marriage but there was also a long-standing Christian tradition about marriage being absent in the age to come. The Lukan Jesus is accordingly described as having said, "Those who belong to this age marry and are given in marriage; but those who are considered worthy of a place in that age and in the resurrection from the dead neither marry nor are given in marriage" (Luke 20:34-35).

In the triple tradition of the Synoptic Gospels, Jesus' logion[63] (Luke 20:34-35) is the conclusion to a controversy between Jesus and a group of Sadducees about a future resurrection.[64] The Sadducees had cited the Jewish practice of levirate marriage[65] as an argument against any future resurrection. Jesus' words are his punch line retort to the then argument of the Sadducees. I have cited Jesus' words in their Lukan version since of the three accounts of the words Luke's version of the saying most resembles the eschatological construct envisioned by Paul in the series of antitheses.

Despite the contextual pertinence of the first antithesis, the five parallel exhortations in 1 Corinthians 7:29b-31a should be taken as a package.[66] They represent ideal modes of behavior but none of the imperatives are to be taken literally. Wimbush suggests that the five-fold relativizing argument points to "accepting involvement in, the structures of the world, with the proviso that concern for 'the things of the Lord' take priority."[67] Wimbush's observation seems to be spot on.

---

[63] Cf. Mark 12:24; Matt 22:30; (Luke 20:34-35).

[64] Cf. Mark 12:18-27; Matt 22:23-33; Luke 20:27-40.

[65] Cf. Deut 25:5. Since it is likely that levirate marriage was not practiced at the time, the Sadducees' argument was clearly hypothetical.

[66] Wimbush suggests that the verses represent an apocalyptic-influenced unit of pre-Pauline material. Cf. Wimbush, *Paul, the Worldly Ascetic*, 47.

[67] Wimbush, *Paul, the Worldly Ascetic*, 96. Observing that Wimbush has concluded rightly, Joseph A. Fitzmyer endorses his interpretation of the exhortations. Cf. Fitzmyer, *First Corinthians*, AYB 32 (New Haven, CT: Yale University Press, 2008), 317.

As far as marriage is concerned, were those who had wives to act as if they were not married, Paul would seem to have concurred with the slogan "It is well for a man not to touch a woman"—the very issue that had warranted such a lengthy and well-reasoned response on his part. Moreover, in verses 3 and 4 of this chapter, the apostle had affirmed married couples' obligations to have sexual intercourse with their spouses. In addition, in both verse 9 and verse 36, Paul affirms the propriety of marriage for unmarried people who would find it difficult to keep their sexual drive under control if they were not to be married. In verses 10-11 and 12-16, Paul urges that married couples remain united rather than separate from one another. The last situation is that of a widow who chooses to remarry after the death of her spouse. The only condition that Paul lays down for her is that she remarry "in the Lord" (*monon en kyriō*, 1 Cor 7:39), not that she enter into a platonic relationship with her spouse. Immediately afterward, the apostle confirms the importance and accuracy of his response with a final, "And I think that I too have the Spirit of God" (*dokō de kagō pneuma theou echein*, 1 Cor 7:40).

Were Paul to suggest in 1 Corinthians 7:29b that husbands and wives treat one another as if their marriage were nonexistent, he would have given the lie to so many things that he had written in this chapter, whose leitmotif is "remain in the condition in which you were called"[68]—not to mention the entire letter. "It is fundamental," says Thiselton, "that Paul is not now advocating a moral asceticism of a kind which he had questioned rather than promoted from 7:2 to 7:28."[69]

Paul's affirmation that the dawning eschaton carries an eschatological challenge to believers in the five areas of their lives mentioned in 7:29b-31a must take into account that the eschaton is not fully upon himself and his readers. The eschatological challenge of the eschaton, hyperbolically expressed in 7:29b-31a, does not mean that Paul's addressees must leave the world (as they would have to do were they not to have an active marriage), never mourn with those who are mourning, never rejoice with those who are rejoicing, never obtain provisions to eat and drink, and treat the world as if it did not exist. Attempting to escape the real world would be at odds with what Paul had written in 1 Corinthians 5:10b, when Paul explicitly rejects leaving this world as a way to deal with the problematic aspects of life, as did those Essenes who withdrew

---

[68] Cf. 1 Cor 7:17, 20, 24.
[69] Thiselton, *First Corinthians*, 578.

from the dwelling of sinful men and women and went to the desert in order to prepare the way of the Lord.[70] Apropos Paul's thought in this regard, there is some similarity between himself and Philo who wrote in regard to created realities, "Whatever should happen, we could never escape or hide ourselves from those, even among things created, that are essential elements of creation . . . a man must needs have all these round him, for no one shall ever be able to escape out of the world [*ou gar exō ge tis tou kosmou pheugein dynēsetai*]" (*Allegorical Interpretation* 3.5).[71]

This reflection can conclude anecdotally. Had Paul intended that his words be taken literally, he would never be able to say, as he did later in this letter, "I rejoice [*chairō*] at the coming of Stephanas and Fortunatus and Achaicus" (1 Cor 16:17). Nor would he have been able to write "Rejoice with those who rejoice, weep with those who weep" (*chairein meta chaironōn laiein meta klaiontōn*, Rom 12:15). And if Christians should act as if they had no possessions, why was Paul so concerned about providing aid for the poor saints in Jerusalem (1 Cor 16:1-4) and why did he apparently dispatch Phoebe to gather the things that he needed for his intended visit to Spain (Rom 16:1-2)?

"Paul's eschatological perspective is such that he recognizes that the Corinthians must face the everyday realities of life. He nonetheless urges them to take some distance from these realities."[72] As Robertson and Plummer said a century ago, the Corinthians must learn "how to sit loose to all earthly ties."[73] Their lives must foreshadow the coming eschaton and anticipate the Parousia of the Lord Jesus Christ.[74] In Fitzmyer's words, "What in Stoic thinking was an aloof reaction to the world of human existence has now been cast in terms of another world dominated by the Christ-event, with a destiny that is different."[75]

[70] Cf. 1QS 8:13–14. The passage cites Isaiah 40:3 as a scriptural warrant for their escape into the desert.

[71] The quotation is from *Philo*, vol. 1, trans. F. H. Colson and G. H. Whitaker, Loeb Classical Library 226 (Cambridge, MA: Harvard University Press, 1929).

[72] Collins, *First Corinthians*, 291.

[73] Robertson and Plummer, *First Corinthians*, 156.

[74] Ciampa and Rosner's paraphrase of the fourth and fifth exhortation well captures their meaning even it loses something of Paul's lexical play. They write: "Those who buy something [ought to live] as if it were not theirs to keep. . . . Those who use the things of the world [ought to live] as if not engrossed in them." Cf. Ciampa and Rosner, *First Corinthians*, 347. *The Common English Bible* renders the fifth exhortation in this fashion: "Those who use the world should be like people who aren't preoccupied with it."

[75] Fitzmyer, *First Corinthians*, 317.

Married people must continue to live like married people, but they must allow the Lordship of Jesus Christ, which will be fully manifest at the Parousia, to dominate the married life that they live.

6

Early Church Legislation

Laying out the argument for clerical celibacy in his short book *The Case for Clerical Celibacy*, Cardinal Alfons Stickler writes, "We know from the Scriptures that the ordination of married men was a normal enough event. Saint Paul, in writing to his disciples Titus and Timothy, prescribed that such candidates could be married only once."[1] He references three passages—namely, 1 Timothy 3:2; 3:12; and Titus 1:6.

Stickler goes on to make reference to the fact that Peter was married, referencing not Jesus' healing of Peter's mother-in-law but Peter's words in Matthew 19:27, "Look, we have left everything and followed you," to which Jesus' responded, as Luke narrates in Luke 18:29-30, "Truly I tell you, there is no one who has left house or wife or brothers or parents or children, for the sake of the kingdom of God, who will not get back very much more in this age, and in the age to come eternal life."[2]

To assist him in making a case for clerical celibacy, Stickler has created a conversation between Peter and Jesus from two different gospel accounts.[3]

---

[1] Stickler, *The Case for Clerical Celibacy*, 12.

[2] Ibid.

[3] Cf. Matt 19:27-30; Mark 10:28-30; Luke 18:28-30. Strikingly Stickler does not make use of the Markan text, the oldest of the three and the one on which Matthew and Luke have based their revisions.

He begins with Matthew's version of Peter's question not only because it was the gospel narrative that had been most commonly used in the Church for centuries but also because it presents Peter as saying that he and the other apostles had left everything—whereas Luke says only that they left their homes. Then Stickler quotes Jesus' response according to Luke. Luke is the only evangelist who describes Jesus as speaking about those who had left their wives. Stickler's version of the conversation is his own literary creation, not one found in the canonical Scriptures.

Later in his study, Stickler introduces a third scriptural text into his case—namely, 1 Corinthians 9:5,[4] which was examined in a previous chapter.

A Norm Established by Paul?

Stickler considers that the texts from 1 Timothy and Titus, the first scriptural texts that he references, are normative. He writes about "the norm which St. Paul gives to Timothy (1 Tim 3:2 and 3:12) and Titus (1:6): candidates, if married, must be *unius uxoris vir*, or married only once (and only to a virgin)."[5] Cochini speaks of "the Pauline principle of *unius uxoris virum*," which he identifies as an "apostolic criterion" whose purpose was "the elimination of candidates with little experience of chastity and not an authorization to have conjugal relations after ordination."[6] Heid, for his part, writes about the *unius uxoris vir*[7] principle being "an unequivocal order from Paul that cannot simply be evaded: clerics should be married only once."[8]

---

[4] Stickler, *Clerical Celibacy*, 94.

[5] Ibid., 92.

[6] Cf. Christian Cochini, *Apostolic Origins of Priestly Celibacy* (San Francisco: Ignatius Press, 1990), 248.

[7] Stickler, Cochini, and Heid take the formula from the Vulgate of Titus 1:6. The Latin phrase is a translation of the Greek *mias gynaikos anēr*. The Latin phrase appears in the early decretals and the writings of some Western Fathers of the Church. In historical studies of clerical celibacy and clerical continence, the phrase is generally cited in its Latin form.

[8] Heid, *Celibacy in the Early Church*, 83.

The Patristic Legacy

Commenting on a 1980 article by Stickler, "High Points in the History of Celibacy,"[9] Cochini observes:

> When St. Paul asks Timothy and Titus to choose as leaders of the Church "husbands of an only wife," he is stipulating conditions guaranteeing that the candidates have the aptitude to practice the perfect continence that will be required of them at ordination. The exegesis of this key passage in the Pauline epistles was authenticated by the popes and the councils from the 4th century on.[10]

Early in the fourth century, Eusebius of Caesarea, wrote, " 'It is fitting [*pros ēkei*],' according to Scripture, 'that a bishop be the husband of an only wife.' But this being understood, it behooves consecrated men and those who are at the service of God's cult, to abstain thereafter from conjugal intercourse with their wives."[11] Some twenty years after the death of Eusebius, Ambrose, bishop of Milan, wrote a pastoral letter to the church of Vercelli in which he stated that, "The Apostle [Paul] . . . orders that [the bishop] be the husband of an only wife, not in order to exclude the one who never took part in the marriage (which is in fact beyond the law), but so that, through conjugal chastity, he keep the grace of his baptism."[12]

As far as the see of Rome is concerned, Innocent I, in letters to Victricius of Rouen and Exupery of Toulouse, dated February 15, 404, and February 20, 405, respectively, cited the principle "the husband of only one wife."[13] Innocent noted that the Apostle did not talk about a man who persisted in his desire to beget. That this was not mentioned allowed Innocent to exclude from his interpretation of Paul's thought the possibility that once-married bishops continue in a sexually active relationship with their wives. Innocent's argument from silence permitted him to suggest that married bishops must cease to have sexual intercourse with their wives.

---

[9] The article in question is "Tratti salienti nella storia del celibato," *Sacra Doctrina* 60 (1970): 585–620.

[10] Cochini, *Priestly Celibacy*, 43.

[11] *Demonstration of the Gospel* 1.9 (GCS 23, 43).

[12] *Epist.* 63, 62–63 (PL 16, 1257a). Reflecting the discipline of his era, Ambrose goes on to say that Paul did not command the bishop to beget children.

[13] Cf. *Epist. ad Victricium episcopum Rothomagensem* 9, 12 (PL 20, 475c–77a); *Epist. ad Exuperium episopum Tolosanum* 1, 2 (PL 20, 496b–98a).

John Chrysostom is arguably the most important of the patristic commentators on Sacred Scripture. Theodore of Mopsuestia was, at one time, one of Chrysostom's fellow students. Later, and as bishop of Mopsuestia, he would become one of the great exegetes of the Antiochene School of biblical interpretation. In contrast with the School of Alexandria, members of the Antiochene School stressed the importance of the literal or historical meaning of the text, albeit not to the detriment of its spiritual and doctrinal meaning.[14]

Among his many writings, Theodore wrote a major commentary on the First Epistle to Timothy,[15] which he attributed to the apostle Paul. In his commentary, Theodore treated the meaning of the phrase *unius uxoris vir* at length. The core of what he wrote, which he describes as a summary on his thought on the matter, is as follows:

> Some have understood "the husband of one wife" as I, too, am inclined to interpret it. Because at that time many legitimately had two wives at once, which they were permitted to do even according to the Mosaic Law.[16] Many had only one lawful wife but did not content themselves with that and joined with other women, whether their slaves or women who manifestly lived in sin. That happens even today among those who are not at all concerned about continence. According to their interpretation, Paul said that man should be selected for the episcopacy who has taken one wife and lived chastely with her, has remained true to her, and with her has kept lust in check. In their opinion a man who has lived thus, and after the loss of his first wife has lawfully married a second time and has lived in the same manner with his second wife as well, according to the guidelines of Paul cannot be refused access to the episcopacy. I take it[17] that this is what Paul said. (*Comm. in 1 Tim.* 3:2)[18]

[14] Cf. John Breck, "Theoria and Orthodox Hermeneutics," *SVTQ* 20 (1976): 195–219; Bradley Nassif, "The 'Spiritual Exegesis' of Scripture: The School of Antioch Revisited," *ATR* 74 (1992): 437–70.

[15] The commentary most likely dates to the second decade of the fifth century.

[16] John Chrysostom and Jerome cite the biblical practice of polygamy as the context of 1 Timothy 3:2. Cf. John Chrysostom, *Hom 10.1 in 1 Tim 3:1-4* (PG 62, 547); Jerome, *Epist.* 69, 5, 1–2 *ad Oceanum* (CSEL 54, 1686, 18–687, 5).

[17] The translation follows Theodore's Greek text. The Latin translation reads "I reject" rather than "I take it" or "I accept." The Latin translation has been influenced by later church practice.

[18] Cf. PG 99, 13–106. Cf. Swete, *Theodori episcopi Monsuesteni*, 2, 103–4.

Theodoret of Cyrrhus, likewise a representative of the Antiochene School, also situates Paul's teaching within the context of polygamy and substantially agrees with Theodore in the interpretation of the meaning of *unius uxoris vir*. The formula was intended to exclude polygamy and extramarital sexual behavior.

That Theodore introduces his commentary on the formula by writing, "some have understood 'the husband of one wife' as I, too, am inclined to interpret it" indicates that the bishop of Mopsuestia was well aware that among his contemporaries early in the fifth century, there existed some diversity of opinion as to the real meaning of *unius uxoris vir*. Indeed there was. In one of his homilies, John Chrysostom, the bishop of Constantinople, said, "Some think that a man ought to be the husband of a wife" (*Tines de hina mias gynaikos anēr ē phasi touto eirēsthai*).[19]

With regard to the idea that the formula requires that a man ought to be married—an opinion that John Chrysostom apparently attributes to others by writing about "some" (*tines*)—Heid writes, "at that time there were also voices, at least among the learned exegetes, who read into the 'husband of one wife' phrase in the pastoral letters an obligation for bishops (clerics) to be married, which of course was not an obligation to marry. That must be considered as a minority opinion."[20]

Three Scriptural Texts

What, then, can be said about the meaning of the phrase *unius uxoris vir*? That is the task to which we must now turn our attention.

The Latin phrase *unius uxoris vir*, a translation of the Greek *mias gynaikos anēr* rendered in the NRSV's English translation as "married only once," appears in this form—that is, with *vir*, "man" or "husband," in the nominative singular—just once in the Vulgate edition of the New Testament—namely, at Titus 1:6:

> [Elders] . . . someone who is blameless, married only once [*unius uxoris vir*], whose children are believers, not accused of debauchery and not rebellious. For a bishop, as God's steward, must be blameless; he must not be arrogant or quick-tempered or addicted to wine or

[19] *Hom 10.1 in 1 Tim 3:1-4* (PG 62, 547). In the fourth-century West, Ambrose and the Ambrosiaster also reject that idea that the phrase requires a man to be married. Cf. Ambrose, *Epist.* 62, to church of Vercelli, 62 (PL 16, 1257a); Ambrosiaster, *Comm. on 1 Tim*, at 3:4-2 (PL 17, 495ab).

[20] Heid, *Celibacy in the Early Church*, 172.

violent or greedy for gain; but he must be hospitable, a lover of goodness, prudent, upright, devout, and self-controlled. (Titus 1:5-8)

A similar phrase, but in the accusative singular, *unius uxoris virum,* a
translation of the Greek *mias gynaikos andra,* appears in a similar context
in the Vulgate at 1 Timothy 3:2:

> Now a bishop must be above reproach, married only once, temper-
> ate, sensible, respectable, hospitable, an apt teacher, not a drunkard,
> not violent but gentle, not quarrelsome, and not a lover of money.
> (1 Tim 3:2-3)

A third formulation of the phrase occurs just ten verses later, where
the author has written, "Let deacons be married only once" (1 Tim 3:12a).
This time the phrase is in the nominative plural, *unius uxoris viri* in Latin,
mias gynaikos andres in Greek.

These three passages are, in fact, the only passages in the New Testament that specifically speak of the marital status of ministers of the
Church. Strikingly the phrase *mias gynaikos anēr,* in its various forms, is
applied to men who are identified in different fashions, "elder" (*presyte-
ros*) in Titus 1:6, "bishop" (*episkopos*) in 1 Timothy 3:2, and "deacons"
(*diakonoi*) in 1 Timothy 3:12.

The three texts are found in just two of the so-called Pastoral Epistles,
1 and 2 Timothy and Titus. Thomas Aquinas described 1 Timothy, the
epistle that contains these last two passages, as "virtually a pastoral rule"
(*quasi regula pastoralis*).[21] Cosmas Magalianus, a Jesuit biblicist of the early
seventeenth century, spoke of the three epistles as "pontifical epistles."[22]
Since the middle of the eighteenth century, 1 Timothy, along with 2 Timothy and the Epistle to Titus, have generally been called the Pastoral
Epistles.[23] The appellation reflects the fact that the epistles are addressed
to Timothy and Titus, two of Paul's closest coworkers. Moreover, 1 Timothy and Titus are concerned with pastoral matters—notably, the organization and regulation of the Church.

---

[21] Cf. *In omnes s. Pauli Apostoli epistolas commentaria* at 1 Timothy 4:1.

[22] Cf. *Opus hierarchici,* Lyons, 1609.

[23] The 1753 and 1755 publications of Paul Anton of the University of Halle, titled
"Exegetical Essays on the Pastoral Epistles of Paul to Timothy and Titus," played an
important role in the adoption of the nomenclature. His essays followed up his university lectures in 1726–27.

Paul's Own Words?

The Fathers of the Church and the early decretalists who cite 1 Timothy 3:2, 12 and Titus 1:6 often cite the phrase *unius uxoris vir* without any reference to its provenance. Those for whom the texts were intended were assumed to know that the words came from Sacred Scripture. When mention is made of their provenance, the words are said to be the words of Paul or, as was common in the patristic era, the words of "the Apostle." The ascription of the phrase to Paul continues in many contemporary writings on the topic of clerical celibacy, such as those of Cochini, Stickler, and Heid.

But does the phrase really come from Paul? Did Paul write the First Epistle to Timothy and the Epistle to Titus? This question must be asked in the light of a discussion that has taken place within biblical scholarship for the past two centuries.[24] Although many evangelical scholars and some few others demur, a scholarly consensus exists today among mainline biblical interpreters that the Pastoral Epistles were not written by Paul, that they are in fact pseudonymous texts.[25] Benjamin Fiore may be cited as representative of the consensus. He writes:

> While echoing Pauline themes and concerns, the PE give their treat-
> ment of them a twist that is characteristic of Pauline communities
> at a later stage of their development. Nonetheless, they carry the
> name of Paul and his associates, known from his letters and the Acts
> of the Apostles, to affirm a relationship and link as well as to draw
> on the authority of the community's founding figure. These observa-
> tions and others detailed below identify the PE as pseudonymous

[24] Cf. Raymond F. Collins, *Letters That Paul Did Not Write: The Epistle to the Hebrews and the Pauline Pseudepigrapha*, GNS 28 (Wilmington, DE: Glazier, 1988), 88–11; *1 and 2 Timothy and Titus*, NTL (Louisville: Westminster/John Knox, 2002), 3–5; Margaret Davies, *The Pastoral Epistles*, New Testament Guides (Sheffield, UK: Sheffield Academic, 1996), 105–10.

[25] Related issues are whether all three texts, 1 Timothy, 2 Timothy, and Titus, were written by the same author and the nature of the relationship between 2 Timothy and Paul. Cf. Jens Herzer, "*Abschied von Konsens? Die Pseudepigraphie der Pastoralbriefe als Herausforderung an die neutestamentliche Wissenschaft*," TLZ 129 (2004): 1267–82. The issue of the origin of 2 Timothy need not detain us in this study since none of the three texts under discussion are found in 2 Timothy. Moreover, the issue of whether 1 Timothy and Titus come from the same hand does not affect the thrust of my study of the texts.

when compared with the letters of undisputed Pauline authorship, referred to as the Pauline *homologoumena*.[26]

In a recent commentary on the Pastoral Epistles, Robert Wall speaks of the "now axiomatic verdict of their deutero-Pauline authorship and post-Pauline social location."[27]

That 1 Timothy and Titus were not written by Paul is, on the surface, of relatively little import for the present study. The texts are canonical and were written by authors who invoked the authority and reputation of the Apostle Paul as they wrote. "The Paul who addresses every reader of these letters is not the historical Paul, but the 'canonical' Paul," writes Wall.[28] The fact that the texts were most probably not written by the Apostle in no way diminishes their authority as Sacred Scripture.

What is important for the purposes of the present study is that, if the pseudonymous texts were not written by Paul, they most likely come from a later era in the history of early Christianity. Their *Sitz-im-Leben* is different from the situation in which the undisputed Pauline letters were written. They come from a different time and reflect a different historical situation in the development of early Christianity,[29] something that would be true even if the Pastorals were written by the Apostle in the waning years of his life.

Most probably, the Pastorals reflect a local situation during the second or perhaps even the third Christian generation.[30] It is almost impossible to date the Pastoral Epistles[31] with any specificity. They were written

---

[26] Benjamin Fiore, *The Pastoral Epistles: First Timothy, Second Timothy, Titus*, SP 12 (Collegeville, MN: Liturgical Press, 2007), 6. The "observations" mentioned by Fiore are considerations that he had previously articulated or would develop later in his commentary.

[27] Robert W. Wall and Richard B. Steele, *1 & 2 Timothy and Titus*, The Two Horizons New Testament Commentary (Grand Rapids, MI: Eerdmans, 2012), 1.

[28] Ibid., 5.

[29] Cf. Fiore, *Pastoral Epistles*, 19.

[30] New Testament scholars tend to use the word generation not in reference to a specific period of time but more in the sense of a dependence of thought. Paul's own writings would represent first generation Christianity, that of his disciples, second-generation Christianity. Works written by the disciples of his disciples are considered third-generation works.

[31] "Epistles" and "letters" are synonymous terms. I generally use "letters" to refer to the undisputed letters of Paul, the Pauline *homologoumena*, and "epistles" to refer to the disputed or pseudepigraphic texts attributed to the apostle.

sometime between the death of Paul in the sixties and the writings of Ignatius in the early second century. Fiore suggests between 80 and 90 CE as the probable time of their composition.[32] There is little reason to quibble with this time frame as providing a working hypothesis for the date of composition of 1 Timothy and Titus, even though the following decade may be the period in which the epistles were composed. At that time in human history, life expectancy is commonly estimated to have been about forty years. The Pastoral Epistles were, in effect, composed a full human generation after the death of Paul. They are, in the words of Jerome Quinn, "a 'characterization' of the great apostle and his teaching for a new generation."[33]

A corollary of the more-than-likely possibility that the Pastoral Epistles were written after Paul's death is the likelihood that the presumed addressees, Titus and Timothy, were also pseudonymous.[34] Moreover, the places in which these disciples of Paul were presumably located— namely, Crete and Ephesus—may have had a representative function.[35] The congregations on Crete may well represent new Jewish Christian communities while Ephesus represents the foundations of the great Pauline mission to the Gentiles in Asia Minor and perhaps elsewhere.

The situation of the Church that the Pastoral Epistles reflect is not that of the missionary situation of Paul and his neophyte communities of believers. The church of the Pastoral Epistles, particularly the churches of 1 Timothy and Titus, is a church that is in the process of getting itself organized for the long haul. Thoughts of an imminent Parousia, so important in the authentic letters of Paul, are no longer on the horizon.

What is expected is the manifestation (*epiphaneia*) of the Lord Jesus Christ but neither 1 Timothy nor Titus contains any suggestion that the glorious manifestation of the Lord will take place in the not too distant

[32] Cf. Fiore, *Pastoral Epistles*, 20.

[33] Cf. Jerome D. Quinn, *The Letter to Titus*, AB 35 (New York: Doubleday, 1990), 19. Beker writes about the "historical distance" between Paul and the Paul of the Pastoral Epistles. Cf. J. Christiaan Beker, *Heirs of Paul: Paul's Legacy in the New Testament and in the Church Today* (Minneapolis: Fortress, 1991), 38.

[34] In which case it might be suitable to speak about the double pseudonymity of the epistles, or, better yet, the double pseudonymity of the epistolary openings of these texts. Cf. Franz Schnider and Werner Stenger, *Studien zum neutestamentlichen Briefformular*, NTTS 11 (Leiden: Brill, 1987), 104–7; Raymond F. Collins, *Letters That Paul Did Not Write*, 92–93; Wall and Steele, *1 & 2 Timothy and Titus*, 10.

[35] Cf. Quinn, *Titus*, 16–17; Quinn and William C. Wacker, *The First and Second Letters to Timothy*, Eerdmans Critical Commentary (Grand Rapids, MI: Eerdmans, 2000), 22.

future.[36] The specter of eschatological urgency that hangs over Paul's words in 1 Corinthians 7 is a nonfactor for the interpretation of 1 Timothy and Titus. Paul's situation in writing to the Corinthians was radically different from the situation in which the Pastoral Epistles were composed.

The *Sitz-im-Leben*

The Pastorals' concern for the organization and good order of the Church is apparent in the first words[37] of the Epistle to Titus: "I left you behind in Crete for this reason, so that you should put in order what remained to be done [*leiponta epidiorthōsē*], and should appoint elders in every town as I directed you" (Titus 1:5).[38] Verses 6-8 of the epistle's first chapter follow immediately. These verses were cited previously in this chapter.

The compound verb *epidiorthoō*, "put in order," which is found in Titus 1:6, occurs just this once in the New Testament.[39] Most of the later uses of the verb are found in Christian literature, perhaps suggesting an influence of the vocabulary of Titus 1:6. Its stem, the verb *diortheuō*, means "put in order." The prepositional prefix *epi-* suggests that the compound verb has the nuance of putting things in order after someone else's activity.[40] That connotation is certainly implied in Titus 1:6. Titus is to

---

[36] Cf. Raymond F. Collins, "From *Parousia* to *Epiphaneia*: The Transformation of a Motif," in *Unity and Diversity in the Gospels and Paul: Essays in Honor of Frank J. Matera*, ed. Kelly Iverson and Christopher W. Skinner, Early Christianity and Its Literature 7 (Atlanta: Society of Biblical Literature, 2012), 273–99.

[37] That is, after the epistolary opening of the text.

[38] Cf. 1 Tim 1:3. Holtz and Redalié note that the situations are comparable. Cf. Gottfried Holtz, *Die Pastoralbriefe*, THKNT 13 (Berlin: Evangelische Verlagsanstalt, 1965), 206–7; Yann Redalié, *Paul après Paul: Le temps, le salut, la morale selon les épîtres à Timothée et à Tite*, Le monde de la Bible (Geneva: Labor et Fides, 1994), 233.

[39] The first aorist subjunctive middle second-person singular form of the verb, *epidiorthōsē*, appears in most of the ancient manuscripts and appears in N-A.[28] The reading *epidiorthōsēs*, in the active voice, appears in some few manuscripts, especially the Codex Alexandrinus. The simple form *diorthōsēs* appears in some ninth-century manuscripts (F, G). A corrector to the sixth-century manuscript D has substituted *epanorthōsēs*, "correct," for the unfamiliar *epidiorthōsēs*. The noun that is cognate with the verb *epidiorthoun* appears in Acts 24:2; 2 Timothy 3:16; and Hebrews 9:10.

[40] Consequently, the verb sometimes has the connotation of making corrections.

organize things after Paul's initial work of evangelization;[41] he is to do so by appointing elders in every town. In the words of Jerome Quinn, "The Pauline paraenetic intervention on the Cretan scene is for the reformation of an existing body of believers, not for the conversion and formation of a new church from the pagans."[42]

Were the Epistle to Titus a real letter[43]—from which the expected epistolary thanksgiving would be remarkably absent—it could be argued that Titus 1:4 expresses the letter's thesis, the epistolary *prothesis*. In which case, organizing the Church would be the principal theme of the letter; what follows would be the exposition of the theme. Should the literary genre of Titus not be that of a real person-to-person letter—a topic to be studied in what follows—Titus 1:5 serves as a preface to the body of the text.

Quinn has argued that the original order of the texts in the minicorpus of the Pastoral Epistles is probably that in which Titus leads off, followed by 1 Timothy and then 2 Timothy.[44] In which case, the elaborate epistolary introduction of Titus (1:1-4) can be taken "as a preface" to the entire collection.[45] It would follow that Titus 1:5 has a broader purpose than simply introducing the purpose of the shortest of the three epistles in the col-

---

[41] Paul may never have visited Crete. Whether he did or not is another detail that lies beyond the scope of the present study.

[42] Quinn, *Titus*, 83. Cf. Redalié, *Paul après Paul*, 233.

[43] That the final greeting of the two epistles, "Grace be with all of you" (*hē charis meta pantōn hymōn*, Titus 3:15b) and "Grace be with you" (*hē charis meth'hymōn*, 1 Tim 6:21b; cf. 2 Tim 4:22b), are in the plural indicates that the epistles were not private letters to the individuals named in the opening greetings.

[44] Witherington, along with Gloer and Stepp, likewise hold that Titus is probably the earliest of the letters. Cf. Ben Witherington III, *Letters and Homilies for Hellenized Christians*, 1: *A Socio-Rhetorical Commentary on Titus, 1–2 Timothy and 1–3 John* (Downers Grove, IL: IVP Academic / Nottingham, UK: Apollos, 2006), 86; W. Hulitt Gloer and Perry L. Stepp, *Reading Paul's Letters to Individuals: A Literary and Theological Commentary on Paul's Letters to Philemon, Titus, and Timothy* (Macon, GA: Smyth and Helwys, 2008), 50–51.

Skeptical about the pseudepigraphic nature of the text, Witherington dates Titus to 64–65 CE, after Paul's release from house arrest in Rome. Were his assessment, and that of Gloer and Stepp, as to the date of the text to be correct, Titus would still reflect a different age and a different situation of the church from that found in the earlier and undisputed letters.

[45] Cf. Quinn, *Titus*, 19–20; Gloer and Stepp, *Reading Paul's Letters*, 50–51.

lection. In some ways, the verse states the purpose not only of Titus but also of 1 Timothy.[46]

Anachronisms

The literature dealing with the related issues of clerical celibacy and clerical continence often refers to the norm established for bishops and deacons in 1 Timothy 3:2 (Titus 1:6) and 1 Timothy 3:12. The nomenclature of the texts, particularly in their modern-language translations, all too easily leads today's reader to think of the bishops and deacons to which the scriptural texts make reference as if they were bishops and deacons of the Church today, such as, for example, those who hold rank of bishop and deacon in the Latin Church of the early twenty-first century. Most translations of the Pastoral Epistles into English translate the Greek *episkopos* as "bishop" and *diakonos* as "deacon." The danger in the use of these translations is that they lead to an anachronistic reading of Scripture.

If there is considerable difference between the situation of the Church of the missionary Paul and that of the Pastorals, there is even more of a distance between the Church of today and the ecclesial situation reflected in the Pastoral Epistles. Both the word *episkopos* and the word *diakonos* were in common use in the Hellenistic Greek of the late first century CE. They had not yet acquired the technical ecclesiastical sense that would be theirs in later Christian centuries.[47]

"Bishop"

An *episkopos* (*epi-skopos*) was literally a "super-visor." Plato the great Greek philosopher, whose writings date back to the early fourth century BCE, used the term in its masculine form to refer to women who served as overseers of young married couples,[48] to people who functioned as

---

[46] This is a conclusion that could be drawn from a reading of the texts in their presumed order of composition. The similarity of contents between Titus and 1 Timothy make it appropriate to see the purpose of 1 Timothy as similar to that of Titus. The situation becomes somewhat more complicated were 1 Timothy to have been composed by someone other than the author of Titus.

[47] Cf. Raymond F. Collins, *1 and 2 Timothy and Titus*, NTL (Louisville: Westminster John Knox, 2002), Excursus 10: Church Order, 326–32.

[48] Cf. Plato, *Laws* 6.784a.

supervisors during athletic events, and to women who fed young children.[49] The term was widely used to designate those who exercised a particular function, not someone who held a specific office. Indeed the terminology was apt only when a person was actually overseeing.

As early as the second century CE Ignatius of Antioch distinguished the *episkopos* from the *presbyteros* ("elder") leading to the later classical doctrine on the threefold hierarchy, bishops, priests, and deacons.[50] In Titus 1:5-9, however, the terms *episkopos* and *presbyteros* were applicable to one and the same person. The terms were virtually interchangeable in New Testament usage,[51] at least with regard to believers in Jesus Christ. There was, nonetheless, an important nuance that distinguished the two terms. The *episkopos* had a function to fulfill, that of oversight. The *presbyteros* was an elder, not necessarily in terms of age, but rather in terms of his wisdom, prudence, and knowledge of a people's tradition.[52] Hence, he was qualified to preach and teach.[53]

"Deacon"

The *diakonos* was a server, someone who assisted others. The noun is related to the verb *diakoneō*, "serve," which was used of a wide variety of actions. The evangelist Mark uses it to describe Simon Peter's mother-in-law serving a meal to Jesus and his companions after she had been cured of her fever (Mark 1:31). As is the case with the word *episkopos*, *diakonos* is a term that describes someone who exercises a function, in this case, someone who is engaged in helping others. The word is neither a title nor descriptive of an office.

Lest the passages in the Pastoral Epistles that mention *episkopoi* and *diakonoi* be misunderstood because they are read anachronistically, I have

---

[49] Ibid., 7.79bd.

[50] Cf. Ignatius, *Magn.* 2; 6:1; *Trall.* 2:1–3; *Phld.* 7:1–3; etc.

[51] Cf. Joseph Barbour Lightfoot, *St. Paul's Epistle to the Philippians* (London: Macmillan, 1869), 95–99; Collins, *Letters That Paul Did Not Write*, 101; George W. Knight III, *Commentary on the Pastoral Epistles*, NIGTC (Grand Rapids, MI: Eerdmans / Carlisle, UK: Paternoster, 1992), 175–77; Jouette M. Bassler, *1 Timothy, 2 Timothy, Titus*, ANTC (Nashville: Abingdon, 1996), 186.

[52] Cf. Philo, *Contemplative Life*, 67.

[53] Cf. 1 Tim 5:17. *Pace* Arichea and Hatton, "elder" (*presbyteros*) is not used in the Pastorals of someone who holds a particular office in the Church. Cf. Daniel C. Arichea and Howard A. Hatton, *A Handbook on Paul's Letters to Timothy and Titus*, UBS Handbook Series (New York: United Bible Societies, 1995), 109, 268.

chosen "overseers" and "servers" in my commentary on the Pastoral Epistles.[54] Wall and Steele render the terms as "administrators" and "servants."[55] There may be other possibilities,[56] but these at least draw attention to the functional nuance of the terms.

Ordination

Another anachronism in the interpretation of the Pastoral Epistles is the language that speaks about the "ordination" of the *episkopoi* and *diakonoi*, as does Stickler in the passage quoted at the beginning of this chapter. Two passages in the Pastorals speak of the imposition of hands (*epithesis tōn cheirōn*) on Timothy.[57] Both passages speak about a gift (*charisma*) in conjunction with the laying on of hands. In 1 Timothy 4:14, it is said that a council of elders (*presbyterion*) imposed hands on Timothy. In 2 Timothy 1:6, it is said that Paul was the one who laid his hands on Timothy. Obviously the two affirmations are not directly contradictory but the discrepancy does give rise to the question of what actually happened.

The gesture of imposing hands on someone can imply a transmission of power and authority but it is premature to speak of the gesture as a ritual or ordination.[58] In 1 Timothy the language of the imposition of hands is used in regard only to Timothy, someone who is never identified either as an *episkopos* nor as a *diakonos* in the Pastoral Epistles,[59] except

[54] Cf. Collins, *1 and 2 Timothy and Titus*, passim.

[55] Cf. Wall and Steele, *1 & 2 Timothy and Titus*, passim.

[56] Luke Timothy Johnson writes about overseers and helpers. Cf. Luke Timothy Johnson, *Letters to Paul's Delegates: 1 Timothy, 2 Timothy, Titus*, The New Testament in Context (Valley Forge, PA: Trinity Press International, 1966), 141–43, 144. "Helpers" and "assistants," for example, also come to mind as appropriate translations of *diakonoi*. Whatever translation of *diakonos* might be chosen should be such that it draws attention to the *diakonoi* serving the community rather than the *episkopos* whom they might assist.

[57] Cf. 1 Tim 4:14; 2 Tim 1:6.

[58] Cf. Raymond F. Collins, "Ordination, Ordain," *NIDB* 4, no. 339–40; see also the extensive discussion in Quinn and Wacker, *First and Second Letters to Timothy*, 392–402, as well as later studies by Hoffius and Schwarz. See Otto Hoffius, "Die Ordination zum Amt der Kirche und die apostolische Sukkession nach dem Zeugnis der Pastoralbriefe," *ZTK* 107 (2010): 261–84; and Roland Schwarz, "Ordination durch Handauflegung in den Pastoralbriefen," *SNTSU* 35 (2010): 145–59.

[59] Cf. Arichea and Hatton, *Paul's Letters to Timothy and Titus*, 106. The silence of the Scriptures did not prevent some Fathers of the Church from writing about the ordi-

when it is said in 1 Timothy 4:6 that he would be a "good servant [*diakonos*][60] of Christ Jesus" if he puts "these instructions" (*tauta*) before the members of the community. Conversely, nowhere does the New Testament affirm that hands have been imposed on those who exercise the functions of *episkopos* and *diakonos*. Apart from Timothy in these two passages, only the believing Samaritans of Acts 8:18 are said to have hands imposed upon them.[61]

In the New Testament the ancient ritual of the imposition of hands is associated with the gift of the Spirit, but it is not an ordination ritual. Indeed, the New Testament does not speak of the "ordination" of any believer in Jesus.

The Household

Titus 1:5 clearly intimates that the epistle is to be of use to "Titus" as he sets about the task of organizing already established communities of urban believers. Capitalizing on the fact of Paul's absence, the author of 1 Timothy writes, "I am writing these instructions to you so that, if I am delayed,[62] you may know how one ought to behave in the household of God [*en oikō theou*], which is the church of the living God [*ekklēsia theou zōntos*]" (1 Tim 3:14-15). In this passage, God's household (*oikos*)[63] is identified as the assembly (*ekklēsia*) of God's people, the Church. The Church is a household.[64]

---

nation of Timothy to the episcopacy. Jerome, for example, writes: "Certainly, when he himself [Timothy] was ordained a bishop [*Episcopus ordinatus est*], he was not much older than my brother is now" when discussing the appropriate age for ordination to the episcopate. Cf. Jerome, *Epist.* 82.8 (PL 22, 740–41).

[60] The NRSV offers "deacon" as an alternative translation to "servant" in a footnote.

[61] Cf. Heb 6:2.

[62] The author's mention of a possible delay is his way of dealing with the fact that Paul is absent. In fact, the apostle is absent because he is deceased.

[63] Herzer argues that the lexeme relates to behavior rather than to structure as such. Cf. Jens Herzer, "Rearranging the 'House of God': A New Perspective on the Pastoral Epistles," in Alberdina Houtman, et al., eds, *Empsychoi Logoi—Religious Innovations in Antiquity: Studies in Honour of Pieter Willem van der Horst*, Ancient Judaism and Early Christianity 73 (Leiden: Brill, 2008), 547–66.

[64] See Collins, *1 and 2 Timothy and Titus*, "Excursus 5: 'The House of God': Theology and Sociology," 102–6; cf. David G. Horrell, "From *adelphoi* to *oikos theou*," *JBL* 120 (2001): 293–311; David C. Verner, *The Household of God: The Social World of the Pastoral Epistles*, SBLDS 71 (Chico, CA: Scholars Press, 1983).

Titus

Titus's task was to organize the Church as the household of God. There was a model close at hand, the familiar example of the Greco-Roman household so well known throughout the Hellenistic world at the end of the first century CE.[65] The presence of the household code in Titus 2:2-10,[66] in which the author respectively addresses older men, older women, young women, younger men, and slaves as to how they are expected to behave, is a reflection of the household structure of the Church. So, too, is the injunction addressed to "Titus" that he should silence rebellious people "since they are upsetting whole families [*holous oikous*] by teaching for sordid gain what it is not right to teach" (Titus 1:11).

An important confirmation of the fact that Titus is to organize the community of the believers is the fact that his primary task is to appoint elders (*presbyteroi*) who would function as overseers (*episkopoi*) in various towns. The author of the epistle specifies that the overseer functions as "God's steward," *theou oikonomos*, literally, God's household manager in these locales.

Why should the members of the household of God adopt mores similar to those of the members of respectable households in the Greco-Roman world? Why should the community of believers adapt the standards of behavior, such as those proposed in the household, that were followed by reputable denizens of the Greco-Roman world? Why should they be like them, those for whom the literary genre of the household code was employed as a means of teaching what was expected of the members of a respectable household?

A motivational clause appended to the responsibilities of believing young women in the household code of Titus 2:2-10 provides a clue to the answer of these questions. Young women are "to love their husbands, to love their children, to be self-controlled, chaste, good managers of the

---

[65] Thus, David Horrell writes, "The author sees proper ordering of the household as an appropriate model both for 'real' households and for the church-as-household." Cf. David G. Horrell, "Disciplining Performance and 'Placing' the Church: Widows, Elders and Slaves in the Household of God (1 Tim 5, 1-6, 2)" in Karl Paul Donfried, ed., *1 Timothy Reconsidered*, Colloquium Oecumenicum Paulinum 18 (Leuven: Peeters, 2008), 109–34, 133. See also David C. Verner, *The Household of God: The Social World of the Pastoral Epistles*, SBLDS 71 (Chico, CA: Scholars Press, 1983).

[66] Collins, *1 and 2 Timothy and Titus*, 336–38.

household, kind, being submissive to their husbands, so that the word of God may not be discredited [*hina mē ho logos tou theou blasphēmētai*]" (Titus 2:4-5). A young woman should act as a good wife should in order that the word of God may be held in high regard. Her duties are similar to those of self-respecting wives in late first-century households; her reason for fulfilling these duties is her concern for the reputation of the word of God.

A remark ostensibly addressed to Titus and inserted into the household code at Titus 2:7-8 provides another clue: "Show yourself in all respects a model of good works, and in your teaching show integrity, gravity, and sound speech that cannot be censured [*akatagnōston*]; then any opponent will be put to shame, having nothing evil to say [*mēden echōn legein peri hemōn phaulon*]." Titus is to model behavior that, when followed, will allow the community to be well-regarded, even by outsiders and opponents.[67]

It is noteworthy that the author uses the ordinary language of ethical discourse to describe the behavior of Titus, just as he did in describing the responsibilities of older men and women, young women and men, and slaves in the course of the passage. With respect to Titus, it is noteworthy that "good works" and the use of hygienic language with regard to his teaching ("sound teaching," *logon hygiē*[68]) are elements belonging to the ethical topoi of the Hellenistic world.[69] As it establishes its place in the Hellenistic world of the late first century CE, the church of the Pastoral Epistles is eager to establish its respectability so that its message gains credibility. The church with its Gospel is seeking to establish its place as a respectable member of Hellenistic society. Lest there be any doubt that this is the author's purpose in writing the Epistle to Titus adds, "Remind them [believers] to be subject to rulers and authorities" (Titus 3:1).

1 Timothy

In regard to all this, 1 Timothy is remarkably similar to Titus. Its concern for order and good behavior in the household of God is evident.

---

[67] Cf. Titus 2:15b.

[68] Cf. Collins, *1 and 2 Timothy and Titus*, 95–96.

[69] Cf. Martha C. Nussbaum, *The Theory of Desire: Theory and Practice in Hellenistic Ethics* (Princeton, NJ: Princeton University Press, 1994), 13–47.

The structure of a household code undergirds the ethical instructions of 1 Timothy 5:1–6:2b.[70] The author writes about good works and the sound words (*hygianousin logois*) of our Lord Jesus Christ (1 Tim 6:3). His teaching on prayer begins with a reminder that rulers and civic authorities are to occupy a special place in the prayers of believers: "First of all, then, I urge that supplications, prayers, intercessions, and thanksgivings be made for everyone, for kings and for all who are in high positions, so that we may lead a quiet and peaceable life in all godliness and dignity" (1 Tim 2:1-12).

As is the case for Titus, so 1 Timothy shows a concern for outsiders' image of the Church.[71] Writing of young widows in 1 Timothy 5:14, the author says, "I would have younger widows marry, bear children, and manage their households, so as to give the adversary no occasion to revile us [*mēdemian aphormēn didonai tō antikeimenō loidorias charin*]." Then writing about slaves, he says, "Let all who are under the yoke of slavery regard their masters as worthy of all honor, so that the name of God and the teaching may not be blasphemed [*hina mē to onoma tou theou kai hē didaskalia blasphēmētai*]" (1 Tim 6:1). These two passages serve as an indication that the author of 1 Timothy is as concerned about the impact of believers' conduct on outsiders as is the author of Titus. Public propriety is one of his major concerns. He does not want the community to be reviled. Neither does he want the name of God—that is, God as revealed to the world, the God confessed in 1 Timothy 2:3-6, and the teaching of the community[72] to be denied.

A Concern for Image

Titus is to model behavior that when emulated by members of the community will bring good repute to the community. Timothy is to do likewise: "Set the believers an example . . . to them, so that all may see your progress [*hina sou hē prokopē phanera ē pasin*]" (1 Tim 4:12, 15). The purpose clause is important. It states that Timothy is to model appropriate behavior to the members of the household of God so that his progress

[70] Cf. Quinn and Wacker, *First and Second Letters to Timothy*, 392–402. These authors describe 1 Timothy 5:1-2 and 6:1-2, respectively, as parts one and two of a "domestic code."

[71] Cf. Yann Redalié, "Come bisogna compartarsi nella casa di Dio (1 Tm 3, 11): L'etica delle lettere pastorali," *Bib* 89 (2008): 435–50.

[72] Cf. Collins, *1 and 2 Timothy and Titus*, "Excursus 4: Faith," 93–99.

might be visible to all. "Progress" (*proskopē*) terminology is Hellenistic, reflecting an important notion of that culture.[73] Quinn and Wacker speak of the "ecumenical emphasis" of "all" (*pasin*). Timothy's progress is a "*typos* for believers; a proclamation of the gospel to *all*."[74] His progress must be visible to all, outsiders as well as insiders.[75]

The idea that outsiders can draw conclusions from the way that the members of God's people act is not a new one in the Judeo-Christian tradition.[76] What is unique to the Pastoral's use of the motif is the idea that the outsiders who regard the members of the household of God can see that these latter follow socially acceptable mores. The letters are permeated with a strong concern for the opinion of contemporary society.[77] In consequence whereof, outsiders should have no reason to demean the living God or take issue with the sound teaching of the Church of the living God.

Literary Genre

First Timothy and Titus were written so that the communities they addressed would be organized on the pattern of a Greco-Roman household and that the members of this household of God would have social respectability in the Greco-Roman world of the late first century.

Ostensibly, they are letters written to individuals, two of the apostle Paul's closest allies in the early Christian mission, but apart from their epistolary openings (1 Tim 1:1-2; Titus 1:1-4) and conclusions (1 Tim 6:21b; Titus 3:15), the two documents are devoid of the epistolary characteristics that normally type a document as a letter. Moreover, the final greetings of both 1 Timothy, "Grace be with you" (*hē charis meth'hymōn*)[78] and Titus, "Grace be with all of you" (*hē charis meta pantōn hymōn*, Titus

---

[73] Cf. Quinn and Wacker, *First and Second Letters to Timothy*, 403–4.

[74] Ibid., 406. Their emphasis.

[75] Cf. Wall and Steele, *1 & 2 Timothy and Titus*, 125.

[76] Cf. Deut 4:6; John 13:35.

[77] Peter Lippert, *Leben als Zeugnis: Die werbender Kraft christlicher Lebensfuhrung nach dem kirchenverstandnis neuetestamentlicher Briefe*, SBM 4 (Stuttgart: Katholisches Biblwerk, 1968); Philip H. Towner, *1–2 Timothy and Titus* (Downers Grove, IL: Intervarsity Press, 1994), 30; Jouette M. Bassler, "Limits and Differentiation: The Calculus of Widows in 1 Timothy 5:3-16," in *A Feminist Companion to the Deutero-Pauline Epistles*, ed. Amy-Jill Levine and Marianne Blickenstaff (Cleveland: Pilgrim Press, 2003), 122–46, 131.

[78] Cf. 2 Tim 4:22b.

3:15b) are in the plural, accentuated in the case of Titus by "all" (*pantōn*). The two texts were intended to be read to a broader public than the opening epistolary formulae would seem to indicate. What then can be said about their literary genre?

In passing, let it be noted that 2 Timothy also concludes with a final greeting in the plural. A quick reading of 2 Timothy reveals that its literary genre is quite different from that of 1 Timothy and Titus. Scholars generally consider that 2 Timothy has something of a testamentary character, making it somewhat resemble the farewell discourses of Second Temple Judaism and early Christianity. It is a posthumous reflection on the life and career of the apostle Paul. Little more needs to be said about this occasionally poignant text since it contains neither the *unius uxoris vir* passages nor mentions of *episkopoi* or *diakonoi*.

Church Order

As far as Titus and 1 Timothy are concerned, the material contained in what would ordinarily be considered as the body of the letter is remarkably similar to later documents on Church order, especially the early second-century *Didache*,[79] the third-century *Didascalia Apostolorum*, the turn-of-the-fourth-century *Apostolic Church Order*, and the fifth-century *Testamentum Domini*. German scholars speak of these documents as examples of a literary genre to which they give the name *Kirchenordungen or Gemeindeordungen*, "church rules" or "congregational rules." Titus and 1 Timothy are probably the oldest exemplars of documents with this literary form. They lie at the origins of what would become, many centuries later, canon law.[80] Just as Paul was a pioneer in developing the apostolic letter,[81] so the anonymous author or authors of Titus and 1 Timothy were pathfinders in developing the literary genre of church law.

---

[79] Some authors date the text to the late first century CE.

[80] Cf. Raymond F. Collins, "The Origins of Church Law," *The Jurist* 61 (2001): 134–56; Nello Casalini, "Corpus pastorale—Corpus constitutionale (La costituzione della chiesa nelle Pastorali)," *SBFLA* 57 (2007): 253–315.

[81] Cf. Helmut Koester, "I Thessalonians—Experiment in Christian Writing," in *Continuity and Discontinuity in Church History: Essays Presented to George Huntston Williams on the Occasion of His 65th Birthday*, ed. F. Forrester Church and Timothy George, Studies in the History of Christian Thought 19 (Leiden: Brill, 1979), 34–44; Raymond F. Collins, *The Birth of the New Testament: The Origin and Development of the First Christian Generation* (New York: Crossroad, 1993), 184–204.

Neither the literary genre of Titus nor that of 1 Timothy—their literary genres are similar to one another—is attested in antiquity. Nonetheless, these texts' way of giving instruction on what needs to be done, as well as the exhortations embedded in the epistles, bears some similarity to that of a Hellenistic papyrus found in Egypt, Tebtunis Papyrus 703.[82]

Mandata Principis

In the papyrus text a senior official gives instructions to a subordinate, an *oikonomos* or manager, on a variety of matters, principally agricultural but also on transportation, finances, and government. A few lines of the papyrus speak about the personal qualities of the manager and his exemplary behavior. The *oikonomos* is to be a model, in the pattern of the senior official, to those over whom he is placed in charge. In antiquity, a listing of virtues was often intended to inspire others to a similar lifestyle.[83] It is interesting to note that the author of Titus specifies the oversight duties of the *episkopos* as those of "God's steward" (*theou oikonomon*[84]).

Luke Timothy Johnson identifies the literary genre of the Tebtunis Papyrus 703 as that of the *mandata principis*, "commandments of a ruler," and finds in this category the literary antecedent of the form of Titus and 1 Timothy.[85] Echoing Johnson, Wall and Steele say that the two epistles are written "in the manner of *mandata principis*."[86] They opine that the regulatory material was to be read publicly whereas the hortatory material was probably kept private. They suggest that the appropriate nomenclature for the genre of the Pastoral Epistles is "apostolic letters of succession."

[82] Cf. Arthur Surridge Hunt and Josiah Gilbart Smyly, *The Tebtunis Papyri* (London: Oxford University Press, 1933), 66–73.

[83] This was also true when a catalogue of virtues appears on a funerary inscription. Cf. Martin Dibelius and Hans M. Conzelmann, *The Pastoral Epistles*, Hermeneia (Philadelphia: Fortress, 1972), 51.

[84] 84 Cf. Titus 1:7. This is the only time that the word *oikonomos* appears in the Pastoral Epistles.

[85] Cf. Luke Timothy Johnson, *The First and Second Letters to Timothy*, AB 35A (New York: Doubleday, 2001), 139–42.

[86] Cf. Wall and Steele, *1 & 2 Timothy and Titus*, 11. See also Bassler, *1 Timothy, 2 Timothy, Titus*, 22; Fiore, *Pastoral Epistles*, 9–10 as well as the extensive reflections of Michel Wolter in *Die Pastoralbriefe als Paulustradition*, FRLANT 146 (Göttingen: Vandenhoeck & Ruprecht, 1988), 156–202.

In passing, it should be noted that only a few verses of the Tebtunis Papyrus are truly parallel with Titus and 1Timothy. Moreover, only a few documents of this type are to be found among the more than fifty thousand papyri that have been unearthed thus far.[87]

Whether Titus and 1 Timothy are to be identified as "mandates of a prince" or not is disputable. What is not disputable is the legislative nature of these texts. It is within this context, the context of the Church's earliest legislation that was developed in order to provide young churches with public respectability, that the Pastorals' "married only once" (*mias gynaikos anēr/unius uxoris vir*) mandate must be examined.

---

[87] See also the nuanced critique of Margaret M. Mitchell, "*PTebt* 703 and the Genre of 1 Timothy: The Curious Career of a Ptolemaic Papyrus in Pauline Scholarship," *NovT* 45 (2002): 344–70.

7

Married Only Once

Applied to leaders of the developing church communities of the first century CE, the phrase "married only once," *mias gynaikos anēr* in the Greek of the New Testament text and *unius uxoris vir* in the Vulgate's Latin translation, appears in just three New Testament passages. These passages are found in the deutero-Pauline Epistle to Titus and the similarly deutero-Pauline First Epistle to Timothy—namely, in Titus 1:6; 1 Timothy 3:2; and 3:12. Stefan Heid considers these passages the key to the practice of clerical continence.[1]

Titus 1:5-9

Any written statement or any oral statement must be interpreted within the context in which it appears. What is arguably the first of the *unius uxoris vir* passages appears within a quasi-legislative text, written to enable the Church to become a well-organized and well-regarded society in the Greco-Roman world of the late first century. The immediate context of the passage in which it is found is Titus 1:5-9. In order to or-

---

[1] With regard to the practice of clerical continence, Heid says, "The key is found in the Pastoral Epistles." See Heid, *Celibacy in the Early Church*, 40. Heid's reflections on the three texts in the Pastorals, pages 40–52 in *Celibacy in the Early Church*, are based on an earlier study, "Grundlagen des Zölibats in der frühen Kirchen," in *Der Zölibats des Priesters*, ed. Klaus M. Beker, Sein und Sendung 9 (St. Otilien: EOS Verlag, 1995), 51–68.

ganize the Church, Titus is to appoint elders in various cities on Crete. The person to be appointed is to be:

> Someone who is blameless, married only once, whose children are believers, not accused of debauchery and not rebellious. For a bishop, as God's steward, must be blameless, he must not be arrogant or quick-tempered or addicted to wine or violent or greedy for gain; but he must be hospitable, a lover of goodness, prudent, upright, devout, and self-controlled. He must have a firm grasp of the word that is trustworthy in accordance with the teaching, so that he may be able both to preach with sound doctrine and to refute those who contradict it. (Titus 1:6-9)

It is noteworthy that the author begins his instructions for the organization of the Church with one that stipulates the appointment of elders (*presbyterous*) in each town (*kata polin*). In the recently established Jewish-Christian community/communities for whose benefit the directive is given, the "elder" would be recognized as a wise man who was knowledgeable about the lore and customs of his people.

Those to be appointed (*katastēsēs*) are to be blameless (*anenklētos*). Barrett notes that all members of the Church be above reproach but that this quality is particularly important for its leaders.[2] The Church's need for public respectability requires that its leaders be seen as blameless. The author of Titus 1:5-9 twice notes that the one to be appointed (an overseer) must be blameless (vv. 6, 7).

As the text unfolds, the author explains that the person under consideration for appointment as an overseer must, first of all, be blameless with regard to his family and household responsibilities. Elders under consideration must have a clean record as heads of their respective families. They are to be "married only once" (*mias gynaikos anēr*)—literally, a "one-woman man." Moreover, their children are to be believers (*tekna echōn pista*)—literally, they are to "have faithful children." Third, these children must "not be accused of debauchery and not rebellious" (*mē en katēgoria asōtias ē anypotakta*)—literally, "not under the accusation of debauchery nor insubordinate."

Thereupon, by way of further explanation,[3] the author turns his attention to the function of the elders to be appointed. He explains that a

---

[2] Cf. C. K. Barrett, *The Pastoral Epistles in the New English Bible* (Oxford: Clarendon Press, 1963), 75.

[3] See the postpositive *gar*, "for," in v. 7.

bishop (*episkopos*), as God's steward (*hōs theou oikonomon*), must possess an entire range of virtues. Reprising the "blameless" (*anenklēton*) of the previous verse, the author says that the overseer, precisely because he is the steward of God, must be blameless. On the negative side, he must not be arrogant or quick-tempered or addicted to wine, or violent or greedy for gain. On the positive side, he must be hospitable, a lover of goodness, prudent, upright, devout, and self-controlled. The accumulation of six vices and six virtues in this fashion echoes the use of catalogues of virtues and vices[4] found in the writings of the moralistic philosophers of the author's day.

The list of qualities to be had and those to be avoided also resembles the duty lists, the *Berufspflichtenlehre* of German exegetes.[5] A topos in ancient literature was the rehearsal of qualities to be had by those in leadership and sensitive positions, such as kings and generals, physicians and midwives.[6] Writing about philosophers, the Stoic Epictetus, whose life partially overlapped with that of Paul, thus making him a contemporary of the Pastorals, says: "You must feel no anger, no rage, no envy, no pity; no wench must look fine to you, no petty reputation, no boy-favorite, no little sweet-cake."[7] Stressing the positive, Onasander, a first-century CE philosopher, writes:

> We must choose a general . . . because he is temperate, self-restrained, vigilant, frugal, hardened to labor, alert, free from avarice, neither too young nor too old, indeed a father of children if possible, a ready speaker, and a man with a good reputation. (*De imperatoris officio* 1)[8]

---

[4] Cf. Raymond F. Collins, "How Not to Behave in the Household of God," *LS* 35 (2011): 7–31.

[5] See, for example, Martin Dibelius and Hans Conzelmann, *The Pastoral Epistles*, Hermeneia (Philadelphia: Fortress Press, 1972), 50–55.

[6] Even a dancer was expected to possess admirable human qualities. Why? Lucian answers: "The praise that he gets from the spectators will be consummate when each of those who behold him recognizes his own traits, or rather sees in the dancer as in a mirror his very self, with his customary feelings and actions" (*The Dance* 81). The citation is from *Lucian. Volume IV*, trans. Austin M. Harmon, Loeb Classical Library 162 (Cambridge, MA: Harvard University Press, 1979).

[7] *Discourses* 3.22.13. Cf. *Epictetus. Discourses Books 3–4. The Enchiridion*, trans. W. A. Oldfather, Loeb Classical Library 218 (Cambridge MA: Harvard University Press, 1928).

[8] Cf. *Aeneas Tacitus, Asclepiodotus, Onasander: With an English Translation by Members of the Illinois Greek Club*, Loeb Classical Library 156 (Cambridge, MA: Harvard University Press, 1977).

Onasander follows up his listing of these sixteen qualities with a brief explanatory commentary on each of them. It is noteworthy that Onasander does not include military ability among the personal qualities that he would require a general to have. Neither does the author of Titus include any function-specific qualities in the list that he provides in 1:6-8. Nonetheless, he appends to his list an additional asset that is related to the office of the *episkopos*: "He must have a firm grasp of the word that is trustworthy in accordance with the teaching, so that he may be able both to preach with sound doctrine and to refute those who contradict it" (Titus 1:9).

Married

Lying within the cultural context of the Pastorals and their lists of responsibilities is the *cura morum* of Roman censors.[9] The primary responsibility of these imperial officials was the census. Their second most important duty was to guide the behavior of the people; they were supervisors of public morality. In this capacity, according to Cicero, they were to forbid people from being unmarried (*caelibes esse prohibento*).[10] It was a matter of public morality that a person not be unmarried. And Cicero wrote some years before the Julian laws on marriage were enacted! Little wonder, then, that the author of Titus requires that an elder to be appointed *episkopos* should be married only once.

John Chrysostom attributes to "some" (*tines*)—that is, to others—the idea that the phrase *mias gynaikos anēr*, "married only once" (NRSV), means that the elder to be appointed *must* be married but once. In fact, that the candidate be married is clearly an obligation. The point could be argued at length. To begin, the author of Titus adduces the requirement as an explanation of the idea that the person to be appointed an overseer should be blameless. Within the society in which the epistle was written, a man who was not married was in public contravention of imperial law and public mores, let alone the Jewish tradition—a factor that must be considered in a document directed to newly established Jewish-Christian communities. In no way would an unmarried adult

---

[9] Cf. Boris A. Pasche, "The *cura morum* of the Roman Censors as Historical Background for the Bishop and Deacon Lists of the Pastoral Epistles," *ZNW* 98 (2007): 105–19.

[10] Cf. Cicero, *De legibus* 3.3.

male be considered "blameless" in the social and cultural conditions of the times in which the Pastoral Epistles were written.

Second, the genre of Titus is that of a legal text. It rehearses duties and obligations. There are no "ifs," "maybes," or "perhaps" in the entire document. The text does not admit of exceptions to the qualities—or qualifies these qualities with conditions—that it spells out for *episkopoi* no more than it admits of exceptions and conditions for older men, older women, young women, young men, and slaves. The duty lists, which resemble Titus's list of qualifications for the elder-overseer, provide these qualifications in straight-out fashion; they do not admit of exceptions.

Third, the immediate context is that of household responsibilities.[11] Titus 1:6 speaks of an elder who is a good husband and a good father. That it speaks of a father's success in rearing his family supposes that he is married. Had he children out of wedlock, his conduct would not have been considered blameless.

The children of the elder to be appointed an overseer are to be believers (*pista*). The adjective *pistos* could mean "loyal" or "faithful," as if the elder's children should be supportive of him[12]; the term *pista* means "faithful" in the sense of "believers" in the context of Titus 1:6. Not only is this the connotation of the adjective in the undisputed Pauline corpus, it is also supported by a similar usage in 1 Timothy 6:2 where it refers to (slaves') masters who are believers and by the reference to the faith (*pistin*) of God's elect in Titus 1:1. As a good Jewish father had the teaching of Torah to his sons as his principal paternal duty, so the believing father should raise his children in the faith of God's elect.[13] John Chrysostom comments: "For he who cannot be the instructor of his own children, how could he be the teacher of others?"[14] That he be a teacher of others is implied in the last verse of the *episkopos*'s profile, where reference is made to his preaching sound doctrine (v. 9). The requirement that the children of an elder be people of faith supposes the existence of a believing family.[15]

---

[11] See also the requirement that the *episkopos* be *philoxenos*, "hospitable" (v. 8), a quality that he should have if he were expected to host the gathering in his own home.

[12] Cf. N. C. Grubbs, "The Truth about Elders and Their Children: Believing or Behaving in Titus 1:6," *Faith & Mission* 22 (2009): 3–13. See Raymond F. Collins, *1 & 2 Timothy and Titus*, NTL (Louisville: Westminister / John Knox, 2002), 321.

[13] Cf. Eph 6:4b.

[14] *Hom. on Titus* 2 (*NPNF* 1 13:524–25).

[15] Cf. Dibelius and Conzelmann, *Pastoral Epistles*, 132.

Within his believing family, the elder's children should also be such that their conduct is neither suspect of debauchery nor insubordinate to their parents and other authorities. In the context of the times in which the Epistle to Titus was written, the words that appear in the last part of Titus 1:6 imply that the elder who might be appointed *episkopos* should have a respectable family. One of our contemporaries might say that his family should not be dysfunctional.

Fourth, the grammar of the sentence must be respected. The principle verb of the clause is the verb *estin*, "is." The elder to be appointed is someone who is married only once. Despite the interpretation laid on his words in later times, the author does not say that the elder may be married, but if married, he may be married only once. Rather he says that the elder must be married. In so doing, he rejected the skewed asceticism that troubled communities of believers at that time[16] and says that the *presbyteros*, in order to be appointed an *episkopos*, should be blameworthy according to the expectations of his society.

That the elder be able to be recognized as a successful *paterfamilias* is particularly important in the light of the function to which he might be appointed, that of "overseer," *episkopos*. In itself, the term is capable of general application[17] but the author specifies that the *episkopos* is to function as "God's steward" (*theou oikonomos*)—that is, God's household manager. The terminology is not used elsewhere in the Pastoral Epistles but the common meaning of *oikonomos* was "household manager."[18] First Timothy 3:16 describes the Church as the household of God. In effect, the elder must be a good household manager in his own family if he is to appointed to oversee the household of God.

That the one to be appointed an overseer is to serve as God's steward may not be without significance in the discussion of the marriage of overseers. At the time, overseers or managers were generally slaves who had responsibility for overseeing and coordinating the work of their fellow slaves in service to their master. With regard to marriage, Columella, a noted first-century CE author, writes, "But be the overseer what he may, he should be given a woman companion to keep him within

[16] Cf. 1 Tim 4:3; 1 Cor 7:1-7.
[17] See above, pp. 113–17. Cf. 1 Tim 4:1-5.
[18] See, for example, Xenophon and Plato.

bounds and yet in certain matters to be a help to him."[19] Almost two centuries earlier, Cato the Elder had written about the duties of a manageress (*vilica*).[20] He noted that if the manager had given the manager a wife to help him, he was to remain faithful to her. He was, in Cato's words, to be "content with her" (*ea esto contentus*).[21]

"Married Only Once"

Within this context what does the phrase *mias gynaikos anēr*, the *unius uxoris vir* of patristic and canonical importance, really mean? Literally, of course, it means a "man of one woman," a one-woman man. Abstracted from its context, the phrase could mean that a man has only one wife, that he not be a (simultaneous) bigamist, a "bigamist" as the term is generally understood today. Members of the Antiochene School of biblical interpretation, as was noted above, took this to be the meaning of the phrase, noting, as Theodore of Mopsuestia did, that having two wives was permitted under Jewish Law.[22]

Another possibility is that the phrase means that a man is to be married once and no more than once—that is, that he should not be a (subsequent) bigamist. This interpretation of the phrase is found in patristic and early canonical writings and is the basis for an ecclesiastical practice that forbids legitimately married priests and deacons from remarrying should their spouses precede them in death. The *Constitutions of the Holy Apostles* cover subsequent bigamy as well as simultaneous bigamy: "It is not lawful for them [a bishop, presbyter, or deacon] . . . to marry a second time, but to be content with that wife which they had when they came to ordination . . . when they are constituted, must be married but once, whether their wives are alive or whether they are dead."[23]

A third possibility is that the phrase means that the elder who is to become an *episkopos* is someone whose marital fidelity is exemplary. This

---

[19] Columella, *Rust.* 1.8.5; cf. Varro, *Agricultural Topics in Three Books* 1.17.5. See John K. Goodrich, "Overseers as Stewards and the Qualifications for Leadership in the Pastoral Epistles," *ZNW* 104 (2013): 77–97, 93–94. See also Xenophon's *Oiconomicos* and Michel Foucault's discussion of this work in *The History of Pleasure: The History of Sexuality*, 2 (New York: Vintage, 1990), 152–65.

[20] Cato, *Agriculture*, 142–43.

[21] Ibid., 143.

[22] See above, p. 165.

[23] *Constitutions* 6:17 (*ANF* 7:457).

interpretation is also found in patristic literature. To cite but one example, Theodore of Mopsuestia writes, "He who marries one wife, lives with her prudently, keeps to her, and directs to her the desire of nature."[24]

Bigamy

Was the *mias gynaikos anēr/unius uxoris vir* phrase written within a social context in which simultaneous bigamy or even polygamy was a real issue? If not, what does the prescription mean?

The Fathers of the Church speak of the biblical tradition allowing a man to have more than one wife. To be sure, in patriarchal times Abraham had Sarah and Hagar as wives[25] and Jacob had the sisters Leah and Rachel as his wives.[26] In later times, Moses married Zephorah as well as an unnamed African woman.[27] In the time of the Judges, Elkanah had two wives, Hannah and Peninnah.[28] These instances of simultaneous bigamy were considered to be warranted by a legitimate desire for offspring to carrying on the family name.

During the period of the monarchy, despite the Deuteronomic prescription that a king should not multiply wives (Deut 17:17), Solomon was reported to have had seven-hundred princesses as wives along with three hundred concubines.[29] To be sure, some of the marriages took place in order to cement political alliances, but Solomon's behavior in accumulating so many sexual partners was censured.[30]

In the first century, bigamy was theoretically acceptable[31]—particularly if a wife had not produced offspring—but Qumran's *Damascus Document* cited Scripture in an attempt to counter the practice. The document argues in favor of monogamy, apparently against the Pharisees, who "are caught twice in fornication: by taking two wives in their lives even

[24] Cf. Henry Barclay Swete, *Theodori episcopi Mopsuesteni: In epistolas B. Pauli commentarii*, vol. 2 (Westmead, England: Gregg International, 1969), 103.

[25] Cf. Gen 16:1-3; 25:1-2.

[26] Cf. Gen 29:15-30.

[27] Cf. Exod 2:21; Num 12:1. This second marriage displeased Moses' siblings, Miriam and Aaron.

[28] Cf. 1 Sam 1:2.

[29] Cf. 1 Kgs 11:3.

[30] Cf. 1 Kgs 11:2, 4.

[31] Josephus notes that some priests, appealing to the example of the patriarchs and citing biblical passages that allowed polygamy (cf. Exod 21:8-11; Deut 21:15; 25:5-10), had more than one wife. Cf. Josephus, *Ant.* 17.1, 2, 14.

though the principle of creation is 'male and female he created them' and the ones who went into the ark 'went in two by two in the ark.'"[32] The text continues, "And about the prince it is written, 'He should not multiply wives to himself.'"[33]

In the Common Era, the Mishnah allowed a man to have five wives,[34] while kings were permitted to have eighteen.[35] The practice, however, seems not to have been common apart from those with great wealth.[36] Monogamy was the common practice of Jewish households.[37] By the tenth century CE, Jewish tradition prohibited a man from having two wives,[38] a prohibition that was already in effect in imperial law since the time of Theodosius in 393.[39]

In the Pastorals' Greco-Roman world, both traditional Greek practice and Roman law effectively prohibited simultaneous bigamy (being married to two wives at the same time). Euripides, for example, said, "We count it as a shame that over two wives one man hold wedlock's reins."[40] For the Greeks, legitimate and physical cohabitation were characteristic of monogamous marriage.[41] Under Roman law, a second marriage would annul a prior marriage, thus making bigamy legally impossible. Among

---

[32] CD 4:20–21, citing Gen 1:27 and Gen 7:9. Cf. 6QD, frg. 1. See Koltun-Fromm, *Hermeneutics of Holiness*, 61.

[33] CD 5:2, citing Deut 17:17. The text continues by excusing David from having violated this precept. "David had not read the sealed book of the law which was in the ark, for it had not been opened in Israel since the day of the death of Eleazar and of Jehoshua, and Joshua and the elders who worshipped Ashtaroth" (CD 5:2-4).

[34] Cf. *m. Yebam.* 11:3.

[35] Cf. *m. Sanh.* 2:4; *b. Sanh.* 21a. Cf. Joseph Blenkinsopp, "The Family in First Temple Israel" in Leo G. Perdue, et al, *Families in Ancient Israel: The Family, Religion, and Culture* (Louisville: Westminster John Knox, 1997), 48–103, esp. 64.

[36] Cf. Leo G. Perdue, "The Israelite and Early Jewish Family: Summary and Conclusions," in Perdue, *Families in Ancient Israel* (Louisville: Westminister John Knox, 1997), 163–222, 185.

[37] Cf. Launderville, *Celibacy in the Ancient World*, 171. Satlow, *Jewish Marriage*, 190; Catherine Hezser, "Part Whore, Part Wife: Slave Women in the Palestinian Rabbinic Tradition," in *Doing Gender—Doing Religion: Fallstudien zur Intersektionalität im frühen Judentum Christentum und Islam*, ed. Ute E. Eisen, Christine Gerber, and Angela Standhartinger, WUNT 302 (Tübingen: Mohr Siebeck, 2013), 303–23, 313, 320.

[38] Cf. Menachem Elon, "Bigamy and Polygamy," *EncJud*² 3, 691–94, esp. 691.

[39] Cf. *Code of Justinian* 1.9.7. The prescription was reiterated in *Novel* 9 in 537. See also John J. Collins, "Marriage, Divorce, and Family in Second Temple Judaism," in Perdue, *Families in Ancient Israel*, 104–61, 122.

[40] *Andromache* 215.

[41] This did not preclude married men's use of prostitutes and *hetaerai*.

ancient societies the monogamy of Greco-Roman society was almost without parallel.[42]

In effect, bigamy and polygamy were virtually nonexistent during the time 1 Timothy and Titus were written within both the dominant Greco-Roman society and among the Jewish population. The reality of marriage at the time would have made it impossible for the author of Titus to have written about an elder who was *mias gynaikos anēr/unius uxoris vir* in order to prohibit a potential overseer from engaging in a nonexistent practice.

A Ban on Remarriage?

The second possibility is that the *mias gynaikos anēr/unius uxoris vir* prescription was designed to prohibit from the role of overseer a man who had been twice married—that is, a man who had taken a second wife after the death or divorce of his spouse. It should be noted that since Titus was intended for a recently founded Christian community (or *communities*), it is not impossible that some neophyte believers had divorced prior to their acceptance of the faith.

The Fathers of the Church often—but not always[43]—interpreted the phrase as if it precluded a person who had married a second wife after the first had died or had been divorced.[44] John Chrysostom, for example, supposing that refraining from a second marriage after the death of one's spouse is a way to honor the deceased, writes, "How could a man who doesn't honor the memory of his wife lead a church?"[45]

Does the phrase in Titus 1:6 really preclude a subsequent second marriage? That is theoretically possible but it would seemingly fly in the face of the teaching of Paul, the revered patronym of the epistle. In his long disquisition on sexual relationships (1 Cor 7), Paul spoke about the situation of widows and widowers, allowing the possibility of their remarrying after the death of their spouses, to wit, "To the unmarried and the

---

[42] Cf. Walter Scheidel, "Monogamy and Polygyny" (Princeton: Stanford Working Papers in Classics, 1999), 1.

[43] The Ambrosiaster, for example, admits the possibility of the second marriage. Cf. *Comm. on 1 Tim*, at 3:2–4 (PL 17, 95ab).

[44] Theodoret of Cyrrhus, for example, alludes to the possibility of a man having dismissed his wife. Cf. *Comm. in 1 Tim*, at 1 Tim 3:2 (PG 82, 804d–805d).

[45] *Hom on 1 Tim II. 1* (PG 62, 553d).

widows I say that it is well for them to remain unmarried as I am. But if they are not practicing self-control [*ouk enkrateuontai*], they should marry. For it is better to marry than to be aflame with passion" (1 Cor 7:8-9).

Restricting his focus to that of a widow, Paul concludes the chapter by writing, "A wife is bound as long as her husband lives. But if the husband dies, she is free [*eleuthera*] to marry anyone she wishes, only in the Lord. But in my judgment she is more blessed if she remains as she is. And I think that I too have the Spirit of God" (1 Cor 7:39-40). This codicil to Paul's reflections on sexual relationships had been written in the context of the expectation of an imminent Parousia and the social context of Roman law, which required younger widows to remarry within a short period after the death of their spouse. For Paul, the issue of her freedom (*eleutheria*) takes precedence over the restraint (*enkrateia*) that he would have preferred while believers were expecting the imminent Parousia.

Titus does not specifically address the issue of another marriage after the death of one's spouse, but 1 Timothy does address the issue, at least with regard to the case of a younger widow. In that instance, the author not only tolerates the second marriage but he almost requires it: "So I would have [*boulomai*] younger widows marry" (1 Tim 5:14a). The reason for this strong counsel is social respectability: "so as to give the adversary no occasion to revile us" (1 Tim 5:14b). Part of the context of this strong exhortation was that a widow between the ages of twenty and fifty was bound to remarry within two years after the death of her spouse according to imperial law.[46]

The author's mentor, the apostle Paul, had allowed for a second marriage even in the situation of the expectation of an imminent Parousia. Moreover, both Paul and the author(s) of the Pastoral Epistles argued against an undue asceticism in sexual matters. In addition, 1 Timothy specifically urges the remarriage of a younger widow for the sake of social respectability in accordance with the law of the realm. Hence, it is hardly likely, in the absence of any further evidence, that the author of Titus 1:8 intended *mias gynaikos anēr/unius uxoris vir* to mean that the elder under consideration as one to exercise the function of overseer should be a person who has not remarried after the death—or possibly divorce—of his spouse.

---

[46] See above, pp. 66–67.

Marital Fidelity

What then about the third possibility—namely, that the *mias gynaikos anēr / unius uxoris vir* prescription requires that the elder to be named as overseer should be a one-woman man in the sense that he must be faithful to his wife?[47]

Socially and culturally, this could be likely. Although Greco-Roman mores strongly endorsed monogamy and Roman law forbade adultery, Greco-Roman society tolerated a married man's dalliances with slaves and prostitutes.[48] Moreover, concubinage was hardly unknown in that society. This sort of sexual congress was not viewed as adultery. Under Roman law, adultery was a matter of a man having sexual intercourse with a married woman, another man's wife, much as it was in the traditional Jewish understanding of adultery. Adultery was an offense against the aggrieved husband[49] who enjoyed exclusive rights to his wife's sexual activity, not so much as a matter of fidelity to her or respect for her, but as a way to ensure the legitimacy of any children born to her. The one thing that was required at the time was that a man's paramours be kept out of the home and away from the man's wife.

Classic is the advice that Plutarch, the Greek philosopher and biographer, gave to married women, telling them to tolerate their husbands' dalliances with slave women because in that way they would be spared direct involvement in their husbands' debauchery.[50] On the other hand, some philosophic moralists condemned such philandering. Thus the Stoic Musonius Rufus criticized a "man who has relations with his own slave girl, a thing that some people consider quite without blame."[51]

In terms of the Christian and literary matrix within which the author of Titus sets out the *mias gynaikos anēr / unius uxoris vir* qualification, it is likely that he had marital fidelity to a single wife in mind. He concludes the short lists of vices and virtues that he stipulates as further

---

[47] Audet compares the phrase to such idiomatic phrases as "the man of one book" or "someone with one idea." He suggests that the connotation of the phrase is that of man's undivided attachment to his wife. Cf. Jean Paul Audet, *Mariage et célibat dans le service de l'Église: Histoire et orientations* (Paris: Éditions de l'Orante, 1967), 95.

[48] Cf. Walter Scheidel, "Monogamy and Polygyny" (Princeton: Stanford Working Papers in Classics), 1999, 3–4, 7; Pomeroy, *Xenophon* Oeconomicus, 35, 297–98. Pomeroy references Xenophon *Oeconomicus* 9.5; 10.12–13; and Pseudo-Demosthenes 59.122..

[49] The "against her" (*ep'autēn*) of Mark 10:11 was truly countercultural.

[50] Cf. Plutarch, "Advice to the Bride and Groom" 16 (*Moralia* 140b).

[51] "On Sexual Relations," frg. 12.

requirements for the overseer by saying that the overseer must be (*dei*, v. 7) self-controlled (*enkrate*, v. 8). This is the only instance of words derived from the *enkrat*-root in the Pastoral Epistles.[52] The adjective suggests control of one's physical appetites, especially one's sexual urges. Lists of virtues and lists of vices were a literary genre mediated to the author(s) of the Pastoral Epistles through the Stoic tradition,[53] which valued such self-control.

Self-control "signifies the free, autonomous and independent person, who does not allow himself to be tempted or diverted by any allurements."[54] As such it is a quality that befits a leader.[55] Philo of Alexandria, for instance, considers self-control to be one of the three characteristics of statesmanship along with the art of shepherding (*poimēnikon*) and household management (*oikonomikon*).[56] Commenting on Palestinian rabbinic attitudes and Xenophon's *Oiconomicos*, Eliezer Diamond writes: "To rule—over one's worker's, one's wife or one's fellow citizens—one must first have demonstrated, through the control of one's passions and impulses, the ability to rule oneself."[57]

Strikingly, the author of Titus says that the overseer must be blameless since he functions as "God's steward" (*theou oikonomos*, v. 7), the manager of God's household. That the overseer is to be self-controlled would seem to confirm that connotation of *mias gynaikos anēr / unius uxoris vir* that the elder to be appointed as overseer be faithful to his wife.[58] Thus, the NEB translates the phrase as "faithful to one wife," capturing well the meaning of the expression *mias gynaikos anēr / unius uxoris vir*.

The words *mias gynaikos anēr / unius uxoris vir* are an expression of a man's morality as much as they are a statement of his social condition

---

[52] Words belonging to the *enkrat-* word group are rarely used in the New Testament. The noun *enkrateia* appears just three times in the New Testament (Acts 24:25; Gal 5:23; 2 Pet 1:6); the verb *enkrateōomai* twice (1 Cor 7:9; 9:25) and the adjective *enkratēs* just once, here in Titus 1:8.

[53] Cf. Raymond F. Collins, *Sexual Ethics and the New Testament: Behavior and Belief*, Companions to the New Testament (New York: Crossroad, 2000), 74, 77–79.

[54] *EDNT* 1, 37.

[55] Polycarp (*Phil.* 5:2) lists self-control as one of the qualities that a *diakonos* should have.

[56] Cf. Philo, *Joseph* 54.

[57] Diamond, " 'And Jacob Remained Alone,' " 54.

[58] Cf. Peter Trummer, "Einehe nach den Pastoralbriefen: Zum Verständnis der Termini *mias gynaikos anēr und henos andros gynē*," *Bib* 51 (1970): 471–84; Sydney Page, "Marital Expectations of Church Leaders in the Pastoral Epistles," *JSNT* 50 (1993): 105–20.

as a married man. The point at issue is not how often a person has been married but how he lives his married life. As Luke Timothy Johnson says, "The value Paul seeks is that of fidelity and respectability."[59]

Pauline Tradition

Understood in this sense, the requirement that the would-be overseer be *mias gynaikos anēr / unius uxoris vir* is consistent with the Pauline tradition. On several occasions, Paul reiterated the traditional Jewish and Roman prohibition of adultery. On my reading of the apostle's exhortation on sanctity in 1 Thessalonians, the oldest of his extant letters, Paul urges the Thessalonian Christians to avoid adultery. He writes, "For this is the will of God . . . that you abstain from fornication; that each of you know how to control your own body in holiness and honor, not with lustful passion, like the Gentiles who do not know God; that no one wrong or exploit a brother or sister in this matter" (1 Thess 4:3-6a).[60] The phrase that no one wrong a brother (*ton adelphon autou*[61]) in this matter is a statement that not violating another Christian's marriage by committing adultery is God's will and a condition of sanctification.

In his First Letter to the Corinthians, he cites "adulterers" (*moichoi*) among ten types of persons excluded from the Kingdom of God.[62] In his Letter to the Romans, in an argument with an imaginary Jewish interlocutor, Paul poses this rhetorical question: "You that forbid adultery, do you commit adultery?"[63] thereby upholding the validity of the sixth

---

[59] Cf. Luke Timothy Johnson, *Letters to Paul's Delegates: 1 Timothy, 2 Timothy, Titus,* The New Testament in Context (Valley Forge, PA: Trinity Press International, 1966), 143.

[60] I hold that "each of you know how to control your own body" is not a statement on ascetic sexual self-control but an expression of God's desire that men marry. Cf. Raymond F. Collins, "This Is the Will of God: Your Sanctification (1 Thess 4:3)," *LTP* 39 (1983): 27–53; "The Unity of Paul's Paraenesis in 1 Thess. 4.3-8: 1 Cor. 7.1-7, A Significant Parallel," *NTS* 29 (1983): 420–29, reprinted in Collins, *Studies on the First Letter to the Thessalonians,* BETL 66 (Leuven: University Press-Peeters, 1984), 299–335; James W. Thompson, *Moral Formation According to Paul: The Context and Coherence of Pauline Ethics* (Grand Rapids, MI: Baker Academic, 2011), 72–79.

[61] Since the phrase concerns adultery within a context in which adultery is viewed as an offense against a cuckolded husband, *adelphon* must be taken as the gender-specific "brother" rather than as the gender-inclusive "brother and sister."

[62] Cf. 1 Cor 6:9.

[63] Rom 2:22.

commandment.[64] Later in the letter, he explicitly cites the sixth commandment, "You shall not commit adultery" (*ou moicheuseis*), listing it first among the four commandments that he cites.[65]

Paul often writes about "fornication" (*porneia*,[66] a general term that connotes sexual misconduct rather than "fornication" in the narrower sense, in which the term is generally taken today). In 1 Corinthians 6:18 and 1 Thessalonians 4:3, he urges his addressees to flee from fornication (*porneia*). In 1 Corinthians 7:2-5, he urges marriage, in which husbands and wives have an active sexual life and similar responsibilities and rights with regard to their sexuality, as a way to combat sexual immorality (*porneia*). There is little doubt that Paul excludes sexual liaisons other than that of a man's sexual union with his wife.

Marital Continence?

Despite Heid's assumption "that the pastoral letters really expected continence of all ministers, whether married or not,"[67] the phrase *mias gynaikos anēr / unius uxoris vir* speaks of marriage, not marital continence. Excluding sexual intercourse from the marriages of ministers of the Church is based on eisegesis of the biblical texts. It is reading something into the texts that the texts themselves do not imply. In no way can the formula be construed as if it banned a man's sexual union with his wife after he became an overseer. The phrase speaks about marriage with a sexual component.[68]

Moreover, abstinence from sexual union with one's wife was unheard of in Judaism, except, perhaps, for those married men who might have joined the community at Qumran.[69] As for Paul, as we have seen, he urges couples who want to avoid extramarital affairs not to deprive one

[64] That is the sixth commandment according to the common Roman Catholic enumeration of the Ten Commandments. Other traditions divide the commandments a bit differently, citing the prohibition of adultery as the seventh commandment.

[65] Cf. Rom 13:9, citing Exod 20:14; Deut 5:18.

[66] Cf. 1 Cor 5:1; 6:13, 18; 7:2; 2 Cor 12:21; Gal 5:19; 1 Thess 4:3. See also 1 Cor 5:9, 10, 11; 6:9, 18; 10:8.

[67] Heid, *Celibacy in the Early Church*, 61.

[68] Siricius' statement that the author does not add "who continues in the desire to have children" (*Epist.* 5.3 [PL 13:160a–1161a]) is clearly gratuitous.

[69] See above, p. 58.

another of their sexual rights "so that Satan might not tempt you because of your lack of self-control [*dia tēn arkasian hymōn*]" (1 Cor 7:5).

In sum, the requirement that an elder to be appointed an overseer must be *mias gynaikos anēr / unius uxoris vir* whose children are believers, not accused of debauchery and not rebellious is a requirement that this elder be married and be faithful to his wife. In marriage, he must have children and be a good family man—and presumably be seen as such by those outside the community. He must have these qualities in order to function as God's steward, as the household manager in the household of God.

1 Timothy 3:1-7

The husband of one wife phrase, *mias gynaikos anēr*, appears again in 1 Timothy 3:2, in a similar context but in the accusative form, *mias gynaikos andra*:

> The saying is sure: whoever aspires to the office of bishop [*episkopēs*] desires a noble task. Now a bishop must be above reproach [*dei oun ton episkopon anepilēmpton einai*], married only once [*mias gynaikos andra*], temperate, sensible, respectable [*kosmon*], hospitable [*philoxenon*], an apt teacher, not a drunkard, not violent but gentle, not quarrelsome, and not a lover of money. He must manage his own household well, keeping his children submissive and respectful in every way—for if someone does not know how to manage his own household well, how can he take care of God's church? He must not be a recent convert, or he may be puffed up with conceit and fall into the condemnation of the devil. Moreover, he must be thought well of by outsiders [*dei de kai marturian kalēn echein apo tōn exōthen*], so that he may not fall into disgrace and the snare of the devil. (1 Tim 3:1-7)

Virtues and Vices

The short list of virtues to be had and vices to be avoided[70] is, for the most part, similar to short catalogues of virtues and vices that are used to list the requisite qualities for an overseer in Titus 1:7-8. The two lists

---

[70] Heid labels the items on the list as "impediments to ordination" (*Celibacy in the Early Church*, 42) and suggests that they served as a questionnaire during a scrutiny

begin in a similar fashion. They open with a comprehensive phrase, the "bishop must be above reproach," although the author of 1 Timothy writes about the overseer being "above reproach" (*anepilēmpton*) while the author of Titus says that the overseer must be "blameless" (*anenklēton*). The two adjectives are basically synonymous but the author of 1 Timothy has a preference for "above reproach" (*anepilēmptos*). The word appears three times in this epistle (1 Tim 3:2; 5:7; 6:14) but in no other passage of the New Testament.

It is noteworthy that, unlike Titus, the author of 1 Timothy emphatically places "married only once" at the head of the list of virtues that he is about to rehearse. Here there is nothing optional about marriage.[71] There is no more an option for an overseer to be married or not than there is for the overseer to have an option to be temperate, sensible, respectable, hospitable, or a good teacher. The *episkopos* "must be" (*dei einai*) the husband of one wife. It is the *dei einai* construction that requires that the phrase "married only once" be in the accusative rather than in the nominative.

The requirement that the overseer be married is consistent with the antiencratist spirit of the epistle. Its author takes issue with those who "forbid marriage and demand abstinence from foods" (1 Tim 4:3). He views marriage and food as having been created by God and argues that "everything created by God is good and nothing is to be rejected" (1 Tim 4:4).

The author's logic in insisting that the overseer be married but once in order that he be above reproach is similar to the logic of Paul's argumentation in 1 Thessalonians and 1 Corinthians where the apostle insists that marriage is a way to avoid sexual misconduct and to be holy (1 Thess 4:3). Being married should lead to conduct that is above reproach, certainly with regard to sexual matters.

The author of 1 Timothy does not speak about an appointment[72] nor does he speak of elders at this juncture in his letter.[73] He concentrates on

---

for ordination (ibid., 46). 1 Timothy 3:10 does indeed make reference to a testing of servers, but the Scripture makes no reference to a similar testing of overseers.

[71] Notwithstanding the clear language of the text, Heid comments: "Here, too, it should be added: on the condition that he is married." See Heid, *Celibacy in the Early Church*, 38. This appears to be a gratuitous addition to Scripture.

[72] Cf. the "appoint" (*katastēsēs*) of Titus 1:5.

[73] Cf. 1 Tim 5:1, 2, 17, 19.

the qualifications required that a man functions well as an overseer in the community and that he be found respectable, well thought of by outsiders. Placing "married only once" (*mias gynaikos andra*) at the head of his list of virtues means that the author considers this quality to be most important if an overseer is to be a blameless individual.

The author defers the overseer's qualities as a household manager until later in the pericope. Nonetheless, the virtue of hospitality (*philoxenon*) appears on his list of the overseer's virtuous qualities just as it does in Titus 1:8.

Household Management

Having run the gamut of the vices that an overseer must avoid, the author of 1 Timothy turns to the overseer's household responsibilities as he says, "He must manage his own household well [*tou idiou oikou kalōs proistamenon*]" (1 Tim 3:4). The qualifiers are important. The household that the overseer must have managed well (*kalōs*) is his own (*tou idiou*). Immediately the author indicates why this qualification is so important: "For if someone does not know how to manage his own household [*ei de tis tou idiou oikou prostēnai ouk oiden*], how can he take care of God's church [*pōs ekklēsias theou epimelēsetai*]?" (1 Tim 3:5). A man's ability to run his own household well qualifies him to run a larger household, God's church. This idea is implicit in Titus' description of the overseer as God's steward, but the author of 1 Timothy expresses the idea with full clarity.

An integral element of the overseer's good management is that he has kept "his children submissive and respectful in every way" (*en hypotagē, meta pasēs semnotētos*). In comparison with Titus' description of the overseer's children, the author of 1 Timothy makes no mention of the offspring's religious adherence and speaks positively rather than negatively.[74] The overseer must have raised his children well, showing that he has been a good leader to them. If the overseer has not been an effective leader of his own children, how can he be a good leader to a larger group?

---

[74] "Not accused of debauchery and not rebellious" is the way that the author of Titus 1:6 describes the children of the would-be overseer.

Marital Fidelity

There is hardly any mention of the overseer's wife in 1 Timothy 3:1-7 but the phrase *mias gynaikos andra* speaks volumes about the overseer's fidelity to her.[75] Marital fidelity and effective household leadership are among the qualities that a man must have if he aspires to become an overseer in the household of God—the Church.

1 Timothy 3:8-13

The third passage in the New Testament that uses the *mias gynaikos anēr* phrase, although in the plural, is found in 1 Timothy 3:12 where it is cited as a qualification of "servers" (*diakonoi*): "Let deacons [*diakonoi*] be married only once."

Servers

Diakonoi do not appear in Titus, perhaps evincing Titus' less developed state of the Church than that witnessed to in 1 Timothy. The noun *diakonos* appears twice in the plural in 1 Timothy 3:8-13 and once in 1 Timothy 4:6, the only passages in which mention is made of servers in the Pastoral Epistles. In 1 Timothy 4:6 the noun *diakonos* is applied to the epistle's patronymic addressee, to whom it is said, "If you put these instructions before the brothers and sisters, you will be a good servant of Christ Jesus [*kalos esē diakonos Christou Iēsou*]."

Cognate with the noun *diakonos*, "server," is the verb *diakoneō*, "serve."[76] The verb appears twice in the passage under consideration—namely, at 3:10 and 3:13—and nowhere else in the minicorpus of the Pastoral Epistles. This use of the language of service suggests its functional connotation, rather than any suggestion of a full-fledged office in the Church. The functional character of the verb is suggested by Paul's own usage. For example, in Philemon 13, the imprisoned Paul says of Onesimus, "I wanted to keep him with me, so that he might be of service [*diakonē*] to me in your place during my imprisonment for the gospel."

---

[75] Cf. Ed. Glasscock, " 'The Husband of One Wife' Requirement in 1 Timothy 3:2," *BSac* 140 (1983): 244–58. Glasscock maintains that "husband of one wife," with its implications, pertains to man's status after his conversion and does not pertain to his preconversion life.

[76] The NRSV, along with the NAB, translates the verb as "serve as deacons." The translation, unfortunately, easily leads to an anachronistic reading of the text.

During his lifetime, the apostle Paul knew of those who functioned as servers in the believing community. He addressed his Letter to the Philippians "to all the saints in Christ Jesus who are in Philippi, with the bishops [*episkopois*] and deacons [*diakonois*]" (Phil 1:1b). And he makes particular mention of a woman named Phoebe whom he commends to God's beloved in Rome, called saints.[77] The apostle identifies Phoebe as "our sister Phoebe, a deacon of the church of Cenchrae [*diakonon*[78] *tēs ekklēsias tēs en Kenchreiais*]" (Rom 16:1).

The Servers' Qualifications

After describing the qualities of the overseer, the author of 1 Timothy turns his attention to the qualities of those who would serve in God's household. He writes:

> Deacons likewise [*diakonous hōsautōs*] must be serious [*semnous*], not double-tongued, nor indulging in much wine, not greedy for money; they must hold fast to the mystery of the faith with a clear conscience. And let them first be tested; then, if they prove themselves blameless [*anenklētoi*], let them serve as deacons [*diakoneitōsan*]. Women likewise [*gynaikas hōsautōs*] must be serious, not slanderers, but temperate, faithful in all things. Let deacons be married only once [*diakonoi estōsan mias gynaikos andres*], and let them manage their children and their households well [*teknōn kalōs proistamenoi kai tōn idiōn oikōn*]; for those who serve well as deacons [*kalōs diakonēsantes*] gain a good standing for themselves and great boldness in the faith that is in Christ Jesus. (1 Tim 3:8-13)

We recognize in this passage lists of qualifications, both virtues to be possessed and vices to be avoided similar to those found in Titus 1:6-9 and 1 Timothy 3:1-7,[79] for both men and women. A brief word about what it means for the overseer and the server to be "blameless" is in order. The Greek of the respective texts uses two different adjectives— *anenklētos* in Titus and 1 Timothy 3:10 and *anepilēmptos* in 1 Timothy 3:2—both of which are translated as "blameless" in the NRSV. Heading the list of vices in 1 Timothy 3:8 is a virtue, "serious" (*semnos*). For all practical purposes, the terms are synonymous. All three terms speak

---

[77] Cf. Rom 1:7.

[78] The epithet is a masculine form, albeit used of the woman Phoebe.

[79] Cf. Collins, "How Not to Behave," 7–31.

about the way that a person is viewed by others but there is an importance nuance that differentiates them.

The terms *anenklētos* and *anepilēmpton* begin with a negative particle and connote the idea that an onlooker could perceive the failure to live up to accepted standards. So that people do not see the elder or overseer as blameworthy, he must be once married and faithful to his wife. His failure to have been married and shown fidelity to his wife would give reason for this leader of the community to be criticized by those within and without the community. The blameworthiness of the server in this regard is ascertained on the basis of the scrutiny that he has undergone.

The adjective *semnos*, on the other hand, is positive in form. The term was most often used in antiquity of the gods, with the connotation of august, revered, awesome. When applied to humans, it means revered or respected. If the one who serves is to be respected within the community that is testing him as well as by outsiders, he must possess the virtues that are listed and avoid those vices that are mentioned. That the servers' faithfulness is also under scrutiny is implied by the phrase, "they must hold fast to the mystery of the faith with a clear conscience."

The reference to women (*gynaikas*) in verse 11 is a reference to female deacons.[80] The list is somewhat different from the list set out for men since Hellenistic society, from the time of Aristotle, believed that some virtues were more appropriate for men and others for women.[81] The list of the female deacon's qualifications does not include the requirement that she be "married only once" (*enos andros gynē*[82]) even though it is more than probable that female deacons were also married.[83] Although it is impossible to enter into the author's mind and discern the reason why he did not explicitly require female deacons to be married only once, it could be that such a prescription would seemingly fly in the face of what he is to recommend for young widows in 1 Timothy 4:14, as well as the prescriptions of the Julian laws for widowed and divorced women under the age of fifty.[84]

[80] Cf. Collins, *I & II Timothy and Titus*, 90–91, 331. See also the note at 1 Timothy 3:11 in the NAB.

[81] Ibid., 91.

[82] See below, pp. 207–9, on 1 Tim 5:9.

[83] Cf. Jürgen Roloff, *Der Erste Brief an Timotheus*, EKKNT 15 (Zurich: Benziger/ Neukirchen: Neukirchener-Vluyn, 1988), 166.

[84] See above, p. 66.

Married Only Once

On the other hand, the list of qualifications for male deacons does include the requirement that they be married only once (*mias gynaikos andres*). Although the terminology of this qualification is similar to that found in Titus 1:6 and 1 Timothy 3:2, the qualification does not appear at the head of the list as it does in the other two instances. As noted above, in both of these instances, the requirement that the overseer be married only once is the first clarifying indication of what it means to be blameless. Whereas it is said that the overseer "must" (*dei*) be "married only once," a matter of obligation, it is written of servers, "let deacons [*diakonoi*, servers] be married only once." The verb *estōsan*, "let be," preceding the *mias gynaikos andres* phrase, is the third-person plural, present imperative of the verb *to be*. "Let them be" is not a permission or an allowance; it is a command and a requirement.[85] Servers are required to be married just as overseers are.

In 1 Timothy 3:8-13, the "husband of one wife" qualification is deferred so that it becomes the first of the server's personal household responsibilities rather the first of the requirements for him as he is being scrutinized prior to be being allowed to "serve" within the community. Marital fidelity is explicitly required of male servers but it is also necessary that they be regarded as overall good family men: "Let them manage their children and their households well" (*teknōn kalōs proistamenoi kai tōn idiōn oikōn*). A single participle is used to speak of the server's responsibility to his children and household. The terseness of the author's description may be due to the fact that, while the server must be well regarded (*semnos*)[86] as a family man, he is not going to function in a capacity that

---

[85] The translation of 1 Timothy 3:12 in the NAB, "Deacons may be married only once and must manage their children and their households well," is at best tendentious. The NAB makes it appear as if there are two principal verbs in the sentence, "may be" and "must" (or "must manage"). The Greek text, however, contains only one principal verb, the imperative *estōsan*. The denotation of the verb is echoed in the "must" of the second clause in the NAB translation. The Greek sentence contains no verb that hints of a concession or allowance. "Manage" is a participial form in Greek (*proistamenoi*). The sentence could be translated in this fashion, "Deacons must be men of one woman, who have managed their children and households well." The REB hits the nail on the head, with its translation of the verse: "A deacon must be the husband of one wife, and good at managing his children and his own household."

[86] Cf. 1 Tim 3:8, 13.

requires managerial skills, such as those required of the steward and overseer in the household of God. Hence, there is no need for the author of 1 Timothy to dwell on the server's managerial skills.

1 Timothy 5:9

As previously stated, the Greek phrase *mias gynaikos anēr*, translated in the NRSV as "married only once" but literally meaning "a man of one woman," appears just three times in the New Testament. All three occurrences are in the Pastoral Epistles—namely, in Titus 1:6 and 1 Timothy 3:2, apropos overseers (*episkopoi*), and in 1 Timothy 3:12, apropos servers (*diakonoi*). Interestingly enough, a similar phrase, *enos andros gynē*, also translated in the NRSV as "married only once," is to be found in 1 Timothy 5:9. The difference in wording between this formula and that found in Titus 1:6; 1 Timothy 3:2, 12 is due to the fact that *enos andros gynē* applies to a woman, a widow (*chēra*). If a widow is to be put on a list of widows who deserve the Church's support she must be a "woman [wife[87]] of one husband," to wit:

> Let a widow be put on the list if she is not less than sixty years old and has been married only once [*enos andros gynē*]; she must be well attested for her good works, as one who has brought up children, shown hospitality, washed the saints' feet, helped the afflicted, and devoted herself to doing service to doing good in every way. But refuse to put younger widows on the list. (1 Tim 5:9-11)

With regard to fidelity in marriage and a second marriage, social expectations for women were different from those for men, both in Greco-Roman and Jewish society. Women were always held to a stricter standard. What, then, does it mean that a real widow[88] should be "married only once"?

[87] The Greek *gynē* literally means woman but, in context it generally connotes "wife."

[88] Cf. 1 Tim 5:3, "Honor widows who are really widows" (*chēras tima tas ontōs chēras*); 1 Tim 5:5, "The real widow [*hē de ontōs chēra*], left alone, has set her hope on God"; 1 Tim 5:16, "so that it can assist those who are real widows" (*tais ontōs chērais*).

The Real Widow

The qualification that a real widow be married only once appears in second place in the list of the widow's virtues and is followed by a rehearsal of the way she raised her children and her service to "the saints," members of the church (1 Tim 5:9). It is noteworthy that the qualification follows after the requirement that she have attained the age of sixty,[89] that she be a senior to whom the Julian laws on widowhood were no longer applicable. This is also the age beyond which further marriage was unlikely.[90]

While this older widow's fidelity to her husband may have been considered noteworthy, the younger widow of child-bearing age was urged to remarry and take care of her family (v. 14), precisely so that the community of believers in God's household not be subject to ridicule and shame. First Timothy 5 also speaks about a third group of widows, those who have children and grandchildren who can take care of them in keeping with traditional norms of filial piety.[91] Other than the fact that this third group consists of women bereft of their husbands at the time, but having living descendants, nothing is said about the possibility or lack thereof of such a widow having married again after the death of her spouse.

Married Only Once

With reference to 1 Timothy 5:9, what is meant when it is said that the real widow, the one to be enrolled, must be *enos andros gynē*, "married only once"? Unlike the rarely attested *mias gynaikos anēr*, "married only once" descriptive of a man, a laudatory form of "married only once" as applied to a woman was well-known in antiquity. A late first-century BCE elegy by Sextus Propertius is indicative in this regard. "Cornelia to Paullus from Beyond the Grave," says:

[89] In Plato's ideal city, sixty was the age at which a woman could become a priestess. Cf. Plato, *Laws* 6.759d. See also Plutarch, *Comparatio Lycurgi et Numae* 26.1–2; Pollianus, 2.11; Demosthenes, *Discourses* 43.62.

[90] So, Oden, who references John Chrysostom and Jerome. Cf. Thomas C. Oden, *First and Second Timothy and Titus*, Interpretation: A Bible Commentary for Teaching and Preaching (Louisville: John Knox, 1989), 156; John Chrysostom, *Letter to a Young Widow*, 2; Jerome, *Epist.* 79.7.

[91] Cf. 1 Tim 5:16. Within Judaism, this dimension of filial piety was codified in the fourth commandment.

I was united to your bed, Paullus, only to leave it so: read it on this stone, she was wedded to one alone [*uni nupta*]. I call as witness the ashes of my forebears, revered by you. . . . My life never altered, wholly without reproach: we lived in honour from the wedding to the funeral torch. . . . Moreover I earned the robe of honour through child-bearing: it was not a childless house that I was snatched from. . . . But if the bed that faces the doorway should be altered, and a careful stepmother occupy my place, boys, praise and accept your father's wife: captivated, she will applaud your good manners. Don't praise your mother too much: thoughtless speech that compares her with the first wife will become offences against her. Or if Paullus, you remember me, content that my shade suffices, and consider my ashes thus worthy, learn to feel now how old age advances, and leave no path open for a widower's cares.[92]

The compound word *monandros* and *univira*[93] are found on a number of Jewish and Gentile inscriptions. The phrases were used to eulogize a good and faithful wife, even in eulogies given by a woman's second husband.[94] Secular usage of the phrase does not, therefore, exclude a second marriage.

Reflecting this usage, Theodore of Mopsuestia comments on the phrase that it applies to a woman, "If she has lived in chastity with her husband, whether she had only one, or whether she was married a second time."[95] Theodoret of Cyrrhus interprets the phrase in similar fashion, to wit,

[92] Propertius, *Elegies*, 4.11. Translation by A. S. Kline (2008), accessible at http://www.poetryintranslation.com/PITBR/Latin/Prophome.htm. See also Valerius Maximus, *Nine Books of Memorable Deeds and Sayings*, 2.1.3. "Women who had restricted themselves to one marriage were honored with the garland of modesty; our ancestors felt that the heart of a married woman was especially incorruptible and trustworthy if she refused to leave the bedroom in which she had lost her virginity, but they believed that to have experienced many marriages was a sign of legalized promiscuity." Henry John Wells, trans., *Valerius Maximus. Memorable Deeds and Sayings: One Thousand Tales from Ancient Rome* (Indianapolis: Hackett, 2004).

[93] Spicq cautions that this word is not the exact equivalent of *enos andros gynē*. See Ceslaus Spicq, *Les épîtres pastorales*, 1, EBib., 4th rev. ed. (Paris: Gabalda, 1969), 402. Cf. *NewDocs* 4, 222; Ben Witherington III, *Letters and Homilies for Hellenized Christians*, 1: *A Socio-Rhetorical Commentary on Titus, 1–2 Timothy and 1–3 John* (Downers Grove, IL: IVP Academic / Nottingham, UK: Apollos, 2006), 269.

[94] Cf. Audet, *Mariage et célibat*, 96.

[95] Cf. Swete, *Theodori episcopi Monsuesteni* 2, 161 (PG 66, 944). Dibelius and Conzelmann label Theodore's interpretation as "correct." Cf. Dibelius and Conzelmann, *Pastoral Epistles*, 75.

"The teaching that a widow should be the wife of only one man is an encouragement to chastity within marriage, not a forbidding of second marriages."[96] John Chrysostom, however, takes the phrase in 1 Timothy 5:9 as one that discourages second marriages. For him it is not so much a matter of a widow showing undivided loyalty to one man as it is a matter of her leisure should she remain unmarried after the death of her husband.[97]

Clearly, some segments of ancient Greco-Roman[98] and Jewish society[99] considered it praiseworthy for a widow not to remarry after the death of her husband. Her willingness to forgo a second marriage was thought to be a sign of her loyalty to her deceased husband. An indication of such loyalty to just one husband was the idea that only widows who had been married a single time were allowed to serve at the altar of Pudicitia.[100]

Accordingly, Lightman and Ziesel[101] maintain that the *univira* epithet functioned in two different ways. In its descriptive form, the epithet served as a formula of social approbation and was used of women who died before their husbands, be they a first or subsequent husband. Used in this fashion, the epithet was used of women from all levels of society. Used, however, in a prescriptive manner and related to various institutional and ritual activities, as it was of those who served as Pudicitia's altar, the term referred to those married women, not necessarily widows, who had been married to a single man. The circles in which this usage was found were those of the social elite.

An Order of Widows?

Origen, the early Alexandrine scholar, held that "real widows" should not be married a second time. His opinion was certainly more rigid and legalistic than were the later views of Theodore of Mopsuestia and John Chrysostom. In a homily on Luke 17:10, Origen remarked, "Anyone twice

---

[96] Cf. Theodoret of Cyrrhus, *Comm. in 1 Tim*, at 1 Tim 5:9 (PG 82, 817).

[97] *Hom 14.1 in 1 Tim* (NPNF 2 10:392).

[98] Cf. *Anthologia graeca* 7, 324.

[99] Spicq cites Jdt 16:22 and Luke 2:36-37 as evidence of the Jewish practice. See Spicq, *Épîtres pastorales*, 1, 402.

[100] Cf. Livy, *Roman History* 10.23.9.

[101] Cf. Majorie Lightman and William Zeisel, "*Univira*: An Example of Continuity and Change in Roman Society," CH 46 (1977): 19–32.

married may be neither a bishop nor a presbyter nor a deacon nor a widow."[102]

With regard to the notion that a real widow must be "married only once," Bassler argues that something more than the death of a spouse is involved. "Celibacy," she says, is the "defining feature of the group" of real widows and speaks of their "vows of celibacy."[103] In fact, in the recent *Wirkungsgeschichte* of 1 Timothy 5:9's "married but once," the interpretation of the phrase appears closely linked with another issue. This is whether "real widows" constituted an order within the nascent Church and whether "real widowhood" was to be seen as a designation of a ministry of Christian service at the time.[104] Authors such as Spicq,[105] Quinn and Wacker,[106] Krause,[107] and Fiore[108] speak of "an order" of widows and suggest that one qualification of becoming a member of the order is that the widow has had only one husband. For example, Quinn and Wacker argue:

> The point of the provision would be quite lost if it referred simply to fidelity in successive marriages, for a widow is a widow and the number of her previous marriages would be irrelevant. The provision is obviously meant to exclude certain widows from the order of real widows with a provision that turns on number, as was the case with preceding provision on age. Widows below sixty are not to be enrolled with the "real widows"; widows of a second marriage are similarly disqualified.[109]

---

[102] Cf. Joseph T. Lienhard, ed., *Origen: Homilies on Luke, Fathers of the Church*, FC, vol. 94 (Washington: Catholic University of America Press, 1996), 75.

[103] Jouette M. Bassler *1 Timothy, 2 Timothy, Titus*, ANTC (Nashville: Abingdon, 1996), 93–94, 96–97.

[104] On this issue, see especially Bonnie Bowman Thurston, *The Widows: A Woman's Ministry in the Early Church* (Minneapolis: Fortress, 1989); "1 Timothy 5:3-16 and Leadership of Women in the Early Church" in *A Feminist Companion to the Deutero-Pauline Epistles*, ed. Amy-Jill Levine and Marianne Blickenstaff (Cleveland: Pilgrim Press, 2003), 159–74, esp. 172.

[105] Cf. Spicq, *Épîtres pastorales*, 1, 532–33.

[106] Jerome D. Quinn and William C. Wacker, *The First and Second Letters to Timothy*, Eerdmans Critical Commentary (Grand Rapids, MI: Eerdmans, 2000), 436.

[107] Cf. Deborah Krause, *1 Timothy* (New York: T&T Clark, 2004), 100–101.

[108] Benjamin Fiore, *The Pastoral Epistles: First Timothy, Second Timothy, Titus*, SP 12 (Collegeville, MN: Liturgical Press, 2007), 104.

[109] Quinn and Wacker, *First and Second Letters to Timothy*, 437.

Commenting on the stringency of the requirements, Krause adds, "it seems fair to wonder if the letter writer's ideal ('real') widow is really a dead widow, or a nonexistent widow."[110]

In my judgment the possibility that there was an order of widows with a ministry of service in the late first century remains a moot question, especially if the order was restricted to sixty-year-old widows. This would definitely be a group of old widows in a society in which life expectancy was forty years of age. Towner correctly observes that "these real widows were in the closing years of their lives, not at a point at which to take up new ministries."[111] That is not to say that they could not continue to perform some services within the church. They were, however, at a venerable stage in life when they would normally look to others to provide for their needs.[112]

A Matter of Translation

Every translation is, as was previously noted, an interpretation and, sometimes, even a falsification. This is the case with translations of lists of the real widows' qualifications in 1 Timothy 5:9-10. The NRSV translates this pair of verses in this way: "Let a widow be put on the list if she is not less than sixty years old and had been married only once; she must be well attested for her good works, as one who has brought up children, shown hospitality, washed the saints' feet, helped the afflicted, and devoted herself to good works in every way."

The wording makes it appear as if having attained the age of sixty and been married but once are coordinate notions and the primary conditions to be fulfilled if a widow is to be enrolled. The translation, with its punctuation, suggests that the text is alluding to some sort of an order of enrolled widows. The NRSV's first "and" as well as the "had been" have, however, no equivalent in Greek. In addition, the Greek text lacks all punctuation, including the semicolon of 1 Timothy 5:9 and the words "she must be" that follow.

[110] Krause, *1 Timothy*, 100.

[111] Philip H. Towner, *The Letters to Timothy and Titus*, NICNT (Grand Rapids, MI: Eerdmans, 2006), 346.

[112] Cf. I. Howard Marshall, *The Pastoral Epistles*, ICC (Edinburgh: T&T Clark, 1999), 593.

In the Greek text, the words from "one who has brought up children" (*ei eteknotrophēsen*) to "devoted herself to good works" (*ei panti ergō agathō epēkolouthēsen*) constitute a series of five conditional clauses, each of which is introduced by *ei*, "if." Arguably the text should be read in this fashion: "let a widow be listed who is no less than sixty, married only once, and well-spoken of because of her good works:[113] rearing children, showing hospitality, washing the saints' feet, helping the afflicted, and devoting herself to every sort of good work."[114] The double reference to "good works" forms a kind of literary inclusion around the intervening four conditional clauses. The clauses that speak of rearing children, showing hospitality, washing the saints' feet, helping the afflicted, and devoting herself to every kind of good work explain what the author means by good works (*ergois kalois*).

In the NRSV, that she be "married only once" appears to be one of two principal conditions required of the widow if she is to be enrolled (perhaps in an order of widows). On my reading of the text, that the widow be "married only once" is one of three conditions to be fulfilled in order for her name to be entered on the list of those to be cared for by the community.

Care for Elderly Widows

The existence of a biblical tradition that demands that care be taken of widows and orphans, those without the male head of household to protect and provide for them, is beyond any reasonable doubt. Passages such as Exodus 22:22; Deuteronomy 14:29; and Zechariah 7:9-10 give evidence of this concern as do such New Testament passages as James 1:7 and Acts 6:1-7.[115] The community of God's people must provide for those widows who are otherwise without anyone to provide for them.

It should be noted that the first words of the passage on widows, 1 Timothy 5:3-16, are "honor widows" (*chēras tima*). Care for widows is

---

[113] The first and last clauses are participial clauses; sandwiched between them is "a one-man woman."

[114] Similarly the NAB, which reads, "Let a widow be enrolled if she is not less than sixty years old, married only once, with a reputation for good works, namely, that she has raised children, practiced hospitality, washed the feet of the holy ones, helped those in distress, involved herself in every good work" (1 Tim 5:9-10).

[115] Cf. Ignatius *Pol.* 4.

the principal theme of the pericope,[116] a theme to which attention is drawn in the opening and closing words. The verb *timaō*, "honor" and the related substantive *timē*, the noun for honor, have to do with material support. The verb is that used in Septuagintal Greek of the fourth commandment, both in Exodus 20:12 and in Deuteronomy 5:16, mandating that adult children, especially males, provide for their elders during their advanced years.[117] The noun *timē* is found in 1 Timothy 5:17, a relatively few verses after the passage under discussion in reference to the support of "elders" within the community.

With this as the horizon for the care of widows enjoined by 1 Timothy 5:3-10, the *enos andros gynē* can read as an indication that the widow to be cared for by the community must be one recognized for the quality of her domestic life and her life as a respectable member of society. Having attained at least the age of sixty, the real widow is one who has married only once, and is well attested for her good works—that is, she has brought up her children and has shown hospitality. Moreover, she must have washed the feet of the saints,[118] helped the afflicted, and done good in every way. "There is," as Dibelius and Conzelmann observe, "no reason whatever to infer a prohibition of a second marriage here."[119]

Within this reading of the text it is arguable that the author's *enos andros gynē*, "married only once," is more of a commentary on the widow's marital fidelity than a reference to the number of times that she has been married. Were *enos andros gynē* to mean that the widow qualifying for enrollment had only a single husband during the course of her life, the implication is that she had enjoyed an unusually long marriage. The median age of widowhood was mid-thirties. Under the Julian laws, a woman whose husband had died before she had turned fifty was expected to remarry.

Support for the moral quality interpretation of the phrase, "married only once," *enos andros gynē*—namely, that the widow to be supported

---

[116] "The main theme is *care* for widows" (his emphasis), writes Towner (*Letters to Timothy and Titus*, 345).

[117] Cf. Raymond F. Collins, "Obedience, Children and the Fourth Commandment— A New Testament Note," *LS* 4 (1972–73): 157–73. Among other things it can be noted that the discussion of this commandment in Mark 7:9-13 and Matthew 15:3-9 deals with the material support of one's parents.

[118] Washing a guest's feet was a traditional gesture of hospitality (cf. Luke 7:44). It may also be that "washing the feet of the saints" is an implicit reference to John 13:12-15.

[119] Dibelius and Conzelmann, *Pastoral Epistles*, 75.

by the Church should have been faithful to her husband—can be found in the fact that the author of 1 Timothy positively urges young widows to remarry (1 Tim 5:14). This bit of paraenesis is consistent with the author's taking issue with those who were against marriage. He argued that marriage is a good created by God and not to be rejected.[120] Does he want to suggest that a widow who follows his advice is unworthy of support from the Church, should her second husband predecease her?

Also to be taken into consideration is the Pauline tradition to which the author lays claim in 1 Timothy 1:1-2a.[121] Even in the context of what he believed to be the impending Parousia, the apostle acknowledged the legitimacy of a widow's remarriage should her passions continue to remain strong (1 Cor 7:8-9). He set down only one condition—namely, that she marry "in the Lord" (1 Cor 7:39) by marrying a believer.

Social respectability is an important feature of the paraenesis of 1 Timothy. The text's author does not explicitly cite this motivational factor in writing about senior widows but in his society a woman's fidelity to her husband was particularly valued. It is that quality that appears to come to the fore in Propertius' *uni nupta* and the *monandros/univira* expression found on ancient epigraphs and in funereal discourse. There is little reason to think that our author's *enos andros gynē* implied anything else.

A Last Thought

One final note: Even if it could be established that the connotation of *enos andros gynē* is that the widow to be enrolled should have had only one husband during her lifetime, the phrase would not be a strong argument for taking the author of 1 Timothy's use of the *mias gynaikos anēr* expression to mean that overseers and servers should not be married once. The fact that ancient standards of marital respectability for women were so different from those for men and the fact that the ancients attributed different virtues to women than they did to men make the application of what pertains to females applicable to males a socially unlikely transition. A widow's single marriage would not mean that overseers and servers were not to remarry if their first wives have died.

---

[120] Cf. 1 Tim 4:1-4.

[121] "Loyal" (*gnēsiō*) in 1 Timothy 1:2a implies that the author is the legitimate heir of Paul. See Collins, *I and II Timothy and Titus*, 24.

Conclusion

This study has had a very limited focus. It has aimed at elucidating the meaning of those New Testament texts that have been used in support of the practice of clerical celibacy and clerical continence, particularly in the Latin church throughout the ages but especially during the patristic era and the period of the first canonical literature on the subject.

As an exegetical study, the pages of this book have been dedicated to the meaning of specific texts within their own literary, historical, and social contexts. The texts chosen for study are those that have been particularly highlighted in two significant monographs on clerical celibacy written in the last half of the twentieth century—namely, the works of Christian Cochini and Stefan Heid. Cochini's study was an important source for the many articles and a short book on the topic by Alphons Maria Stickler, who devoted a good part of his academic career to the study of clerical celibacy and the related practice of clerical continence.

The principal concern of these three authors has been the history of the development of the related practices, particularly from the perspective of the writings of some of the Fathers of the Church, the canons of several councils (for the most part, regional church councils), and the early papal decretals. These historical sources were, in and of themselves, not the focus of the current study. They served the purposes of this study insofar as they witnessed to the use of a limited number of scriptural texts that were cited in support of the developing practice and discipline.

What this study has endeavored to do is to analyze time-honored scriptural texts with the aid of contemporary historical, literary, and linguistic methods. Use of these methods enables us to better understand what the first Christian generations understood when they heard these words of Scripture. Taken from the historical circumstances in which they were written and the literary contexts in which they are found, these texts were heard again in different historical circumstances and embodied in different literary contexts in such a way that a new interpretation was attributed to them. This new interpretation was often far removed from the meaning of the texts in the first years of the Christian church.

Words were retained but their meaning was changed. Taking the texts out of their literary context often meant that little attention was paid to the remainder of the scriptural book in which these texts are found. Taking the texts out of their historical context meant that they acquired a timelessness that they did not originally have. Ultimately the historical reality of revelation was neglected and the law of the incarnation was ignored.

The texts that served as the subject of our study were those most frequently cited in the historical sources for the ecclesiastical practice of clerical continence, from which the Western Church's discipline of clerical celibacy has emerged. These same texts understandably recur in contemporary historical studies, but they are generally not subject to the same rigors of historical and literary research as are the patristic and early canonical texts in which they occur.

From the gospels come such passages as "we have left everything and followed you" (Mark 10:28; Matt 19:27) and "there are eunuchs who have made themselves eunuchs for the sake of the kingdom of heaven" (Matt 19:12). From the letters of the apostle Paul come exhortations such as "do not deprive one another except perhaps by agreement for a set time, to devote yourselves to prayer" (1 Cor 7:5)—a passage often cited in abbreviated form as "deprive one another to devote yourselves to prayer—and "let even those who have wives be as if they had none" (1 Cor 7:29). The letters also contain such self-referential passages as "I say that it is well for them to remain unmarried as I am" (1 Cor 7:8) and "do we not have the right to be accompanied by a believing wife, as do the other apostles and the brothers of the Lord and Cephas?" (1 Cor 9:5). From epistles attributed to Paul, but arguably not written by him, comes the famous *unius uxoris vir* adage whose classic interpretation, *propter continentiam futuram*, is attributed to Pope Siricius I. The phrase itself is found in 1 Timothy 3:2, 12 and Titus 1:6.

This short overview of the principal scriptural texts cited in the historical sources and current literature suggests that the texts can be gathered together and analyzed in three groups—namely, (1) the gospel narratives about Jesus and his disciples, (2) the letters written by Paul, especially his First Letter to the Corinthians, and (3) the Pastoral-Epistles, especially the quasi-legislative First Letter to Timothy and the Letter to Titus.

Jesus and the Gospels

The gospel stories about Jesus and his disciples are literary narratives. The most ancient of these is the Gospel according to Mark.[1] The fact that they are narratives, *stories*, must be taken into account if they are to be read and heard with due understanding. The reading of a story demands its own hermeneutic.

The gospel stories were not written as historical accounts—certainly not by the standards of contemporary historiography—but they are the principal sources available to us as we endeavor to know what Jesus and his disciples did, to know what he said to his disciples and they to him. As stories rather than as modern biographies or histories, the gospels often do *not* provide us with the details we would like. Any story—and this certainly includes the gospel stories—is selective. Authors pick and choose what they want to write in the light of their aim. The aim of the gospel stories is ultimately theological. The Synoptic stories, in particular, attempt to portray the claim of the Kingdom of God on Jesus of Nazareth and those who listened to him.

Jesus' own life story bears witness to the Kingdom of God, which "has come near," as Jesus proclaimed at the beginning of his public ministry (Mark 1:15). For the sake of the kingdom, Jesus adopted a celibate lifestyle, to which a single New Testament text bears witness—namely, Matthew 19:12. Excoriated for his celibate lifestyle, Jesus defended himself with a startling image. He speaks about those who have who have made themselves eunuchs for the sake of the kingdom of heaven.

The coming of the kingdom colored all that Jesus did and said, even with regard to marriage. He had reason to defend himself with regard to his lifestyle because contemporary society took it for granted that men should be married. Faithful Jewish men were expected to marry not only because marriage led to progeny but also because marriage was incumbent upon God's people to whom the Lord had said, "Be fruitful and multiply" (Gen 1:28).

---

[1] Markan priority is the reason why I have generally referenced Mark first when a saying or incident is to be found in more than one gospel.

That marriage was, in fidelity to God's command, the normal and normative way of life for first-century Jewish men is not to be overlooked when Jesus issued the call to discipleship, "Follow me" (Mark 1:17). Rabbinic texts, often attributed to the Schools of Hillel and Shammai, the great rabbis whose influence on first-century CE Jewish culture was so strong, sought to understand the specifics of a religious response to God's "Be fruitful and multiply." The celibate lifestyle was not among the appropriate responses under consideration. Marriage was a social reality, the purpose of which was procreation. In turn, this suggests that marriage without sexual intercourse was not marriage in the way that people understood it. The rabbinic texts were written long after the gospels were written, but, like the gospels, they were conservative in nature. They attempted to preserve the tradition and, in so doing, attest to the culture of marriage in first-century Jewish Palestine, albeit from later perspectives.

At that time—the time of Jesus—Palestine was under Roman domination. Among the evangelists, Luke particularly drew attention to the Roman reality of the world in which Jesus lived and preached. Roman laws on marriage had been enacted a few decades before Jesus came on the scene. These laws had as their primary purpose to increase population among the Roman elite. It is virtually impossible to know whether and to what extent the laws were enforced in the provinces, but they were the law of the Empire and contributed a culture of marriage for the sake of progeny that existed in Jesus' day.

In this context, it is all but certain that Simon Peter was not the only disciple of Jesus to have been married. Were they not to have been considered contraveners of God's will, all of Jesus' disciples would have married. The sources are silent about their marriages but, as has been noted, the sources are selective and were written not to provide biographical data about the members of Jesus' company but to provide an impression of the claim of the coming kingdom on them. In order that the gospel be proclaimed, Jesus' disciples left their homes, families, and livelihood, but the separation appears not to have been permanent.

As for Cephas, their spokesperson and eventual leader, Paul affirms that he was accompanied by his wife as he fulfilled the mission of preaching the Gospel. The sometimes fanciful and often graphic apocryphal literature of later years builds on the tradition that Peter was indeed a married man, with family.

Paul and His Letters

Peter and Paul were contemporaries.[2] We know far more about Paul than we do about Peter—not only because of what Luke writes about Paul in the Acts of the Apostles but also, and especially, because of what he himself has written in letters to various churches. The letters are revealing in many different ways. One thing they reveal is that their author was a faithful Jew—a trait confirmed by Luke in Acts—whose *Weltanschaung*, his overall view of reality, was colored not only by his belief in Jesus as Lord but also by a conviction that Jesus was to appear, as Christ and Lord, in the not-too-distant future.[3]

This future appearance of Jesus, the Parousia, provided a Christian slant for Paul's apocalyptic Judaism. The world to come would feature the presence of Jesus as Lord. The expectation of an imminent end-time— "the appointed time has grown short," he writes to the Corinthians (1 Cor 7:29)—provides an eschatological lens through which Paul's letters must be seen if they are to be understood.

About a quarter of a century after Jesus' death and resurrection some members of the Church of God at Corinth wrote a letter to Paul in which they mentioned an idea that so troubled them that they wanted Paul's clarification. The troubling thought was that "it is well for a man not to touch a woman" (1 Cor 7:1). Some people in their community had apparently adopted this as a supposedly Christian principle. It may be that this came from a misunderstanding of Paul's message about the world to come. If the time was as short as Paul implied, if the end times already impinged upon their existence, then marriage and sex were out of the question for a believer.

In the seventh chapter of his First Letter to the Corinthians, Paul gives a detailed response to the concern that the troubled Corinthians had voiced. Far from being the sexual ascetic that many of our contemporaries see him to be, Paul was a realist with regard to human sexuality. He realized that sexual passions were strong, so his first bit of advice was that people should be married. Each man should have his own wife and each woman should have her own husband.[4] He goes on to say that sexual intercourse belongs to the reality of marriage and that each of the spouses owes to the other the satisfaction of her or his sexual needs.

---

[2] Cf. 1 Cor 9:5; Gal 2:7-14.
[3] Cf. 1 Thess 4:15, 17.
[4] Cf. 1 Cor 7:2.

Abstinence from marital intercourse can be allowed but only on the fulfillment of three conditions—namely, (1) that the purpose of the time of abstinence be prayer, (2) that the partners mutually agree to the abstinence, and (3) that the period of abstinence be for a relatively short period of time, after which they should resume a normal marital life. In setting down these conditions, Paul anticipates three ideas that will later be found in rabbinic texts. At bottom, Paul's ideas on the reality of marriage derive from his Jewish culture.

Jewish rabbis allowed for a short period in which a man might not have sexual intercourse with his wife. They accepted the possibility that sometimes a man's occupation might require a physical separation from his wife but they did not want this period of time to be unduly prolonged. It was to be as short as possible. Some rabbis raised the issue of a period of physical separation for the sake of prayer, accepting its legitimacy on the condition of spousal agreement.

The advice on marriage and marital intercourse in 1 Corinthians 7 that reflects the Jewish matrix of Paul's thought is primarily addressed to married couples. "Let each one remain in the condition in which you were called"[5] is a principle that comes repeatedly to the fore in the chapter. If couples are married, then they should continue to live and act as married couples. The coming of the eschaton and their call to be believers should not deter them from the way of life that had been theirs when they were called. Eschatological enthusiasm should not put them in a situation where they might be tempted by Satan.

Paul's words of advice were directed to the community at large whose members were married. The apostle made no special provisions for the leadership of the community, those who exercised the charisms about which he writes in chapters 12 and 14 of the letter. At no point does he suggest that these charismatic leaders forgo sexual intercourse with their spouses.

Paul's advice to those not yet married continues to be formulated in the light of the "remain in the condition in which you were called" principle. It is well, the apostle writes to virgins, the nonmarried, to remain as they are.[6] It is his own bit of advice. He acknowledges that he has no commandment of the Lord in this regard.[7]

---

[5] Cf. 1 Cor 7:17, 20, 24.
[6] Cf. 1 Cor 7:26.
[7] Cf. 1 Cor 7:25.

Paul's advice stems from his opinion about the impending crisis, the eschaton, which he expects to occur in a relatively short period of time. Paul does not enter into details but the Jewish matrix of his thoughts on marriage and sexuality suggest that the imminent eschaton would render marriage and the exercise of sexual intercourse within marriage as socially unfruitful. The impending crisis would not allow for any children to be born of the marriage to grow to adulthood, when they could become responsible members of society.

Paul does not say that his advice to those not yet married, the *parthenoi*, as he calls them, is specifically directed to those charismatically called to leadership within the community. His words about remaining in the condition in which they were called—meaning their not-yet-married situation—are his words of advice for all not yet married believers in the community at Corinth.

Even in face of the impending eschaton, marriage is not to be considered a sin. Passions may be strong and sexual immorality is to be resolutely avoided. Therefore, Paul suggests that a remark he addressed "to the unmarried and widows" is applicable to the not yet married as well. "It is better to marry than to be aflame with passion"[8] is a realistic principle for all to follow. Nevertheless, says Paul, in the relatively short time remaining before the eschaton, someone who marries does well but the person who refrains from marriage will do better.

The eschatological perspective that, along with a Jewish understanding of marriage, dominates Paul's thought on marriage and sexuality, leads him to convey a sense of eschatological urgency as he writes, "Let even those who have wives be as though they had none, and those who mourn as though they were not mourning, and those who rejoice as though they were not rejoicing, and those who buy as though they had no possessions, and those who deal with the world as though they had no dealings with it" (1 Cor 7:29-31). As is often the case with many of the New Testament's eschatological sayings, the saying is tinged with a bit of hyperbole. Earlier in his letter Paul had reminded his addressees that they lived in this world and that they were not to take the advice of a previous letter as if it meant that they had to leave this world.[9]

[8] Cf. 1 Cor 7:8.
[9] Cf. 1 Cor 5:10.

Were the apostle's addressees not to mourn with those wept and not to rejoice with those who were rejoicing, not to buy things that were needed and have no dealings with the world, indeed, were they not to marry at all, they would have to leave the world. It was not Paul's intention that the believers in Corinth should leave this world. Mourning and weeping, buying and dealing with the world, and marrying were the way that the believer was to live until the end time. Indeed, in what may have been the last of his extant letters, Paul told God's holy people in Rome, "Rejoice with those who rejoice, weep with those who weep,"[10] These words would be utter nonsense were 1 Corinthians 7:29-31 to be anything other than the hyperbolic, eschatologically phrased challenge that it is.

As for Paul himself, it is likely that he heeded his own advice. As a faithful and zealous Jew of the Pharisaic persuasion, he would have heeded God's command to be fruitful and multiply. His zeal for the Law would not have allowed him to refrain from marrying. That he was once married is implicitly confirmed in 1 Corinthians 7 when Paul compares himself not to the not yet married, the *parthenoi*, but to those who had once married but no longer were, the *agamoi kai chērai*, the unmarried and widows.

Paul would not remarry for the end was at hand, the time was short. Another comparison between himself and others that the apostle makes confirms his unmarried status at the time that he wrote to the Corinthians. Speaking of the rights that he was willing to forgo, among which was his right to receive financial support from the Corinthians, Paul asks a pertinent rhetorical question, "Do we not have the right to be accompanied by a believing wife, as do the other apostles and the brothers of the Lord and Cephas?"[11]

The negatively phrased rhetorical question posed by one who was a master of rhetoric demanded an affirmative response. No one had to speak the answer aloud but all who listened to the reading of Paul's letter knew that he was affirming his right to be accompanied by a believing woman as his wife. He had the same rights as the other apostles and brothers of the Lord, the same rights as Peter who did not fail to avail himself of the use of his rights.

[10] Cf. Rom 12:15.
[11] Cf. 1 Cor 9:5.

The Pastoral Epistles

It has been said that the Pastoral Epistles are key to an understanding of the origins of the discipline of priestly continence from which the Western discipline of clerical celibacy has emerged.[12] There are three pertinent texts—namely, those in which a bishop is required to be "married only once" (1 Tim 3:2), a deacon is required to be "married only once" (1 Tim 3:12), and an elder to be named bishop was required to be "married only once" (Titus 1:6).

The Fathers of the Church and the early decretalists considered 1 Timothy and Titus to have been written by the apostle Paul whose name they bear. Contemporary biblical scholars, however, consider the texts to have been written under Paul's aegis in an attempt to show that the apostle's teaching was relevant for an age different from the one in which he lived. They suppose a situation different from those that the apostle encountered at Corinth and elsewhere. While their primary purpose may have been to retain the doctrinal purity of Paul's teaching even as it was being actualized in a new situation, a purpose of almost equal importance was their concern for the organization and good reputation of believing communities in the Greco-Roman world toward the end of the first century CE.

In order that this latter purpose be fulfilled, 1 Timothy and Titus set out the qualities that the leaders of the church, primarily the top-tiered leaders who served as overseers or supervisors (*episkopoi*), should have. Those who assisted in church leadership, the servers (*diakonoi*), were expected to have similar qualities. These qualities were set down in lists that resemble the catalogues of virtues and vices created by the philosophic moralists of the day. Such lists were used to encourage people to live a life of virtue and eschew a life of vice. In effect, they served as a standard of what was considered upright and respectable behavior.

It is likely that the Epistle to Titus was written before the First Letter to Timothy. Its author created his own version of the popular list in order to say that any elder to be considered for appointment as an overseer of a community of believers should be a person who was deemed respectable in the social world of Greco-Roman society. Any idea of an imminent Parousia, so important for Paul, was no longer on his horizon. His hori-

---

[12] See Heid, *Celibacy in the Early Church*, 40.

zon was less temporal[13] than it was social; he was concerned that others look upon the community of believers and find a group of people that they could respect.

They should be able to find as their leader a person who was above reproach. As the author of Titus spells out, the implications of the leader of the community being above reproach, the first thing that he specifies is that an elder who was eligible for an appointment as an *episkopos* should be married only once (Titus 1:6). In similar fashion, the author of 1 Timothy specifies that the *episkopos* should be married only once (1 Tim 3:2). The requirement that a server or assistant be married only once (1 Tim 3:12) is buried further down on the list of qualifications that a server should have, but a closer look at the text reveals that the author has divided the list of qualifications into two groups and that he be married only once heads up the second part of the list.

There are two important issues to be considered with regard to the Pastorals' "married only once"—*mias gynaikas anēr* in Greek and *unius uxoris vir* in the Latin Vulgate and subsequent Western discussion. These are, respectively, the obligatory nature of the requirement and the specific meaning of the wording.

As for the obligatory nature of the requirement, all three texts that use the expression speak of the requirement as something that is mandatory. There are no conditions attached. It is no more optional for the leader of the community to be married only once than it is optional for him to be a lover of goodness (Titus 1:8) or an apt teacher (1 Tim 3:2). Any attempt to introduce conditions, as if the text read, "if he is married, he should be 'married only once,'" is an example of eisegeis, reading into the text something that is not there.

The second issue that warrants consideration is the meaning of the "married only once" phrase, three words in English, three words in the original Greek, and three words in the Western (Latin) interpretive tradition of the Greek. The Greek is somewhat more ambivalent than is the English-language translation, "married only once." The Greek actually

---

[13] The point should not be pushed overly far. Although the idea of an imminent Parousia is not found in the Pastoral Epistles, their author(s) use the language of appearance (*epiphaneia*) in such a way that the existence of a believing community is situated between two appearances of the Lord Jesus Christ. The texts attest to a hope in a future appearance but give no indication that this future appearance is in the proximate future.

reads "a one-woman man." Such a rendering of the text points more readily to the problem of interpretation than does "married only once."

What does it mean to be a "one-woman man" in a society where the Greek *gynē*, meaning "woman," can specifically and in context mean "wife"? Does the requirement that a leader of the Church be a "one-woman man" mean that he should have but a single wife during the course of his life even if he had divorced his wife or she him, or his wife had predeceased him? Does the requirement of being a "one-woman man" mean that he should not take a second woman as wife while the first is still living, thus avoiding bigamy? Or does the requirement of being a "one-woman man" mean that he does not have another woman or other women on the side?

From a purely linguistic point of view the three-word expression, *mias gynaikas anēr* phrase, variously translated as *"unius uxoris vir"* and as "married only once," admits of all three interpretations. The interpreter must turn to the context of the expression in order to ascertain what the expression means. The narrow literary context is clear enough. It is a catalogue of virtues.

Broader contexts must therefore be taken into consideration. In an ever-widening circle, these broader contexts are (1) the teaching of the Pastorals on marriage, (2) the legacy of Paul on marriage and sexual immorality, and (3) the social situation in which not only Paul wrote his authentic epistles but also the social situation of those who wrote in his name. When these several factors are taken into consideration the requirement that a leader of the church be married only once means that he be married and that he remain faithful to his wife.

Unfortunately—at least from a contemporary perspective—the author(s) of the Pastorals does not use the specific language of marriage, the root *gam-*, in setting down the requirement. Had he done so and explicitly stated that a leader of the Church who had lost his wife through death should adopt a countercultural approach and not remarry after the loss of his wife, we would know that he meant to exclude a second marriage. But Paul allows for the possibility of a second marriage after the death of a spouse. And 1 Timothy not only allows but urges the remarriage of a young widow. Accordingly, the wider context of the "married only once" precludes the possibility that it bans a lifestyle that Paul had allowed.

Had the author(s) of the Pastorals used the specific language of marriage, with words derived from the root *gam-*, we would have known that he was speaking about marriage and not about a Platonic relationship with the woman to whom the community leader was once married.

Absent the use of specific marital language, the "married only once" requirement of Titus 1:6 and 1 Timothy 3:2, 12 means that Church leaders were required to be married and that they be faithful to their respective spouses. The Pastorals codified, as it were, the social requirement of Jesus' first disciples who heeded the Lord's command to "be fruitful and multiply." This allowed them to have their wives at their side as they led the church and proclaimed the Gospel of salvation.

Bibliography

General Bibliography

Aasgaard, Reider. *"My Beloved Brothers and Sisters!" Christian Siblingship in Paul.* ECC 285. London: T&T Clark, 2005.

Abegg, Martin, Jr., Peter Flinch, and Eugene Ulrich. *The Dead Sea Scrolls Bible: The Oldest Known Bible Translated into English for the First Time.* San Francisco: Harper, 1999.

Anderson, R. Dean, Jr. *Glossary of Greek Rhetorical Terms: Connected to Methods of Argumentation, Figures and Tropes from Anaximenes to Quintilian.* CBET 24. Leuven: Peeters, 2000.

Arens, Eduardo. "Was Paul Married?" *TBT* 66 (1973): 1188–91.

Arichea, Daniel C., and Howard A. Hatton. *A Handbook on Paul's Letters to Timothy and Titus.* UBS Handbook Series. New York: United Bible Societies, 1995.

Audet, Jean Paul. *Mariage et célibat dans le service de l'Église: Histoire et orientations.* Paris: Éditions de l'Orante, 1967.

Avery-Peck, Alan J., Jacob Neusner, and Bruce Chilton, eds. *Judaism in Late Antiquity, 5: The Judaism of Qumran: A Systematic Reading of the Dead Sea Scrolls, 1: Theory of Israel.* Leiden: Brill, 2000.

Baer, Richard L. *Philo's Use of the Categories Male and Female.* ALGHJ 3. Leiden: Brill, 1970.

Bailey, Kenneth E. *Paul through Mediterranean Eyes: Cultural Studies in 1 Corinthians.* Downers Grove, IL: Inter Varsity Press Academic, 2011.

Barbero, Mario. "A First-Century Couple, Priscilla and Aquila: Their House Churches and Missionary Activity." PhD thesis. The Catholic University of America, Washington, DC, 2001.

Bartchy, S. Scott. MAΛΛON XPHSAI: *First-Century Slavery and the Interpretation of 1 Corinthians 7:21.* SBLDS 11. Missoula, MT: Scholars Press, 1971.

Bassler, Jouette M. "Limits and Differentiation: The Calculus of Widows in 1 Timothy 5:3-16." In Levine and Blickenstaff, *A Feminist Companion to the Deutero-Pauline Epistles,* 122–46.

Bauckham, Richard. *Gospel Women: Studies of the Named Women in the Gospels.* Grand Rapids, MI: Eerdmans, 2002.

Beker, J. Christiaan. *Heirs of Paul: Paul's Legacy in the New Testament and in the Church Today*. Minneapolis: Fortress, 1991.

Beker, Klaus M. *Der Zölibats des Priesters*. Sein und Sendung, 9. St. Otilien: EOS Verlag 1995.

Bernstein, Moshe J. "Women and Children in Legal and Liturgical Texts from Qumran." *DSD* 11 (2004): 191–211.

The Biblical Foundations of the Doctrine of Justification: An Ecumenical Follow-Up to the Joint Declaration on the Doctrine of Justification. Mahwah, NJ: Paulist, 2012.

Bieringer, Reimund, ed. *The Corinthian Correspondence*. BETL 125. Leuven: University Press / Peeters, 1996

Biondi, Biondo. *Storia di Roma*, 20: *Il Diritto Romano*. Bologna: Licinio Cappelli, 1957.

Birge, Mary K. *The Language of Belonging: A Rhetorical Analysis of Kinship Language in First Corinthians*. CBET 31. Leuven: Peeters, 2004.

Blenkinsopp, Joseph. "The Family in First Temple Israel." In Perdue, *Families in Ancient Israel*, 48–103.

Blinzler, Josef. "*Eisin eunouchoi:* Zur Auslegung von Mt. 19, 12." *ZNW* 48 (1957): 254–70; revised and, with additional bibliographic note, reprinted as "Zur Ehe unfaähig . . ."—Auslegung von Mt 19, 12." In idem. *Aus der Welt und Umwelt des Neuen Testaments. Gesammelte Aufsätze*. Stuttgart: Katholisches Bibelwerk, 1969, 20–40.

———. "Justinus Apol. I 15, 4 und Matthäus 19, 11–12." In *Mélanges bibliques en hommage au R. P. Béda Rigaux*, edited by Albert M. Descamps and André de Halleux. Gembloux: Duculot, 1970, 45–55.

Blue, Bradley B. "The House Church at Corinth and the Lord's Supper: Famine, Food Supply and the *Present Distress*." *CTR* 5 (1991): 221–39.

Bockmuehl, Markus. *Simon Peter in Scripture and Memory: The New Testament Apostle in the Early Church*. Grand Rapids, MI: Baker Academic, 2012.

Bond, Helen K. "Gamaliel." *NIDB* 2, 520.

Borg, Marcus J., and John Dominic Crossan. *The First Paul: Reclaiming the Radical Visionary behind the Church's Conservative Icon*. New York: Harper One, 2009.

Boyarin, Daniel. *Carnal Israel: Reading Sex in Talmudic Culture*. Berkeley: University of California Press, 1993.

———. *Dying for God: Martyrdom and the Making of Christianity and Judaism*. Stanford, CA: Stanford University Press, 1999.

Boyle, Isaac. *The Ecclesiastical History of Eusebius Pamphilius*. Grand Rapids, MI: Baker Book House, 1988.

Bray, Gerald. *1–2 Corinthians*. ACCS. New Testament 7. Downers Grove, IL: Inter Varsity Press, 1999.

Breck, John. "Theoria and Orthodox Hermeneutics." *SVTQ* 20 (1976): 195–219.

Brooks, Stephenson H. *Matthew's Community: The Evidence of His Special Sayings Material*. JSNTSup. Sheffield: JSOT, 1987.

Brown, Jeannine K. *The Disciples in Narrative Perspective: The Portrayal and Function of the Matthean Disciples.* Atlanta: Society of Biblical Literature, 2002.

Brown, Peter. *The Body and Society: Men, Women and Sexual Renunciation in Early Christianity.* Lectures on the History of Religions, N.S. 13. New York: Columbia University Press, 1988.

Brown, Raymond E. *The Community of the Beloved Disciple.* New York: Paulist, 1979.

———. *An Introduction to the Gospel of John.* Edited by Francis J. Moloney. ABRL. New York: Doubleday, 2003.

Broyde, Michael J., and Michael Ausubel, eds. *Marriage, Sex, and Family in Judaism.* Lanham, MD: Rowman & Littlefield, 2005.

Brunt, P. A., and J. M. Moore. *Res Gestae Divi Augusti: The Achievements of the Divine Augustus.* London: Oxford University Press, 1967.

Caird, G. B. *The Language and Imagery of the Bible.* London: Duckworth, 1980.

Campbell, Ken M., ed. *Marriage and Family in the Biblical World.* Downers Grove, IL: Inter Varsity Press, 2003.

Caragounis, Chrys C. " 'Fornication' and 'Concession'? Interpreting 1 Cor 7:1-7." in Bieringer, *Corinthian Correspondence*, 543–59.

Casalini, Nello. "Corpus pastorale—Corpus constitutionale (La costituzione della chiesa nelle Pastorali)." *SBFLA* 57 (2007): 253–315.

Chapman, David W. "Marriage and Family in Second Temple Judaism." In Campbell, *Marriage and Family*, 182–240.

Charlesworth, James H. *The Beloved Disciple: Whose Witness Validates the Gospel of John?* Valley Forge, PA: Trinity Press International, 1995.

Chilton, Bruce D., and Jacob Neusner. "Paul and Gamaliel." In *In Quest of the Historical Pharisees*, edited by Jacob Neusner and Bruce D. Chilton, 175–223. Waco, TX: Baylor University Press, 2007.

Cholij, Roman. *Clerical Celibacy in East and West.* 2nd ed. Leominster: Gracewing, 1990.

Church, F. Forrester, and Timothy George, eds. *Continuity and Discontinuity in Church History: Essays Presented to George Huntston Williams on the Occasion of his 65th Birthday.* Studies in the History of Christian Thought 19. Leiden: Brill, 1979.

Cochini, Christian. *Apostolic Origins of Priestly Celibacy.* San Francisco: Ignatius Press, 1990; *Origines apostolique du célibat sacerdotal.* Paris: Lethielleux, 1981.

Cohen, Jeremy. *"Be Fertile and Increase, Fill the Earth and Master It": The Ancient and Medieval Career of a Biblical Text.* Ithaca, NY: Cornell University Press, 1989.

Cohick, Lynn H. *Women in the World of the Earliest Christians: Illuminating Ancient Ways of Life.* Grand Rapids, MI: Baker Academic, 2009.

Collins, John J. (Jesuit scholar). "Chiasmus, the 'ABA' Pattern and the Text of Paul." In *Studiorum paulinorum congressus internationalis catholicus*, 2. AnBib 19. Rome: Pontifical Biblical Institute, 1961, 575–84.

Collins, John J. (Yale professor). "Marriage, Divorce, and Family in Second Temple Judaism." In Perdue, *Families in Ancient Israel*, 104–161.

————. *Beyond the Qumran Community: The Sectarian Movement of the Dead Sea Scrolls*. Grand Rapids, MI: Eerdmans, 2010.

Collins, Raymond F. *The Birth of the New Testament: The Origin and Development of the First Christian Generation*. New York: Crossroad, 1993.

————. *Divorce in the New Testament*. GNS 38. Collegeville, MN: Liturgical Press, 1992.

————. "From *Parousia* to *Epiphaneia*: The Transformation of a Motif." In *Unity and Diversity in the Gospels and Paul: Essays in Honor of Frank J. Matera*, edited by Kelly Iverson and Christopher W. Skinner. Early Christianity and Its Literature 7. Atlanta: Society of Biblical Literature, 2012, 273–99.

————. "How Not to Behave in the Household of God." *LS* 35 (2011): 7–31.

————. *Introduction to the New Testament*. New York: Doubleday / London: SCM, 1983.

————. *Letters That Paul Did Not Write: The Epistle to the Hebrews and the Pauline Pseudepigrapha*. GNS 28. Wilmington, DE: Glazier, 1988.

————. "Obedience, Children and the Fourth Commandment—A New Testament Note." *LS* 4 (1972–73): 157–73.

————. "Ordination, Ordain." *NIDB* 4, 339–40.

————. "The Origins of Church Law." *The Jurist* 61 (2001): 134–56.

————. "Paul's Damascus Experience: Reflections on the Lukan Account." *LS* 11 (1986): 99–118.

————. *Sexual Ethics and the New Testament: Behavior and Belief*. Companions to the New Testament. New York: Crossroad, 2000.

————. "A Significant Decade: The Trajectory of the Hellenistic Epistolary Thanksgiving." In *Paul and the Ancient Letter Form*, edited by Stanley E. Porter and Sean A. Adams. Pauline Studies (Past 6). Leiden: Brill, 2010, 159–84.

————. *Studies on the First Letter to the Thessalonians*. BETL 66. Leuven: University Press / Peeters, 1984.

————. " 'This Is the Will of God: Your Sanctification,' (1 Thess 4:3)." *Laval théologique et philosophique* 39 (1983): 27–53.

————. "The Transformation of a Motif: 'They Entered the House of Simon and Andrew' (Mark 1, 29)." SNTSU 18 (1993): 5–40.

————. "The Unity of Paul's Paraenesis in 1 Thess. 4.3-8: 1 Cor. 7.1-7, A Significant Parallel." *NTS* 29 (1983): 420–29.

Constas, Nicholas. *Proclus of Constantinople and the Cult of the Virgin: Homilies 1–5 Texts and Translations*. VCSup 66. Leiden: Brill, 2003.

Conway, Colleen M. "Beloved Disciple." *NIDB* 1, 422–23.

Coppens, Joseph, ed. *Priesthood and Celibacy*. Milan-Rome: Ancora, 1972.

Crouzel, Henri. "Celibacy and Ecclesiastical Continence in the Early Church: The Motives Involved." In Coppens, *Priesthood and Celibacy*, 451–502.

Cullmann, Oscar. *Peter, Disciple, Apostle, Martyr: A Historical and Theological Study*. Philadelphia: Fortress, 1953.

Culpepper, R. Alan. *John the Son of Zebedee: The Life of a Legend.* Studies on Personalities of the New Testament. Columbia, SC: University of South Carolina Press, 1994.

Danby, Herbert. *The Mishnah translated from the Hebrew with Introduction and Brief Explanatory Notes.* London: Oxford University Press, 1933.

Davies, Margaret. *The Pastoral Epistles.* New Testament Guides. Sheffield, UK: Sheffield Academic, 1996.

DeConick, April D. *Holy Misogyny: Why the Sex and Gender Conflicts in the Early Church Still Matter.* New York: Continuum, 2011.

Deming, Will. *Paul on Marriage and Celibacy: The Hellenistic Background of 1 Corinthians 7.* 2nd ed. Grand Rapids, MI: Eerdmans 2004.

Denaux, Albert, ed. *New Testament Textual Criticism and Exegesis: Festschrift Joel Delobel.* BETL 161. Leuven: Leuven University Press / Peeters, 2002.

Descamps, Albert M., and André de Halleux. *Mélanges bibliques en homage au R. P. Béda Rigaux.* Gembloux: Duculot, 1970.

Diamond, Eliezer. "'And Jacob Remained Alone': The Jewish Struggle with Celibacy." In *Celibacy and Religious Traditions,* edited by Carl Olson, 41–64. New York: Oxford University Press, 2008.

Dimant, Devorah, and Uriel Rappaport, eds. *The Dead Sea Scrolls: Forty Years of Research.* STDJ, 10. Leiden: Brill/Jerusalem: Magnes Press and Yad Ben Zvi, 1992.

Donahue, John R. *The Theology and Setting of Discipleship in the Gospel of Mark: The 1983 Père Marquette Theology Lecture.* Milwaukee: Marquette University Press, 1983.

Donfried, Karl Paul, ed. *1 Timothy Reconsidered.* Colloquium Oecumenicum Paulinum 18. Leuven: Peeters, 2008.

Dorff, Elliot N. "The Jewish Family in America: Contemporary Challenges and Traditional Resources." In *Marriage, Sex, and Family in Judaism,* edited by Michael J. Broyde and Michael Ausubel, 214–43. Lanham, MD: Rowman & Littlefield, 2005.

Duval, Yves-Marie. *La décrétale Ad Gallos Episcopos: son texte et son auteur.* VCSup 73. Leiden: Brill, 2005.

Ehrman, Bart D. *The Orthodox Corruption of Scripture: The Effect of Early Christological Controversies on the Next of the New Testament.* Oxford: Oxford University Press, 1993.

Eisen, Ute E., Christine Gerber, and Angela Standhartinger, eds. *Doing Gender–Doing Religion: Fallstudien zur Intersektionalität im frühen Judentum, Christentum und Islam.* WUNT 302. Tübingen: Mohr Siebeck, 2013.

Elon, Menachem. "Bigamy and Polygamy." *EncJud*[2] 3, 691–94.

Engberg-Petersen, Troels. "Philo's *De Vita Contemplativa* as a Philosopher's Dream." *JSJ* 30 (1999): 40–64.

Epp, Eldon John. *Junia: The First Woman Apostle.* Minneapolis: Fortress, 2005.

———. "Text-Critical, Exegetical, and Socio-cultural Factors affecting the Junia/Junias Variation in Romans 16:7." In Denaux, *New Testament Textual Criticism,* 227–91.

Fascher, Erich. "Zur Witwerschaft des Paulus und der Auslegung von 1 Cor 7." *ZNW* 28 (1929): 62–65.

Feldman, Louis H. *Josephus's Interpretation of the Bible.* Berkeley: University of California Press, 1998.

Finlan, Stephen. *The Family Metaphor in Jesus' Teaching: Gospel and Ethics.* Eugene, OR: Cascade, 2009.

Fiorenza, Elisabeth Schüssler. *In Memory of Her: A Feminist Theological Reconstruction of Christian Origins.* New York: Crossroad, 1984.

Ford, Josephine Massingberd. *A Trilogy on Wisdom and Celibacy.* Cardinal O'Hara Series 4. Notre Dame, IN: University of Notre Dame Press, 1967.

Foucault, Michel. *The History of Pleasure: The History of Sexuality,* 2. New York: Vintage, 1990.

García Martínez, Florentino, and Eibert J. C. Tigchelaar. *The Dead Sea Scrolls.* 2 vols. Leiden: Brill, 1997–98.

Gardner, Jane F. *Family and* Familia *in Roman Law and Life.* Oxford: Clarendon 1998.

Gillman, Florence Morgan. *Women Who Knew Paul.* Zacchaeus Studies. Collegeville, MN: Liturgical Press, 1992.

Glasscock, Ed. " 'The Husband of One Wife' Requirement in 1 Timothy 3:2.' " *BSac* 140 (1983): 244–58.

Goodrich, John K. "Overseers as Stewards and the Qualifications for Leadership in the Pastoral Epistles." *ZNW* 104 (2013): 77–97.

Gorday, Peter. *Colossians, 1–2 Thessalonians, 1–2 Timothy, Titus, Philemon.* ACCS: New Testament 9. Downers Grove, IL: Inter Varsity Press, 2000.

Grubner, Mayer I. "Women in the Religious System of Qumran," in Avery-Peck, *Judaism in Late Antiquity,* 173–96.

Grubbs, N. C. "The Truth about Elders and Their Children: Believing or Behaving in Titus 1:6." *Faith & Mission* 22 (2009): 3–13.

Gryson, Roger. *Les Origines du célibat ecclésiastique du premier au septième siècle.* Recherches et synthèses. Section d'histoire 2. Gembloux: Duculot, 1970.

Gundry, Robert H. *The Use of the Old Testament in St. Matthew's Gospel.* NovTSup 18. Leiden: Brill, 1967.

Gundry-Volk, Judith M. "Controlling the Bodies: A Theological Profile of the Corinthian Sexual Ascetics (1 Cor 7)." In Bieringer, *Corinthian Correspondence,* 519–41.

Hamidovic, David. *"Écrit de Damas": Le manifeste des esséniens.* Collection de la Revue des Études Juives, 51. Leuven: Peeters, 2011.

Heger, Paul. "Celibacy in Qumran—Hellenistic Fiction or Reality? Qumran's Attitude Toward Sex," *RevQ* 101 (2013) 21–90.

Heid, Stefan. *Celibacy in the Early Church: The Beginning of Obligatory Continence for Clerics in East and West.* San Francisco: Ignatius Press, 2000.

———. "Grundlagen des Zölibats in der frühen Kirchen." In *Der Zölibats des Priesters,* edited by Klaus M. Beker, 51–68.

Heil, John Paul. *The Rhetorical Role of Scripture in 1 Corinthians*. Studies in Biblical Literature. Atlanta: Society of Biblical Literature, 2005.

Hemer, Colin J. *The Book of Acts in the Setting of Hellenistic History*. Edited by Conrad H. Gempf. WUNT 49. Tübingen: J. C. B. Mohr (P. Siebeck), 1989. Reprinted: Winona Lake, IN: Eisenbrauns, 1990.

Hengel, Martin. *Saint Peter: The Underestimated Apostle*. Grand Rapids, MI: Eerdmans 2010.

Herzer, Jens. "Abschied von Konsens? Die Pseudepigraphie der Pastoralbriefe als Herausforderung an die neutestamentliche Wissenschaft." *TLZ* 129 (2004): 1267–82.

———. "Rearranging the 'House of God': A New Perspective on the Pastoral Epistles." In Houtman, *Empsychoi Logoi*, 547–66.

Hezser, Catherine. "Part Whore, Part Wife: Slave Women in the Palestinian Rabbinic Tradition." In *Doing Gender-Doing Religion: Fallstudien zur Intersektionalität im frühen Judentum, Christentum und Islam*, edited by Ute E. Eisen, Christine Gerber, and Angela Standhartinger, 303–23. WUNT 302. Tübingen: Mohr Siebeck, 2013.

Hoffius, Otto. "Die Ordination zum Amt der Kirche und die apostolische Sukkession nach dem Zeugnis der Pastoralbriefe." *ZTK* 107 (2010): 261–84.

Holland, Glenn. "Celibacy in the Early Christian Church." In *Celibacy and Religious Traditions*, edited by Carl Olson, 65–84. New York / Oxford: Oxford University Press, 2008.

Holmes, Michael W. *The Apostolic Fathers in English*. 3rd ed. Grand Rapids, MI: Baker Academic, 2006.

Horrell, David G. "Disciplining Performance and 'Placing' the Church: Widows, Elders and Slaves in the Household of God (1 Tim 5, 1-6, 2)." In Donfried, *1 Timothy Reconsidered*, 109–34.

———. "From *adelphoi* to *oikos theou*." *JBL* 120 (2001): 293–311.

Horsley, Richard A. "Spiritual Marriage with Sophia." *VC* 33 (1979): 30–54.

Houtman, Alberdina, et al., eds. *Empsychoi Logoi*—Religious Innovations in Antiquity: *Studies in Honour of Pieter Willem van der Horst*. Ancient Judaism and Early Christianity 73. Leiden: Brill, 2008.

Hübner, Hans. "Zölibat in Qumran?" *NTS* 17 (1971): 153–67.

Hunt, Arthur Surridge, and Josiah Gilbart Smyly. *The Tebtunis Papyri*. London: Oxford University Press, 1933.

Hunter, David G. "Clerical Marriage and Episcopal Elections." In *Episcopal Elections in Late Antiquity*, edited by Johan Leemans, Peter Van Nuffelen, Shawn W. J. Keough, and Carla Nicolaye. Berlin: De Gruyter, 2011, 183–202.

———. *Marriage, Celibacy, and Heresy in Ancient Christianity: The Jovinianist Controversy*. Oxford Early Christian Studies. Oxford: Oxford University Press, 2007.

Irmscher, Johanne, and Georg Strecker. "The Pseudo-Clementines." In Schneemelcher, *New Testament Apocrypha*, vol. 2, 483–541.

Iverson, Kelly, and Christopher Skinner, eds., *Unity and Diversity in the Gospels and Paul: Essays in Honor of Frank J. Matera*. Early Christianity and its Literature 7. Atlanta: Society of Biblical Literature, 2012.

Jenkins, Claude. "Origen on I Corinthians." *JTS* 9 (1908): 231–47.

———. "Origen on I Corinthians. III." *JTS* 9 (1908): 500–514.

Jeremias, Joachim. "Nochmals: War Paulus Witwer?" *ZNW* 28 (1929): 321–23.

———. "War Paulus Witwer?" *ZNW* 25 (1926): 310–12.

Johnson, Luke Timothy. *The Literary Function of Possessions in Luke—Acts*. SBLDS 39. Missoula, MT: Scholars Press, 1977.

Käsemann, Ernst. *Perspectives on Paul*. NTL. Philadelphia; Fortress, 1971.

———. "The Theological Problem Presented by the Motif of the Body of Christ." In idem. *Perspectives on Paul*. NTL. Philadelphia; Fortress, 1971, 102–21.

Keener, Craig S. *Paul, Women and Wives: Marriage and Women's Ministry in the Letters of Paul*. Peabody, MA: Hendrickson, 1992.

Keller, Marie Noël Keller. *Priscilla and Aquila: Paul's Coworkers in Christ Jesus*. Paul's Social Network: Brothers and Sisters in Christ. Collegeville, MN: Liturgical Press, 2010.

Kodell, Jerome. "The Celibacy Logion in Matthew 19:12." *BTB* 8 (1978): 19–23.

Koester, Helmut. "I Thessalonians—Experiment in Christian Writing." In Church, *Continuity and Discontinuity in Church History*, 34–44.

Koltun-Fromm, Naomi. *Hermeneutics of Holiness: Ancient Jewish and Christian Notions of Sexuality and Religious Community*. Oxford: Oxford University Press, 2010.

Koperski, Veronica. "Women in Romans." In Schnelle, *Letter to the Romans*, 441–51.

Koskenniemi, Heikki. *Studien zur Idee und Phraseologie des griechischen Briefes bis 400 n. Chr*. Annales Academicae scientiarum Fennicae. Series B, 102, 2. Helsinki: Suomalaisen Tiedeakatemia, 1956.

Kovacs, Judith L. *1 Corinthians Interpreted by Early Christian Commentators*. The Church's Bible. Grand Rapids, MI: Eerdmans, 2005.

Kraemer, Ross Shepherd. *Unreliable Witnesses: Religion, Gender, and History in the Greco-Roman Mediterranean*. New York / Oxford: Oxford University Press, 2011.

Launderville, Dale. *Celibacy in the Ancient World: Its Ideal and Practice in Pre-Hellenistic Israel, Mesopotamia, and Greece*. Collegeville, MN: Liturgical Press, 2010.

Légasse, Simon. *Paul Apôtre: Essai de biographie critique*. Paris: Cerf/Fides, 1991.

Legrand, Lucien. "St. Paul and Celibacy." In Coppens, *Priesthood and Celibacy*, 427–50.

Lenchak, T. "What's Biblical about . . . Celibacy?" *TBT* 48 (2010): 41–42.

Levine, Amy-Jill, and Marianne Blickenstaff, eds. *A Feminist Companion to the Deutero-Pauline Epistles*. Cleveland: Pilgrim Press, 2003.

Lightman, Majorie, and William Zeisel. "Univira: An Example of Continuity and Change in Roman Society." *CH* 46 (1977): 19–32.

Liotta, Filippo. *La Continenza di Chierici nel pensiero canonistico classico (da Graziano a Gregorio IX)*. Quaderni di Studi Senesi 24. Milan: Gioffrè, 1971.

Lippert, Peter. *Leben als Zeugnis: Die werbender Kraft christlicher Lebensfuhrung nach dem kirchenverstandnis neuetestamentlicher Briefe*. SBM 4. Stuttgart: Katholisches Biblewerk, 1968.

Loader, William. *The Dead Sea Scrolls on Sexuality: Attitudes towards Sexuality in Sectarian and Related Literature at Qumran*. Grand Rapids, MI: Eerdmans, 2009.

———. *Philo, Josephus, and the Testaments on Sexuality: Attitudes towards Sexuality in the Writings of Philo and Josephus and in the Testaments of the Twelve Patriarchs*. Grand Rapids, MI: Eerdmans, 2011.

———. *The Pseudepigrapha on Sexuality: Attitudes towards Sexuality in Apocalypses, Testaments, Legends, Wisdom and Related Literature*. Grand Rapids, MI: Eerdmans, 2011.

———. *Sexuality and the Jesus Tradition*. Grand Rapids, MI: Eerdmans, 2005.

———. *Sexuality in the New Testament: Understanding the Key Texts*. Louisville: Westminster John Knox, 2010.

Malul, Meir. *Knowledge, Control and Sex: Studies in Biblical Thought, Culture and Worldview*. Tel-Aviv/Jaffa: Archeological Center Publications, 2002.

Marguerat, Daniel. "L'Esprit de famille: un parcours matthéen." In Van Oyen and Wénin, *La Surprise dans la bible*, 157–75.

Marín, Francisco. "Un ricurso obligado a la tradición presinóptica." *EstBib* 36 (1977): 205–16.

Marucci, Corrado. *Parole di Gesù sul divorzio: ricerche scritturistiche previa ad un risonsamento teologico, canonistico e pastorale della dottrina cattolica dell' indissolubilità del matrimonio*. Aolisiana 16. Naples: Morelliana, 1982.

Matta, Yara. *À cause du Christ. Le retournement de Paul le Juif*. LD 256. Paris: Cerf, 2013.

Matthews, Christopher R. *Philip, Apostle and Evangelist: Configurations of a Tradition*. NovTSup. 105. Leiden: Brill, 2002.

McArthur, Harvey. "Celibacy in Judaism at the Time of Christian Beginnings." AUSS 25 (1987): 163–81.

Meier, John P. *A Marginal Jew: Rethinking the Historical Jesus*, 1: *The Roots of the Problem and the Person*. ABRL. New York: Doubleday, 1991.

———. *A Marginal Jew: Rethinking the Historical Jesus*, 3: *Companions and Competitors*. ABRL. New York: Doubleday, 2001.

Menoud, Philippe-H. "Mariage et célibat selon saint Paul." *RTP* 1 (1951): 21–34.

Metzger, Bruce M. *A Textual Commentary on the Greek New Testament*. 2nd ed. Stuttgart: Deutsche Bibelgesellschaft / United Bible Societies, 1994.

Mitchell, Margaret M. "*PTebt* 703 and the Genre of 1 Timothy: The Curious Career of a Ptolemaic Papyrus in Pauline Scholarship." *NovT* 45 (2002): 344–70.

Molinari, Andrea Lorenzo. "*I Never Knew the Man*": *The Coptic Acts of Peter (Papyrus Berolinensis 8502.4), Genre and Legendary Origins*. BCNH. Sect. Ét. 5. Quebec: Laval University Press—Leuven: Peeters, 2000.

———. "Women Martyrs in the Early Church: Hearing Another Side to the Story." *Priscilla Papers* 22 (2008): 5–10.

Moloney, Francis J. *Disciples and Prophets. A Biblical Model for the Religious Life*. London: Darton, Longman and Todd, 1980.

———. *"A Hard Saying": The Gospel and Culture*. Collegeville, MN: Liturgical Press, 2001.

———. *A Life of Promise: Poverty, Chastity, Obedience*. Eugene, OR: Wipf & Stock, 2001.

———. "Matthew 19:3-12 and Celibacy. A Redactional and Form Critical Study." *JSNT* 2 (1979): 42–60.

———. *Mark: Storyteller, Interpreter, Evangelist*. Peabody, MA: Hendrickson, 2004.

Morris, Ian, and Walter Scheidel, eds. *The Dynamics of Ancient Empires: State Power from Assyria to Byzantium*. New York: Oxford University Press, 2009.

Murphy-O'Connor, Jerome. *Keys to First Corinthians: Revisiting the Major Issues*. Oxford: Oxford University Press, 2009.

———. *Paul: A Critical Life*. Oxford: Clarendon, 1996.

Nassif, Bradley. "The 'Spiritual Exegesis' of Scripture: The School of Antioch Revisited." *ATR* 74 (1992): 437–70.

Neirynck, Frans. *Duality in Mark: Contributions to the Study of the Markan Redaction*. Leuven: Peeters-Leuven University Press, 1988.

Neusner, Jacob, and Bruce D. Chilton, eds. *In Quest of the Historical Pharisees*. Waco, TX: Baylor University Press, 2007.

Niederwimmer, Kurt. *Askese und Mysterium: Über Ehe, Ehescheidung und Eheversicht des christlichen Glaubens*. FRLANT 113. Göttingen: Vandenhoeck & Ruprecht, 1975.

Novak, David. "Jewish Marriage: Nature, Covenant and Contract." In *Marriage, Sex, and Family in Judaism*, edited by Michael J. Broyde and Michael Ausubel, 61–87. Lanham, MD: Rowman & Littlefield, 2005.

Nussbaum, Martha C. *The Theory of Desire: Theory and Practice in Hellenistic Ethics*. Princeton, NJ: Princeton University Press, 1994.

Oepke, Albrecht. "Probleme der vorchristlichen Zeit des Paulus." *TSK* 105 (1933): 387–424.

Olson, Carl, ed. *Celibacy and Religious Traditions*. New York: Oxford University Press, 2008.

Osiek, Carolyn, and David L. Balch. *Families in the New Testament*. Family, Religion and Culture. Louisville: Westminster John Knox, 1997.

Owens, M. D. "Should Churches Ordain the Divorced and Remarried? An Examination of *Mias gynaikos aner* in the Pastoral Epistles." *Faith & Mission* 22 (2005): 42–50.

Page, Sydney. "Marital Expectations of Church Leaders in the Pastoral Epistles." *JSNT* 50 (1993): 105–29.

Pasche, Boris A. "The *cura morum* of the Roman Censors as Historical Background for the Bishop and Deacon Lists of the Pastoral Epistles." *ZNW* 98 (2007): 105–19.

Perdue, Leo G., et al. *Families in Ancient Israel. The Family, Religion, and Culture.* Louisville: Westminster John Knox, 1997.

Perdue, Leo G. "The Israelite and Early Jewish Family: Summary and Conclusions." In idem, *Families in Ancient Israel,* 163–222.

Perkins, Pheme. *Peter: Apostle for the Whole Church.* Studies on Personalities of the New Testament. Columbia, SC: University of South Carolina Press, 1994.

Pesch, Rudolf. *Simon Petrus: Geschichte und geschichtliche Bedeutung des erste Jüngers Jesu Christi.* Päpste und Papstum 15. Stuttgart: Anton Hiersemann, 1980.

Pietersma, Albert, and Benjamin G. Wright, eds. *A New English Translation of the Septuagint.* Oxford: Oxford University Press, 2007.

Pomeroy, Sarah B. *Families in Classical and Hellenistic Culture: Representations and Realities.* Oxford: Clarendon, 1997.

———. *Xenophon* Oeconomicus: *A Social and Historical Commentary.* Oxford: Clarendon, 1994.

Pontifical Biblical Commission. *The Interpretation of the Bible in the Church. Origins* 23 (1994): 497, 499–524.

Quesnell, Quentin. "Made Themselves Eunuchs for the Kingdom of Heaven (Mt 19, 12)." *CBQ* 30 (1968): 335–58.

Redalié, Yann. "Come bisogna compartarsi nella casa di Dio (1 Tm 3, 11): L'etica delle lettere pastorali." *Bib* 89 (2008): 435–50.

———. *Paul après Paul: Le temps, le salut, la morale selon les épîtres à Timothée et à Tite.* Le monde de la Bible. Geneva: Labor et Fides, 1994.

Renan, Ernest. *Saint Paul.* New York: Carleton, 1869.

Robinson, James M., Paul Hoffmann, and John S. Kloppenborg, eds. *The Critical Edition of Q.* Hermeneia. Minneapolis: Fortress / Leuven: Peeters, 2000.

Roetzel, Calvin J. *Paul: The Man and the Myth.* Studies on the Personalities of the New Testament. Minneapolis: Fortress, 1999.

Rothstein, David. "Gen 24:12 and Marital Law in 4Q271:3: Exegetical Aspects and Implications." *DSD* 12 (2005): 189–204.

Rotondi, Giovanni. *Leges publicae populi Romani: Elenco cronologica con una introduzione sull' attività legislativa dei comizi romani.* Hildesheim: Georg Olms, 1966. A photographic reproduction of the 1912 Milan edition.

Sand, Alexander. *Reich Gottes und Eheverzicht imn Evangelium nach Matthäeus.* SBS 109. Stuttgart: KBW, 1983.

Satlow, Michael. *Jewish Marriage in Antiquity.* Princeton, NJ: Princeton University Press, 2001.

Schäferdiek Kurt, "The Acts of John." In Schneemelcher, *New Testament Apocrypha,* 2, 152–209.

Schechter, Solomon. *Documents of Jewish Sectaries. Edited from Hebrew Manuscripts in the Gairo Genizah Collection Now in the Possession of the University Library, Cambridge,* 1. Cambridge: University Press, 1910.

Scheidel, Walter. "Sex and Empire: A Darwinian Perspective." In *The Dynamics of Ancient Empires: State Power from Assyria to Byzantium*, edited by Ian Morris and Walter Scheidel. New York: Oxford University Press, 2009, 255–324.

———. "Monogamy and Polygyny." Princeton: Stanford Working Papers in Classics, 1999.

Schiffman, Lawrence H. "Laws Pertaining to Women in the Temple Scroll." In *The Dead Sea Scrolls: Forty Years of Research*, edited by Devorah Dimant and Uriel Rappaport. STDJ 10. Leiden: Brill / Jerusalem: Magnes Press and Yad Ben Zvi, 1992, 210–28.

Schneemelcher, Wilhelm. "The Acts of Peter" in Schneemelcher, *New Testament Apocrypha*, 2, 271–321.

———, ed. *New Testament Apocrypha, 2: Writings Related to the Apostles, Apocalypses and Related Subjects*. Rev. ed. Translated and edited by R. McL. Wilson. Louisville, Westminster John Knox, 2003.

Schnelle, Udo. *Apostle Paul: His Life and Theology*. Grand Rapids, MI: Baker Academic, 2005.

———, ed. *The Letter to the Romans*. BETL 226. Leuven: Peeters, 2009.

Schnider, Franz, and Werner Stenger. *Studien zum neutestamentlichen Briefformular*. NTTS 11. Leiden: Brill, 1987.

Schwarz, Roland. "Ordination durch Handauflegung in den Pastoralbriefen." SNTSU 35 (2010): 145–59.

Shemesh, Aharon. "4Q271.3: A Key to Sectarian Matrimonial Law." *JJS* 49 (1998): 244–63. An expanded version of Shemesh's study was published in Hebrew, in Jerusalem, in 2001.

Spencer, F. Scott. "Eunuch," *NIDB* 2, 355–56.

Stepp, Perry L. *Leadership Succession in the World of the Pauline Circle*. New Testament Monographs 5. Sheffield: Sheffield Phoenix Press, 2005.

Stickler, Alfons M. "The Evolution of the Discipline of Celibacy in the Western Church from the End of the Patristic Era to the Council of Trent." In Coppens, *Priesthood and Celibacy*, 503–97.

———. "La continenza dei Diaconi specialmente nel primo millennio della Chiesa." *Salesianum* 26 (1994): 275–302.

———. "Tratti salienti nella storia del celibato." *Sacra Doctrina* 60 (1970): 585–620.

———. *The Case for Clerical Celibacy: Its Historical Development and Theological Foundations*. San Francisco: Ignatius Press, 1995.

Swete, Henry Barclay. *Theodori episcopi mopsuesteni: In epistolas B. Pauli commentarii*, 2 vols. Cambridge: Cambridge University Press, 1880, 1882. Reprinted by Westmead, Farnborough, Hants, England: Gregg International, 1969.

Taylor, Joan E. "Philo of Alexandria on the Essenes: A Case Study on the Use of Classical Sources in Discussion of the Qumran-Essene Hypothesis." *The Studia Philonica Annual* 19 (2007): 1–28.

——. *Jewish Women Philosophers of First Century Alexandria: Philo's Therapeutae' Reconsidered*. London: Oxford University Press, 2004.

Thompson, James W. *Moral Formation according to Paul: The Context and Coherence of Pauline Ethics*. Grand Rapids, MI: Baker Academic, 2011.

Thurston, Bonnie Bowman. "1 Timothy 5:3-16 and Leadership of Women in the Early Church." In Levine and Blickenstaff, eds. *A Feminist Companion to the Deutero-Pauline Epistles*, 159–74.

——. *The Widows: A Woman's Ministry in the Early Church*. Minneapolis: Fortress, 1989.

——. *Women in the New Testament: Questions and Commentary*. Companions to the New Testament. New York: Crossroad, 1998.

Treggiari, Susan. *Roman Marriage: Iusti Conjuges from the Time of Cicero to the Time of Ulpian*. Oxford: Oxford University Press, 1991.

Trummer, Peter. "*Einehe nach den Pastoralbriefen: Zum Verständnis der Termini mias gynaikos anēr und henos andros gynē.*" *Bib* 51 (1970): 471–84.

Tucker, J. Brian. "*Remain in Your Calling*": *Paul and the Continuation of Social Identities in 1 Corinthians*. Eugene, OR: Pickwick Publications, 2011.

Van der Horst, Pieter W. "Celibacy in Early Judaism." *RB* 109 (2002): 390–402.

Van Oyen, Geert, and André Wénin, eds. *La Surprise dans la bible. Hommage à Camille Focant*. BETL 147. Leuven: Peeters, 2012.

Verner, David C. *The Household of God: The Social World of the Pastoral Epistles*. SBLDS 71. Chico, CA: Scholars Press, 1983.

Vogels, Heinz-Jürgen. *Priester dürfen heiraten: Biblische, geschichtliche und rechtliche Gründe gegen den Pflichtzölibat*. Bonn: Köllen, 1992.

Wassen, Cecilia. *Women in the Damascus Document*. SBLABib 21. Boston: Brill, 2005.

Watson, Jo-Ann Ford. "Philip." *ABD* 5, 310–12.

Wimbush, Vincent L. *Paul, the Worldly Ascetic: Response to the Lord according to 1 Corinthians 7*. Macon, GA: Mercer, 1987.

Winter, Bruce W. "1 Corinthians 7:6-7: A Caveat and a Framework for 'The Sayings' in 7:8-24." *TynBul* 48 (1997): 57–65.

——. "Secular and Christian Responses to Corinthian Famines." *TynBul* 40 (1989): 86–106.

Witherington, Ben, III. *What Have They Done with Jesus? Beyond Strange Theories and Bad History—Why We Can Trust the Bible*. Grand Rapids, MI: Eerdmans, 2004.

Wolter, Michel. *Die Pastoralbriefe als Paulustradition*. FRLANT 146. Göttingen: Vandenhoeck & Ruprecht, 1988.

Wray, T. J., and Gregory Mobley. *The Birth of Satan: Tracing the Devil's Biblical Roots*. New York: Palgrave Macmillan, 2005.

Yarbrough, O. Larry. *Not Like the Gentiles: Marriage Rules in the Letters of Paul*. SBLDS 80. Atlanta: Scholars, 1985.

Yaron, Reuven. "The Climactic Tricolon." *JJS* 37 (1986): 153–59.

Yieh, John Y. H. "Philip." *NIDB* 4, 499–500.

Zhekov, Yordan Kalev. *Defining the New Testament Logia on Divorce and Remarriage in a Pluralistic Context*. Eugene, OR: Pickwick, 2009.

Zias, Joseph E. "The Cemeteries of Qumran and Celibacy: Confusion Laid to Rest?" *DSD* 7 (2000): 220–53.

Bibliography of Scriptural Commentaries

Allen, Willoughby C. *A Critical and Exegetical Commentary on the Gospel according to Matthew*. ICC. 3rd ed. Edinburgh: T&T Clark, 1912.

Anderson, Francis L., and David Noel Freedman. *Micah*. AB 24E. New York/London: Doubleday, 2000.

Barrett, C. K. *The Pastoral Epistles in the New English Bible*. Oxford: Clarendon Press, 1963.

———. *The First Epistle to the Corinthians*. BNTC. Peabody, MA: Hendrickson, 1993.

Bassler, Jouette M. *1 Timothy, 2 Timothy, Titus*. ANTC. Nashville: Abingdon, 1996.

Beavis, Mary Ann. *Mark*. Paideia. Grand Rapids, MI: Baker Academic, 2011.

Blenkinsopp, Joseph. *Isaiah 46–66*. AB 19B. Doubleday: New York, 2003.

Boring, M. Eugene. *Mark: A Commentary*. NTL. Louisville: Westminster John Knox, 2006.

Bovon, François. *Luke 1: A Commentary on the Gospel of Luke 1:1–9:50*. Hermeneia. Minneapolis: Fortress, 2002.

Brown, Raymond E. *The Gospel according to John I–XII*. AB 29. Garden City, NY: Doubleday, 1966.

Bruce, F. F. *1 and 2 Corinthians*. NCB. London: Oliphants, 1971.

Byrne, Brendan. *Romans*. SP 6. Collegeville, MN: Liturgical, 1996.

Ciampa, Roy E., and Brian S. Rosner. *The First Letter to the Corinthians*. The Pillar New Testament Commentary. Grand Rapids, MI: Eerdmans, 2010.

Collins, Adela Yarbro. *Mark*. Hermeneia. Minneapolis: Fortress, 2007.

Collins, Raymond F. *1 and 2 Timothy and Titus*. NTL. Louisville: Westminster John Knox, 2002.

———. *First Corinthians*. SP 7. 2nd ed. Collegeville, MN: Liturgical Press, 2006.

———. *Second Corinthians*. Paideia. Grand Rapids, MI: Baker Academic, 2013.

Conzelmann, Hans. *1 Corinthians: A Commentary on the First Epistle to the Corinthians*. Hermeneia. Philadelphia: Fortress, 1975.

———. *Acts of the Apostles*. Hermeneia. Philadelphia: Fortress, 1987.

Cranfield, C. E. B. *The Epistle to the Romans*. Vol. 2. ICC. Edinburgh: T&T Clark, 1979.

Davies, William D., and Dale C. Allison. *A Critical and Exegetical Commentary on the Gospel according to Matthew*. 3 vols. ICC. Edinburgh: T&T Clark, 1988, 1991, 1992.

De Boer, Martinus C. *Galatians*. NTL. Louisville: Westminster John Knox, 2011.

Dibelius, Martin, and Hans Conzelmann. *The Pastoral Epistles*. Hermeneia. Philadelphia: Fortress, 1972.

Dunn, James D. G. *Romans*. WBC 38. 2 vols. Dallas: Word Books, 1988.

Fee, Gordon D. *The First Epistle to the Corinthians*. NICNT. Grand Rapids, MI: Eerdmans, 1987.

Fiore, Benjamin. *The Pastoral Epistles: First Timothy, Second Timothy, Titus*. SP 12. Collegeville, MN: Liturgical Press, 2007.

Fitzmyer, Joseph A. *The Gospel according to Luke I–IX*. AB 28. Garden City: Doubleday, 1981.

———. *The Gospel according to Luke X–XXIV*. AB 28A. Garden City, NY: Doubleday, 1985.

———. *Romans*. AB 33. New York: Doubleday, 1993.

———. *The Acts of the Apostles*. AB 32. New York: Doubleday, 1998.

———. *First Corinthians*. AYB 32. New Haven, CT: Yale University Press, 2008.

Focant, Camille. *The Gospel according to Mark: A Commentary*. Eugene, OR: Pickwick, 2012.

Gloer, W. Hulitt, and Perry L. Stepp. *Reading Paul's Letters to Individuals: A Literary and Theological Commentary on Paul's Letters to Philemon, Titus, and Timothy*. Macon, GA: Smyth and Helwys, 2008.

Gnilka, Joachim. *Das Evangelium nach Markus*. 5th ed. EKKNT 2. 2 vols. Zürich: Benizger / Neukirchen-Vluyn: Neukirchener Verlag, 1998.

Gourgues, Michel. *Les Deux letters à Timothée—La Lettre à Tite*. Commentaire biblique: Nouveau Testament. Paris: Cerf, 2009.

Gundry, Robert H. *Mark: A Commentary on His Apology for the Cross*. Grand Rapids, MI: Eerdmans, 1993.

Haenchen, Ernst. *The Acts of the Apostles: A Commentary*. Philadelphia: Westminster / Oxford: Blackwell, 1971.

Hagner, Donald A. *Matthew 14–28*. WBC 33B. Dallas: Word, 1995.

Hawthorne, Gerald F., and Ralph P. Martin. *Philippians*. WBC 43. Rev. ed. Nashville: Thomas Nelson, 2004.

Hillers, Delbert R. *Micah*. Hermeneia. Philadelphia: Fortress, 1984.

Holtz, Gottfried. *Die Pastoralbriefe*. THKNT 13. Berlin: Evangelische Verlagsanstalt, 1965.

Hooker, Morna D. *The Gospel according to Saint Mark*. BNTC. Peabody, MA: Hendrickson, 1991.

Jewett, Robert. *Romans: A Commentary*. Hermeneia. Minneapolis: Fortress, 2007.

Johnson, Luke Timothy. *Letters to Paul's Delegates: 1 Timothy, 2 Timothy, Titus*. The New Testament in Context. Valley Forge, PA: Trinity Press International, 1966.

———. *The Gospel of Luke*. SP 3. Collegeville, MN: Liturgical Press, 1991.

——. *The Acts of the Apostles*. SP 5. Collegeville, MN: Liturgical Press, 1992.

——. *The First and Second Letters to Timothy*. AB 35A. New York: Doubleday, 2001.

Keener, Craig S. *1–2 Corinthians*. New Cambridge Bible Commentary. Cambridge: Cambridge University Press, 2005.

Knight, George W., III. *Commentary on the Pastoral Epistles*. NIGTC. Grand Rapids, MI: Eerdmans / Carlisle, UK: Paternoster, 1992.

Krause, Deborah. *1 Timothy*. Readings: A New Biblical Commentary Series. London: T&T Clark, 2004.

Lightfoot, Joseph Barbour. *St. Paul's Epistle to the Philippians*. London: Macmillan, 1869. Most recently edited and republished in 1994 by Crossway, Wheaton, IL and Nottingham, UK.

Lohmeyer, Ernst. *Das Evangelium des Markus*. 17th ed. KEK 1. Göttingen: Vandenhoecjk und Ruprecht, 1997.

Longenecker, Richard N. *Galatians*. WBC 41. Dallas: Word, 1990.

Luz, Ulrich. *Matthew 8–20*. Hermeneia. Minneapolis: Fortress, 2001.

Marcus, Joel. *Mark 8–16*. AYB 27A. New Haven, CT: Yale University Press, 2009.

Marshall, I. Howard. *Commentary on Luke*. NIGTC. Grand Rapids, MI: Eerdmans, 1978.

——. *The Pastoral Epistles*. ICC. Edinburgh: T&T Clark, 1999.

Martyn, J. Louis. *Galatians*. AB 33A. New York: Doubleday, 1997.

Matera, Frank J. *Galatians*. SP 9. Collegeville, MN: Liturgical Press, 1992.

Meyers, Carol L., and Eric M. Meyers. *Zechariah 9–14*. AB 25C. New York: Doubleday, 1993.

Moloney, Francis J. *The Gospel of John*. SP 4. Collegeville, MN: Liturgical Press, 1998.

——. *The Gospel of Mark: A Commentary*. Peabody, MA: Hendrickson, 2002.

O'Brien, Peter T. *Commentary on Philippians*. NIGTC. Grand Rapids, MI: Eerdmans, 1991.

Oden, Thomas C. *First and Second Timothy and Titus*. Interpretation: A Bible Commentary for Teaching and Preaching. Louisville: Westminister John Knox, 1989.

Orr, William F., and James A. Walther. *I Corinthians*. AB 32. New York: Doubleday, 1976.

Quinn, Jerome D. *The Letter to Titus*. AB 35. New York: Doubleday, 1990.

Quinn, Jerome D., and William C. Wacker. *The First and Second Letters to Timothy*. Eerdmans Critical Commentary. Grand Rapids, MI: Eerdmans, 2000.

Reumann, John. *Philippians*. AYB 33B. New Haven, CT: Yale University Press, 2008.

Robertson, Archibald, and Alfred Plummer. *A Critical and Exegetical Commentary on the First Epistle of St. Paul to the Corinthians*. ICC. 2nd ed. Edinburgh: T&T Clark, 1914.

Roloff, Jürgen. *Der Erste Brief an Timotheus*. EKKNT 15. Zurich: Benziger / Neukirchen Vlujyn: Neukirchener Verlag, 1988.

Senft, Christoph. *La première épître de Saint Paul aux Corinthiens.* CNT 2/7. 2nd ed. Geneva: Labor et Fides, 1990.

Spicq, Ceslaus. *Les épîtres pastorales*, 1. *EBib.* 4th revised edition. Paris: Gabalda, 1969.

Thiselton, Anthony C. *The First Epistle to the Corinthians: A Commentary on the Greek Text.* NIGTC. Grand Rapids, MI: Eerdmans, 2000.

Thurston, Bonnie B. "Phillipians." In Bonnie B. Thurston and Judith M. Ryan, *Philippians and Philemon.* SP 10. Collegeville, MN: Liturgical Press, 2005, 3–163.

Towner, Philip H. *1–2 Timothy & Titus.* The IVP New Testament Commentary Series. Downers Grove, IL: Inter Varsity Press, 1994.

———. *The Letters to Timothy and Titus.* NICNT. Grand Rapids, MI: Eerdmans, 2006, 346.

Wall, Robert W., and Richard B. Steele. *1 & 2 Timothy and Titus.* The Two Horizons New Testament Commentary. Grand Rapids, MI: Eerdmans, 2012.

Witherington, Ben, III. *Letters and Homilies for Hellenized Christians*, 1: *A Socio-Rhetorical Commentary on Titus, 1–2 Timothy and 1–3 John.* Downers Grove, IL: Inter Varsity Press Academic: Apollos, 2006.

———. *Paul's Letter to the Romans: A Socio-Rhetorical Commentary.* Grand Rapids, MI: Eerdmans, 2004.

Index of Scripture References

Index of Classical, Jewish, and Patristic Sources

4QD, *Damascus Document*

4QDᵃ	55, 56, 57
4QDᵇ	55, 57
4QDᶜ	55, 58
4QDᵈ	55, 57
4QDᵉ	55, 56, 57, 58
4QDᶠ	55, 56, 57, 58
4QDᵍ	55, 57
4QpapDʰ	55, 58
4Q1	50, 56
4QGen	50
4QpapGen	50

4QMMT, the Halakhic Letter

42	99

4Q491–496 58

5QD, *Damascus Document*
55, 58

6QD, *Damascus Document*
55, 57

11QPsᵃ, Psalm Scrollᵃ
50

11QTᵃ, *Temple Scrollᵃ*

	55
2:14–15	53
26:11	54
27:2	54
27:4	54
29:5	54
37:12	54
39:7–8	54
40:5–6	54
42:1–4	54
42:14	54
45:7–12	53
46:7	54
47:3	54
47:8–9	54
48:13–14	54
48:15–17	53

50:10–15	53
51:6	54
51:7	54
53:16–10	54
54:2–3	54
54:4–5	54
54:19–21	53
55:15–21	53
56:18–19	53
57:2	54
57:15–19	53
58:19	54
60:17–18	53
62:9–10	53
63:10–15	53
64:4	54
64:5	54
64:6	54
64:10	54
65:7–15	53
66	54
66:1–8	54
66:1	54
66:3	54
66:5	54
66:8–11	54
66:12–16	54

11QTᵇ, *Temple Scrollᵇ*

	54
12:4–5	53
13:2	53
14:17–21	53
16:1–7	53

CD, Cairo Genizah Copy of the *Damascus Document*

1–16	55
4:20–5:11	55
4:20–5:1	55
4:20–21	50, 192
4:20	58
5:1–2	56
5:2–4	192
5:2	192

Index of Modern Authors

Index of Topics